COMPUTER POWER

FOR YOUR

SMALL BUSINESS

A Guide From Home Office Computing Magazine

Nick Sullivan

amacom

AMERICAN MANAGEMENT ASSOCIATION

*This publication is designed to provide accurate and authoritative
information in regard to the subject matter covered. It is sold with the
understanding that the publisher is not engaged in rendering legal,
accounting, or other professional service. If legal advice or other expert
assistance is required, the services of a competent professional person
should be sought.*

Library of Congress Cataloging-in-Publication Data

Sullivan Nick.
    Computer power for your small business : a guide from Home office
computing magazine / Nick Sullivan.
      p. cm.
    Includes index.
    ISBN 0-8144-7740-2 (pbk.)
     1. Small business—Data processing. 2. Home office computing.
I. Title.
    HF5548.2.S839   1991   90-53218
    658.02'2'0285—dc20   CIP

Cover Design: Vincent Ceci

Printing number

10 9 8 7 6 5 4 3 2 1

COMPUTER POWER

FOR YOUR

SMALL

BUSINESS

CONTENTS

Preface
Give Your Business the Electronic Edge

This is the first computer book that covers the main facets of running a business—and the first business book that describes how to get more out of your computer. It shows how you can use technology to build and run a better business.

This book is for all people who want to make better use of the computer as a business tool—but especially for the many professionals who are running their own small businesses. For these independents or small-business owners, who are without corporate support staffs, broadening computer horizons is just as important as expanding business skills. You don't learn that in business school or in the school of hard knocks.

In researching this book, I've referred to and relied on the published articles and hands-on experience of the editors and writers of *Home Office Computing*, the monthly magazine that shows professionals how they can use computers, telephones, and fax machines to give their businesses an electronic edge.

As a senior editor on the magazine, I've interviewed many businesspeople, read their letters, and fielded their queries over the phone. They want product information—what's good, and what's good value? And they want to know how to use this information to solve their problems. "How do I generate a targeted mailing list? How do I publish a newsletter? How do I track my cash flow?" As I wrote, I heard these questions in my head.

The first and last chapters focus on equipment, but most of the book describes software applications: business plans, project planning, communications, reports and presentations, adding graphics, newsletters, mailing lists, financial record keeping, time and information management, tax preparation, and other topics.

For each task, I point to MS-DOS and Macintosh products that have been given high ratings by the magazine's reviewers, editors, and readers. Many of these products have been reviewed several times with each new release. They stand out from hundreds of come-and-go products because they're effective, worth the money, easy to use, popular, and well supported by manufacturer or publisher. Not every product scores high points in every category, but its cumulative score makes it an "editors' pick."

Each chapter features a "Spotlight On" section, which highlights the most popular and effective software for a given task. Rather than include a laundry list of features that are apt to change with new releases, I capsulize the key benefits that set a given program apart.

You shouldn't necessarily buy one of these products without seeing or using it, but you should pencil it in on your short list. If you want more information, the publishers' phone numbers are listed at the end of the book.

For a given task or application, such as electronic mail, I describe the business benefits, how others are using it, and the required equipment, software, and skills. I also list additional resources. Reading one chapter in one book on a given task won't make you an expert user, but it will give you an entry point. And getting started is often the hardest part of applying a computer to your business needs.

Don't know anything about creating a slide presentation? Spend five minutes reading Chapter 9, and you'll know what it requires, and whether you should try it yourself or hire an expert. Baffled by the number of accounting and financial packages on the market? Read Chapter 18 and you'll know how to narrow your search.

The average professional uses a computer primarily for one task. Most people deal with words or numbers, so they know word processors or spreadsheets. Graphic artists and publishers know drawing and publishing programs. Any one of these professionals may use other software, such as communications for electronic mail or a database to store addresses, but most don't milk the machine for all it's worth. That's fine in a big company, where every task is handled by a specialist. But in a one-person or small business, you don't have enough time, money, or people to handle the ceaseless flow of information that crosses your desk.

Try something new! A small business has to make good use of technology to stay competitive. You may already feel like an octopus juggling research, production, marketing, fulfillment, and office tasks—but dedicate one arm to the computer. You may shorten your day, cut your costs, and improve your profits.

Use this book as a springboard. Turn to those chapters that address your needs. You'll learn how computers can help your business, how difficult or expensive each task is, and what you need to know to shop for a given product. From there, you're on your own—like lots of other independent businesspeople.

Nick Sullivan

Acknowledgments

In writing this book, I synthesized the research and wisdom of numerous people, primarily the writers and editors of *Home Office Computing*. I also drew from the experience of many of the businesspeople the magazine writes about every month. These businesspeople are too numerous to thank by name, although many are mentioned in the book.

I can, however, thank the writers. For information on business plans and taxes, I relied on the research and writing of Steve Edwards, Linda Stern, and David Hallerman; for project management, Brooks Hunt and Karen Novak; for type, graphics, word processing, and desktop publishing, Roger Hart, Steve Morgenstern, and Leslie Simons; for presentations and newsletters, Robin Raskin; for communications, Afred Glossbrenner, Ernest Perez, and John Wasik; for managing information and finances, Robert Cullen, Lis Fleming, Robert Gehorsam, Steve Miller, Jack Nimersheim, and Michael Thomsett; for mailing lists, Lynie Arden and Charles Bermant; for databases and spreadsheets, Rob Krumm and Charles Gajeway.

Every editor on *Home Office Computing* contributed to this book. David Hallerman originally edited many of the application-oriented magazine articles that provided the backbone of the book and read the final manuscript for accuracy. Technical editors Lance Paavola, Steven C. M. Chen, and Ted Stevenson edited many of the magazine's original product reviews and read other manuscripts for accuracy and content. Karen Kane edited financial articles and software reviews. Bernadette Grey read all articles for style and content, as well as the first draft of the book manuscript. And Claudia Cohl, editor-in-chief, directed all this activity, insuring that the magazine and thus the book will present practical technology solutions to common business problems.

Thanks to artists Peter Samek and Franck Levy for permission to use their original art, and to Ash Jain and Tim Berry for preparing computer printouts expressly for the book.

Myles Thompson, acquisitions editor at AMACOM, suggested the idea for this book to *Home Office Computing*. Priscilla Tate Austin read the initial outline for the book, and her comments helped me trim it into a workable table of contents. Eva Weiss, the book's editor, then helped me turn megabytes of notes and ideas into book form.

Finally, thanks to my wife, Deborah, and girls, Sarah J. and Lucy, for their sweet, unstinting support while I burned the midnight oil to complete the manuscript.

PART I
Planning a Business

Chapter 1
The Electronic Office

Choose the right computer and printer to anchor your business. Then hook the computer to the phone lines to make it fly.

> Watching masses of peasants scything a field 300 years ago, only a madman would have dreamed that the time would soon come when the fields would be depopulated, when people would crowd into urban factories to earn their daily bread. And only a madman would have been right. Today it takes an act of courage to suggest that our biggest factories and office towers may, within our lifetimes, stand half empty, reduced to use as ghostly warehouses or converted into living space. Yet this is precisely what the new mode of production makes possible: a return to the cottage industry on a new, higher, electronic basis, and with it a new emphasis on the home as the center of society.
>
> Alvin Toffler, *The Third Wave*

Two carpenters with the same basic set of tools can build dramatically different things. One may build a post-and-beam barn of fir, while the other perfects a six-panel pine door. Both use hammer and saw, level and square.

Two professionals with the same basic tools can also work toward different ends. One may produce bright-colored financial charts, while the other churns out simple press releases. Both use computer and printer, fax and phone.

"The electronic office makes all this possible," says Ash Jain, head of the Irvine Resources Group, who began publishing the *Macintosh Market Report* from his home in Irvine, California, in 1988. "I can reach anyone, anywhere, anytime."

Steve McGowan, a marine consultant in Dartmouth, Massachusetts, can receive a bid from a boatyard in Holland, sign on to a database to retrieve an up-to-date currency exchange rate, then fax the proposal to his client in New Zealand.

Bill Vick, an executive recruiter who works out of a back bedroom in his home in Plano, Texas, has built up the international side of a $250,000 business. "The president of a Japanese multinational flew to Dallas to have dinner with me the other night," says Vick, who can reach virtually every kind of technological tool by swiveling his desk chair. "I get a kick out of that."

The stories of what one person with the right tools and a bit of gumption can do are by now legion. Stories of computer nightmares, of time and money down the drain, are equally widespread. Obviously, the technology won't run a business, any more than hammers and saws will build a house. Success requires an investment of time to learn how to use the technology and apply it to your specific business tasks.

People like Jain, McGowan, and Vick have done both, and they use computers to run every facet of their businesses—from research to production to communications. To stay competitive today, every independent and small business has to master and apply the tools. You cannot count on labor and hard work to get the job done in a world where social trends, consumer tastes, and corporate needs are as changeable as spring winds.

This chapter describes the basic electronic tools needed to conduct business in the 1990s. For $5,000 to $10,000—less than the cost of a four-door station wagon—you can assemble virtually the same production and communications tools that are used in big companies. You start with a computer and printer, preferably a laser printer. And you can't do without a two-line phone and a fax machine. That gives you the equipment to create, analyze, and edit materials; print them out; and send them to others.

Once the equipment is in place, software will transform the computer into a number cruncher, letter writer, graphics designer, slide presenter, or mailing list manager. Most of the succeeding chapters describe ways to use the computer tools to suit your particular business.

MS-DOS VS. MACINTOSH

This book focuses on two types of personal computers: IBM-compatible and Macintosh. Why choose one system over the other? Two years ago the difference between the two rival operating systems was immense: Next to a graphic Macintosh, the character-based MS-DOS clone often seemed like a relic from the Fred Flinstone era. But now that speed and memory are cheaper and MS-DOS software is becoming more and more graphic (running under *Windows*, *GEM*, and *DeskMate*), the gap has narrowed considerably (see Figure 1-1).

The case for an IBM-compatible is primarily its lower cost. Because that market is more competitive, prices are much lower. More machines are sold, and thus more software is developed. You certainly have a wider

Figure 1-1.

Choose your electronic desktop: Macintosh or MS-DOS. The Macintosh Finder (*pictured*) shows folders that hold all programs and files in a certain category; click on Write, then MS *Word* in the Write window, and you see icons representing the contents of the folder.

The *Windows* desktop is similar—so similar that Apple sued Microsoft for copying its "look and feel." The major difference between the two environments is that all Macintosh programs operate under the same principles; only MS-DOS software written specifically for *Windows* will work with *Windows*.

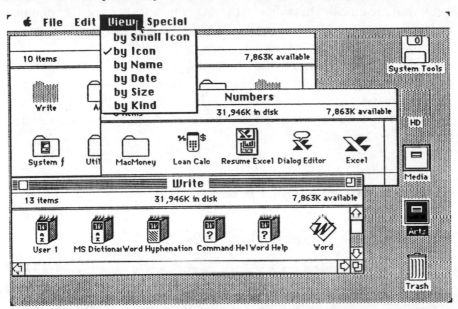

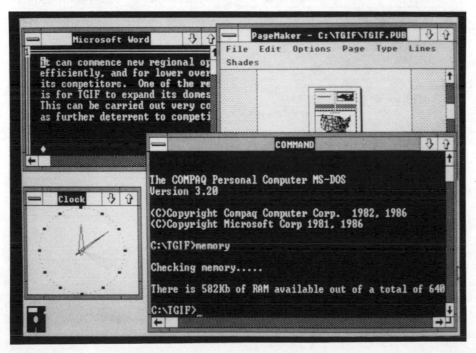

selection of both software and add-ons if you buy an IBM-compatible. And if you need sheer speed, the fastest IBM-compatibles are faster than the fastest Macintoshes.

The case for the Macintosh is that it's easier to use. And that's not just an advertising slogan. Almost all software operates the same basic way, so once you're comfortable with the computer you can learn and use more software more quickly. In addition, the Macintosh is still a better computer for graphic artists and publishers, since its operating system allows you to mix, match, and move different files more easily.

The truth, however, is that it's more important to decide how powerful a computer you need—primarily in terms of speed and memory (see Figure 1-2). All brand name computers work well and have a solid software base. The decision about which brand to buy comes down to your own preferences and biases.

Figure 1-2. Which Computer Is Best For You?

Take This Self-Test

To help you figure out which computer is best for you and your business, Home Office Computing devised this simple test. Answer the six questions that follow. If most of your responses fall into the first column, you probably need a Productivity Booster. If your answers fall into the second column, you need a Workhorse. And so on. If the right choice isn't apparent, give more weight to the first three questions as you decide on a purchase.

PRODUCTIVITY BOOSTER	WORKHORSE	SPEED DEMON	STATE-OF-THE-ART
IBM PC AND COMPATIBLES			
10- or 12-MHz 286-based	16-MHz 286-based or 20-MHz 386SX-based	20-MHz 386SX-based or 25-MHz 386-based	33- or 40-MHz 386-based
MACINTOSH			
Mac SE	Mac SE/30 or Mac IIcx	Mac IIci	Mac IIfx

1. How will you use the computer?

Text Applications	Light Numerical Applications	Heavy Numerical and	Graphics Applications
Word Processing (text only) Telecommunicating Small Database[1]	Accounting Programming Financial Planning Number Crunching Statistical Analysis	Word Processing (text and graphics) Large Database[2] Financial Planning Number Crunching Statistical Analysis	CAD/CAM Desktop Publishing Desktop Presentations

2. Do you plan to use MultiFinder, OS/2, Windows/3.0, or multitasking software?

No	No	Yes	Yes

3. What kind of business growth do you expect?

Little growth	Growth within three years	Substantial growth within two years	Substantial growth within one year

4. What's your computing level?

Beginner	Intermediate	Intermediate	Power User

5. How much time to you plan to spend computing?

A few hours a week	Up to two hours a day	About three hours a day	More than four hours a day

6. How much money are you willing to spend on a computer system?

Up to $2,500	Up to $4,500	Up to $7,000	Up to $10,000

[1]Fewer than 500 records and 15 fields.   [2]More than 1,000 records and 15 fields

MS-DOS COMPUTERS

About three out of four business computers in use today are modeled after the IBM PC or the IBM PS/2. These computers are often called IBM clones or MS-DOS computers, after the MS-DOS operating system, which an estimated 16 million computers around the world are running. Many of these computers also run Operating System/2 (OS/2), a newer and more high-powered operating system that allows you to run several programs at a time. IBM, however, is no longer as dominant as it once was; other firms, such as Compaq, Tandy, Dell, AST, and Epson, are all major players.

The four main classes of IBM-compatible computers are 286, 386, 386SX, and 486 systems—named after the Intel 80286, 80386, and 80386SX microprocessors that power them. (There are portable as well as desktop versions of all these systems.) The basic—though not the only—difference between them is speed.

286 Computers

At the end of the last decade, the 286 computer (based on the original IBM PC AT) was the de facto standard in both big and small businesses. The 286 computer runs most MS-DOS software and much OS/2 software, although there's a growing list of 386-specific MS-DOS programs. The 286 computer—running at a speed of ten megahertz (MHz) or more—is suited for a wide range of business tasks, with the exception of making intense numerical calculations, sorting huge databases, or working with complex graphic applications.

386 Computers

Despite the rugged efficiency of the 286 computer, the 386 or stripped-down 386SX has a longer life expectancy, in part because extra speed is a real asset in running today's graphic-based software. Various models run at 20 MHz, 25 MHz, 33 MHz, and more—so fast that you sometimes can't read type as it whizzes past you on the screen. Because of its internal design and processing speed, the 386-based computer is best suited for running OS/2 and *Presentation Manager*, the graphic mouse-driven interface that makes an IBM look like a Macintosh. The 386's speed also makes it ideal for any graphics-oriented work, such as desktop publishing or computer-aided design.

Consider the following example: You're working with a desktop publishing program on a 286, and it takes ten seconds to redraw the screen each time you move from page to page. If it only takes five seconds on the

386 and the screen is redrawn sixty times per hour, that means a savings of five minutes per hour, or up to forty minutes per day.

An 80386SX-based computer is basically a slower, stripped-down version of a standard 386 computer, running at speeds of 16 and 20 MHz. In addition to the slower clock speed, the SX computers can't process as much data at the same time as 386 computers. Nonetheless, SX computers can run all 386 software and are better suited to run OS/2 and *Presentation Manager* than the slower 286s. Why buy a 386SX instead of a 386? They cost considerably less.

MACINTOSH

The Mac was once cute and different. Its icons, mouse, 3.5-inch disk drive, silhouette, and small screen all set it apart. Now the Mac is merely the minority business computer that sells at a premium price and is constantly forced to prove its worth. But establishing it as a business computer is what Apple wanted.

Macintosh computers are divided into two main groups: those based on the Motorola 68000 microprocessor (Plus, SE, and Portable) and those based on the Motorola 68030 microprocessor (SE/30, IIx, IIcx, IIci, and IIfx). The 68030 models are a better choice for business use. They operate at speeds of 16 Mhz to 40 Mhz.

Some Macintoshes are sold as one-piece units with a built-in black-and-white monitor, while others include expansion slots and can be used with a variety of monitors.

All Macintoshes include MultiFinder as part of the operating system, which allows you to open several programs at once and switch between them. Thus, to switch from a word processor to a spreadsheet you don't have to close one and open the other, but merely click the mouse to jump to the next window.

With MultiFinder operative, you can use your laser printer or send an electronic file by modem while you write a letter or perform any other task. Obviously, this feature is an immense productivity booster. To run Multi-Finder, you need 2 megabytes (MB) of memory, and preferably 4 MB.

The other major plus of the Macintosh operating system is that you can cut and paste text and graphics between applications, with little worry about file formats. You could, for example, mark a section of your spreadsheet and copy it into a letter you were composing with your word processor, and then print the letter. While you can do the same with some MS-DOS applications, especially with *Windows*, you cannot do it universally. But, as noted above, that is changing fast.

Finally, Macintosh models SE and later can read MS-DOS data disks (as long as they're 3.5-inch disks), which is important in offices with both types of computers.

MONITORS

People generally don't set out to buy monitors; they set out to buy computers, and computers come with monitors. But you'll be staring at that monitor for thousands of hours, so it pays to get one you like.

The standard monitor for MS-DOS computers is the VGA monitor, which is extremely sharp and colorful. VGA monitors display 256,000 colors, and up to 256 at a time (depending, of course, on your software). VGA monochrome monitors turn colors into gray scales and can display up to sixty-four shades at a time. Compared to the older amber or green phosphor monitors, VGA monitors are often called "paper-white," because they display black text on a white screen. That alone—without the higher resolution—makes them more readable.

Because VGA color monitors are so sharp, they're adequate for text-oriented work. With earlier CGA and EGA color monitors, which are still sold, text is often fuzzy.

Macintosh Monitors

The standard Macintosh monitor was once the nine-inch black-and-white screen that's built into the compact models. However, some of the compact models and all of the modular models have slots so that you can choose a different kind of monitor—a larger monochrome, color, portrait, or two-page monitor.

Except for the Macintosh IIci, adding a monitor to these systems also requires a video card, just as on an MS-DOS system. The number of colors available is determined by the type of video card used. For example, an eight-bit color card can support 256 colors, and a twenty-four-bit card can support as many as sixteen million colors.

Full-Page Monitors

One problem with standard-sized computer monitors is that you can't see the whole page that you're working on. If you will print on a standard 8.5-by 11-inch piece of paper, you see on-screen only a small portion of the final page at one time. Many word processing and other programs have a page-preview mode that shows you a miniature facsimile of what the printed page will look like, but to edit you have to return to the normal screen display. Full-page—or large-screen—monitors were designed to overcome this problem.

Full-page monitors fall into two groups: Portrait monitors (taller than they are wide) are designed to display a single page at a time; landscape monitors (wider than they are tall) are designed to display two pages side by side (see Figure 1-3). Both types offer extremely high-resolution displays, although some distort images around the edges of the screen.

Graphic artists, desktop publishers, and engineers benefit from full-screen displays, since seeing the whole picture in maximum detail is vital to each. A less obvious application for full-page monitors involves the increasingly popular graphical user interface (GUI) environments of *Windows*, OS/2 *Presentation Manager*, *GEM*, and Macintosh. With a larger screen you can display several applications in on-screen windows simultaneously, giving each enough space to present a meaningful amount of information.

Perhaps least obvious is the dramatic benefit that users of character-based applications, such as word processing and spreadsheet software, can derive from a larger display. Seeing a full page of work at a glance eliminates

Figure 1-3.

Depending on your application, you might want to use a two-page monitor (*left*) or a full-page, or portrait, monitor (*right*)—both of which are much larger than standard monitors. The monitors shown here are for the Apple Macintosh, but similar monitors are plentiful for MS-DOS computers.

a lot of scrolling time. Since you scan larger sections of your work, you can make connections between different parts of your document more easily.

Before buying a large-screen monitor, you should make sure that the software you use will support it. Not all software includes drivers for all monitors. The big-name packages (such as Lotus *1-2-3*, *PageMaker*, *Ventura Publisher*, *WordPerfect*) and the GUIs (such as *Windows* and *GEM*) support most full-page monitors.

LASER PRINTERS

If the monitor is the point of interaction between you and the computer, the printer is the connection between your computer work and the outside world. And nothing short of commercial typesetting beats a laser printer.

Laser printers are fast and quiet, and they produce high-quality print. These three attributes will add spark and sparkle to your business. The laser's speed saves you time; its quiet allows you to conduct phone conversations while the printer is working; and its text and graphics output approaches typeset quality.

In 1990, the Hewlett-Packard LaserJet Series IIP was the first laser printer to break the $1,000 price barrier. The IIP prints four pages a minute, compared with six or eight on more expensive models. By comparison, the fastest 24-pin dot-matrix printers grind out text in near-letter-quality mode at about 1.5 pages per minute. Since HP is the leader in the laser market, its dramatic pricing is forcing other manufacturers to follow suit.

Unlike dot-matrix printers, which primarily use perforated computer paper, lasers use single sheets of paper (generally copier paper) stacked in a paper tray. Often you can add a second tray to handle legal-size paper. Lasers also print labels and envelopes more easily than dot-matrix printers; however, they are not impact printers and cannot print multipart forms.

There are two main types of laser printers: PostScript and non-PostScript. The latter are primarily Hewlett-Packard compatibles and use the Hewlett-Packard Printer Control Language (HP PCL). However, the HP LaserJet Series III models add many PostScript features, as described later.

PostScript Printers

PostScript printers, such as the Apple LaserWriter, are sophisticated (and expensive) printers that come equipped with a wide variety of fonts, making them ideal for professional publishing tasks. Since most Macintosh software supports PostScript, Macintosh users should consider PostScript printers primarily. Another option is a QuickDraw printer, such as the Apple Laser

Writer IISC, which isn't a PostScript printer but is supported by the Macintosh's built-in QuickDraw routines.

PostScript is a page-description language (developed by Adobe Systems) that provides precise control over virtually every detail on a printed page. PostScript printers come equipped with a large number of scalable typefaces. Users can specify type in any of these faces and styles (roman, italic, bold, and bold italic), and almost any size; PostScript creates the characters on the fly during the printing process. Most PostScript printers come with Adobe's standard starter set of eleven typefaces that make up thirty-five styles. In addition, Adobe has developed a huge library of typefaces that can be purchased separately.

PostScript is compatible with professional typesetting equipment. A newsletter or catalog designed in PostScript can be proofed on a laser printer and then sent to a PostScript typesetter for final output. The proof and the final will be very similar (although the line breaks may differ slightly), except that the typeset page will have higher resolution.

While the resolution of a laser printer is 300 by 300 dots per inch (dpi), or 90,000 dpi, professional typesetting machines use a matrix of 1,200 by 1,200 (or higher), or at least 1,440,000 dpi. However, when text is printed in standard sizes—say, 10-point or 12-point—the difference in quality is barely perceptible. With much smaller or larger type, or graphics, the discrepancy is much more apparent.

PostScript printers cost considerably more than HP-compatible printers. The manufacturers pay licensing fees to Adobe, and the printers require more memory—at least 2MB and often 4MB.

Hewlett-Packard Printers

Just as the gap between Macintosh and MS-DOS computers is narrowing, so is the gap between PostScript and non-PostScript printers. The old Hewlett-Packard LaserJet Series II models came with far fewer fonts than PostScript printers—and they couldn't be scaled to create larger or smaller type sizes. But that changed with the HP LaserJet Series III, whose AutoFont feature scales type. The printer can also smooth curved type, thereby eliminating many of the jagged edges. And, you can convert it to a full-fledged PostScript printer by adding a cartridge.

Most MS-DOS software supports HP printers, so MS-DOS users are certainly safe with HP-compatible printers. However, more and more MS-DOS software also supports PostScript printers, and more and more printers support both modes. Thus, it's possible that an MS-DOS user would want to buy a dual-purpose printer. And it's almost always possible to convert a non-PostScript printer into one, by adding either hardware or software (for more on this, see Chapter 5).

INK-JET PRINTERS

Before laser prices dropped so dramatically, ink jets were a more attractive alternative than they are now. However, they still are considerably less expensive than lasers and produce a high-quality type that is nearly as good as laser output.

Ink-jet printers, notably the Hewlett-Packard DeskJet (for MS-DOS computers) and the Hewlett-Packard DeskWriter (for Macintosh), are certainly a big improvement over dot-matrix printers. Their output is better, and they are quieter and faster.

Ink jets create images of dots, just as do dot-matrix and laser printers, by firing tiny drops of liquid ink at the paper. If you look closely, you'll see more jagged contours on 300 dots-per-inch text produced by an ink jet than on a laser; liquid ink inevitably spreads out a little in the paper fiber. Liquid ink is also water soluble, so it runs if you wet it.

COMMUNICATIONS

The cornerstone to a smooth communications system, of course, is a good phone system. But that means more than a good phone. You need enough phone lines to handle the traffic—voice calls, fax calls, and modem calls. Depending on your volume, you need two or three phone lines into your office. And—since voice and data are like oil and water—you may need a way to automatically switch calls between the two (see Chapter 11).

If you have a fax machine, you may think you don't need a modem. While both devices can be used to send and receive memos and letters, the modem connects your computer to the telephone lines. And in an age of advanced computer communications—with more and more work produced and sent through computers—that is a big plus. Whatever you send or receive arrives in electronic form, ready for editing.

Modems

Modems are either external devices, connecting to the computer's serial port, or internal boards that plug into an empty slot. On the back of the modem are two phone jacks—one for a line to your phone, the other for a line to the outside line. Modems dial the phone, connect you to an electronic-mail service or another computer, and send files from your computer to the remote computer.

You give commands to the modem—which number to dial, how fast to send a file, and so on—through communications software. Like a computer, a modem is useless without software. Besides communications software, an increasing number of software packages let you use your modem as an automatic telephone dialer: Just enter numbers from your Rolodex and use the modem's autodial feature to automatically place voice calls (see Chapter 11 and Chapter 14 for more information).

Speed

Virtually all modems are so-called "Hayes-compatible," modeled after Hayes modems. Since all modems operate the same basic way, and the technology is well tested and reliable, you can shop for modems based on price and speed. A 1200-baud modem sends the equivalent of three double-spaced pages of text per minute, and a 2400-baud modem about six pages per minute.

An increasing number of 9600-baud modems are in use, although they generally require fiber-optic telephone lines for data integrity. And since both sending and receiving modems must operate at the same speed, you often won't be able to use the rarer 9600-baud modem at full speed. Today, the 2400-baud modem is the most widely used and makes the most sense for general use.

A GOOD MACHINE IS *NOT* HARD TO FIND

If you run your own business, you need an electronic toolkit to stay competitive. And the computer is the cornerstone of that toolkit. Finding a good computer is easy—most computers work well. The technical kinks were worked out long ago. On the other hand, choosing a computer can be confusing, since it's so hard to differentiate among the many reliable models. Often what sways the buyer is not the product's features, but the reliability of the manufacturer and the strength of its dealer network. In other cases, a buyer is looking for one particular feature that only a handful of computers offer.

Consider these two rules of thumb: Find a computer that does what you need done now, not one that *might* accomplish your tasks in the future; and buy a little more horsepower than you think you need, since your needs will probably expand with your skills and your business. If you like the IBM-compatible world, train your eyes on the 386 and 386SX models; if you like the Macintosh, focus on those with the Motorola 68030 microprocessor or better. Both these machines will be at the center of computing activity for the next few years.

OFFICE SETUP RESOURCES

Working From Home: Everything You Need to Know to Live and Work Under the Same Roof, by Paul and Sarah Edwards, Jeremy P. Tarcher, 436 pp., 1989; $24.95.

This comprehensive guide to making it on your own includes tips for getting and keeping business, and it describes the equipment you need to work independently.

Home Offices and Workspaces, by the editors of Sunset Books and *Sunset* Magazine, Lane Publishing, 96 pp., 1986; $7. This book includes large, full-color photos of workspace; advice on choosing space-saving furniture, shelving, and equipment; plus pictures and plans for furniture you can build for yourself.

The Home Office Book, How to Set Up an Efficient Personal Workspace in the Computer Age, by Mark Alvarez, Goodwood Press, 304 pp., 1990; $14.95. This self-published book covers all aspects of office setup, including furniture, lighting, and design. Its four chapters on computer hardware, computer software, computer peripherals, and electronic equipment provide quick overviews of what you need to get going. But the author, who says he is "not a computer expert," doesn't go into too much detail.

386 Computer Buyer's Guide and Handbook, by Edwin Rutsch, Modular Information Systems, 453 pp., 1988; $29.95. The author, who has written a number of books on buying IBM-compatible computers, does a good job of explaining the more technical features of 386 machines (such as wait states and cache memory) and how they affect performance. The book also includes reviews of major 386 computers. Obviously, the reviews are useful only if the book is fairly current, so check to see when the latest edition was published.

The Book of Fax, by Daniel Fishman and Elliot King, Ventana Press, 176 pp., 1990; $9.95. This "impartial guide to buying and using facsimile machines" is useful for people with heavy fax needs—either special graphic requirements, or advanced polling and broadcasting needs. The book covers all fax machine features, computer-generated faxes, the "cellular/fax connection," and offers some innovative ideas about how to use your fax machine.

Home Office Computing, Scholastic Inc., published monthly, $19.97 per year. Each month the magazine runs a feature on a given hardware and software category, and reviews more than forty new products. The magazine covers phones, fax machines, and "office essentials," as well as all types of computer equipment and shows by example how you can apply this technology to your business needs.

SPOTLIGHT ON: General Business Computers

Cost: $2,500 and up.

Learning Curve: Medium; computers are much easier to master than they were a few years ago, primarily because the operating systems and applications software are so much better; many come with "front-end" software that insulates you from the techy operating system. The difficult part is finding software that solves your business problems.

Required Equipment (for Full system): Computer with 40MB hard disk drive (or larger); VGA monitor (for MS-DOS systems); laser printer; modem highly recommended.

Recommended Manufacturers: Apple, AST, Compaq, CompuAdd, Dell, Epson, Everex, IBM, Tandy.

Buying Tips: Be certain to test the keyboard and view the display (VGA is the best bet) before buying; be sure you get a twelve- or fifteen-month warranty and see if the manufacturer offers an on-site contract; buy MS-DOS version 4.01 (or higher), which supports large hard-disk drives and provides a DOS shell that makes many DOS functions easier to use.

Chapter 2
The Business Plan: Your Road Map to Success

Put your business on a solid foundation by creating a full financial and market plan with specialized software.

Sometimes, I think, the things we see
Are shadows of the things to be;
That what we plan we build. . . .

Phoebe Cary, *Dreams and Realities*

The first step in any new business is writing a business plan. Just as a good poker player makes choices—based on probabilities—that affect the outcome in a card game, so do a businessperson's choices affect the direction of any business.

Many people starting small businesses, especially one- or two-person outfits, might think they don't need to write or follow a business plan. After all, many service professionals don't need outside financing, and the need to produce a loan proposal prompts many business plans.

A business plan, however, isn't important only to high-powered MBAs, large businesses, or heavily financed start-up companies. Business plans can offer you a clear road map in your drive to success, and are the link between your personal goals and operating plans for the business.

The world is full of businesspeople who know their businesses, their products, and their markets but who don't know how to put this information on paper. As Stanley Rich, coauthor of *Business Plans That Win $$$*, succinctly puts it, "Those who fly by the seats of their pants often get torn pants."

Preparing a business plan is an exercise that will focus your attention on where you are now, where you want to go, and how you can get there. It will help you understand the risks, rewards, and requirements of your business. The business plan is an evolving document that lists specific goals and steps to achieve them.

The thought of drawing up a business plan—with the complex math and pages of text—can be forbidding. You've got to describe your company and product or service, analyze the market and the competition, outline your operations and management, and generate a financial forecast far enough in advance to show a break-even point. But specialized software can ease the task.

Dan Gunther, who started Cell-Comm USA, a cellular phone agency in Tennessee, had produced several business plans for other companies by hand before doing one on his computer. "The computer-generated plan was more professional and detailed than the others," says Gunther, who used *Venture—The Entrepreneur's Handbook* (Star Software). "The software walked me through and forced me to examine areas I hadn't considered. I showed my finished plan to a high-level bank executive who said it was the best plan he'd seen in 40 years." Gunther and his partner, Chris Moorhead, used the plan to raise $100,000 in start-up capital from individual investors.

This chapter examines business plan software, describes several sources of census and other demographic data that you can use to draw up a market study, and shows how you can use the power of a spreadsheet to analyze the impacts of a poor, good, or strong economy on your plan.

BUSINESS PLAN SOFTWARE

Although a wide range of financial planning software is available, and you can use spreadsheets to design financial models (see Chapter 3), very little software walks the user through a full business plan from start to finish. True business plan software includes templates for sales and marketing forecasts, break-even analysis, cash flow, and cash balance sheets. And it includes outlines and often boilerplate text to help you with the descriptive portion of the plan.

You can choose from two main types of business plan software. Templates for popular spreadsheets, such as Lotus *1-2-3* or *Excel*, create financial models. These packages typically include booklets and outlines for creating the written part of the plan, although you have to use your own word processor. A stand-alone program creates financial models without a spreadsheet and includes a built-in word processor. The type of software you choose depends in large part on whether or not you already use and are comfortable with a spreadsheet.

Business Plan Toolkit

The best spreadsheet template is *Business Plan Toolkit* (Palo Alto Software), with versions for Lotus *1-2-3* (MS-DOS) and Microsoft *Excel* (Macintosh).

While MS-DOS users have a wider selection of business plan software, *Toolkit* is the primary Macintosh program.

The various templates guide you through the planning process so that even if you don't know how to write spreadsheet formulas or forecasting models, you can obtain professional results—in formats that bankers, accountants, and investors instantly recognize and understand.

The excellent documentation emphasizes a three-step approach: (1) high-quality planning based on market and competitive research; (2) setting specific goals; and (3) detailing the tasks, responsibilities, and deadlines for realizing those goals. The documentation also makes a good case for producing concise presentations with charts and graphs instead of detailed prose.

Each template has an associated chart, table, or graphic for you to complete (see Figure 2-1). The program creates a number of subsidiary worksheets so that you can break the task into small chunks, which makes the process less intimidating. You then feed summary results into the main plan. The *Business Plan Outline* workbook shows you how to integrate these financial reports into an overall business plan, which you create with your word processor.

The downside to such financial templates is that you must be adept enough with your spreadsheet to customize the template to suit your own business.

Figure 2-1.

When compiling a business plan, a chart can convey your long-term outlook better than plain figures. This chart was generated by *Business Plan Toolkit*.

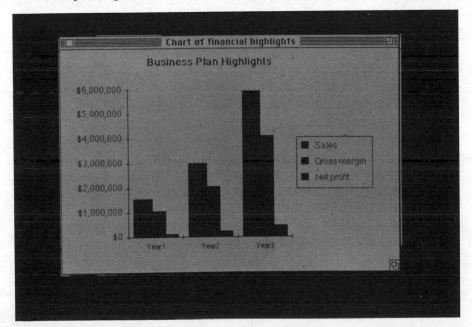

Venture—The Entrepreneur's Handbook

Venture—The Entrepreneur's Handbook, whose business plan module is based on the *Entrepreneur's Handbook*, developed by the faculty of the University of Southern California's Department of Business, is a complete business plan generator (for MS-DOS). *Venture* runs under the *DeskMate* interface, developed by Tandy, which adds pulldown menus, icons, cut-and-paste transfer between all modules, and allows optional mouse operation—all of which make the program easy to navigate through. (For more information on *DeskMate* and other MS-DOS graphic interfaces, see Chapter 20.)

Venture's question-and-answer format guides you through each step of a plan. Before starting, you indicate whether your business is in the service, manufacturing, retail, or distribution sector. Then you complete a feasibility study, which determines if your idea is strong enough to pursue.

After you answer questions, you can transfer the information to the program's built-in word processor for formatting or move it to the spreadsheet to complete the financial sections.

If you want to create a powerful business plan, then *Venture* will more than meet your needs. However, its real strength lies in its ability to manage your business. Given the time and personnel constraints on small companies, it's too easy to put the plan on the shelf and move on to the full-time task of managing. Since *Venture*'s built-in check writer, double-entry general ledger, and word processor are designed as everyday work tools, you'll always be a menu selection away from your business plan.

Venture's legal and financial templates are also strong points. For example, the program includes a nondisclosure agreement for the word processor, pro forma income statements for the spreadsheet, and an entrepreneur's bibliography for the file manager, plus a sample chart of accounts for the general ledger. The weakest part of the package is the documentation, which is difficult to read and doesn't include a business plan tutorial. The company offers a demonstration tape, so you can evaluate the software before buying it.

VenturPlan

VenturPlan is also a stand-alone business plan generator for MS-DOS computers, although it lacks the mouse-and-icon interface. Three versions are sold—for service businesses, retailers, and manufacturers. The program consists of ten independent but closely linked modules. You can start in any section, and the program moves the relevant information into the other modules so that you don't have to reenter it.

Probing questions coax information from you, to aid in completing a market plan. A resource section in the manual directs you to government and industry information sources; it also includes a sample business plan. An on-line "Advisor" provides sample paragraphs and advice for completing many of the sections.

Clearly, since business plan software depends on word processors and spreadsheets, you can accomplish the same ends with those stand-alone programs. But business plan software offers a road map for businesspeople who are unaccustomed to the style, format, and financial formulas required in business plans. The software or the documentation—or both—pepper you with questions and ideas. In effect, you are interacting with a business plan consultant as you work. You turn over all possible stones before you start your business—so they won't come loose and trip you up once you start your business.

OBTAINING MARKET DATA

One of the key elements of any business plan is an analysis of the potential market for your proposed product or service. The more you can quantify your market—by identifying the number of businesses in a given area that need your product or the number of people fitting certain demographic characteristics—the stronger your plan.

You can often find market data—from the government, market research firms, or financial services institutions—at the library. But you'll find it much quicker to use your computer to search electronic databases. To do so, you'll need a modem and a subscription to an electronic information service. (For more details, see Chapter 13.)

For example, using *Dun's Direct Access* (Dun & Bradstreet) and a modem, you can access specific marketing information on more than six million U.S. businesses in the Dun & Bradstreet database. If you want to identify all businesses in the computer maintenance field with over fifty employees in New York City, *Dun's Direct Access* would search the database and produce a list of businesses that meet those criteria. Such information is useful not only to a salesperson looking for new prospects, but also to a business planner who wants to judge the size of a given market. Similar information is also available on CompuServe, through its Business Demographics Reports.

CompuServe is an even better source of consumer demographic data. Besides CENDATA, a compilation of U.S. Census statistics, CompuServe carries a wide range of neighborhood demographic data, the same kind used by advertisers and retailers to help determine product distribution or store placement (see Figure 2-2).

If you were developing a service to reach retirees, you would turn to the ACORN report (see Figure 2-3), a service developed by MRI, a market

Figure 2-2.

On CompuServe, an electronic information service you access by modem, you can examine demograhic data for any zip code. The report shown is just a sample.

1986 NEIGHBORHOOD REPORT
ZIP CODE: 12345
ANYCOUNTY, U.S.A.

	1980	1986
TOTAL POPULATION	38946	45648
TOTAL NUMBER OF HOUSEHOLDS	12370	15190
AVERAGE AGE	30.1	32.0
AVERAGE HOUSEHOLD INCOME	$25688	$39406

AGE GROUPS:

0–4	7.1%
5–11	11.1%
12–16	9.6%
17–21	10.0%
22–29	11.6%
30–44	26.0%
45–54	11.1%
55–64	7.1%
65 +	6.4%
	100.0%

HOUSEHOLD INCOME:

$ 0–14999	12.8%
$15000–24999	13.9%
$25000–34999	17.9%
$35000–49999	28.3%
$50000–74999	20.0%
$75000 +	7.1%
	100.0%

TYPES OF HOUSEHOLDS:

SINGLE PERSON	14.2%
MALE	5.6%
FEMALE	8.6%
FAMILY	82.9%
NON-FAMILY	2.9%
	100.0%

OCCUPATION:

EXECUTIVE	17.4%
PROFESSIONAL	14.7%
TECHNICAL	3.1%
SALES	14.0%
CLERICAL	19.6%
PRIVATE	0.3%
SERVICE	9.2%
FARMING	0.8%
CRAFT	10.5%
OPERATOR	7.5%
LABORER	2.9%
	100.0%

OCCUPIED HOUSING UNITS:

OWNED	77.9%
RENTED	22.1%
	100.0%

AVERAGE HOME VALUE	$69823
AVERAGE RENT	$280

RACE:

WHITE	97.2%
BLACK	1.8%
OTHER	1.0%
	100.0%

OCCUPIED HOUSING BUILT IN:

1975–1980	25.3%
1970–1974	25.6%
1960–1969	28.1%
1950–1959	8.2%
1940–1949	2.2%
PRE–1940	10.7%
	100.0%

Figure 2-3.

CompuServe offers in-depth descriptions of different demographic groups, which you can use to determine the market potential for a given product or service. As shown below, if you choose Mature Adults in Stable Neighborhoods, you'll see another menu outlining segments of that group. Choose Golden Year Retirees and you'll get a full description of that segment's life-style and buying patterns.

ACORN USER'S GUIDE

1 Introduction
2 Links to MRI and Gallup Data
3 Group A: Wealthy Metropolitan Communities
4 Group B: Trend Setting, Suburban Neighborhoods
5 Group C: Young Apartment Dwellers and College
6 Group D: Big City Urban Neighborhoods
7 Group E: Hispanic and Multi-Racial Neighborhoods
8 Group F: Black Neighborhoods
9 Group G: Suburban Middle-Class Families
10 Group H: Blue Collar Families in Small Towns
11 Group I: Mature Adults in Stable Neighborhoods
12 Group J: Seasonal and Mobile Home Communities
13 Group K: AGRICULTURAL-ORIENTED COMMUNITIES
14 Group L: OLDER, DEPRESSED FACTORY TOWNS
15 Group M: SPECIAL POPULATIONS

ACORN GROUP I

1 Group Description
2 Type I29: Golden-Year Retirees
3 Type I30: Adults in Pre-War Housing
4 Type I31: Small Town Families
5 Type I32: Nostalgic Retirees & Adults
6 Type I33: Home Oriented Senior.Citizens
7 Type I34: Old Families in Pre-War Homes

Enter choice I2

DEMOGRAPHIC: Group I is characterized by an older-than-average age distribution. Over 27% are at least 65, and over 44% are over 55. As a result, family size is a low 2.7. These elderly are white and more mobile.

SOCIOECONOMIC: I29s are relatively wealthy for an elderly group. Incidence of college graduates is 26% above average, the institutionalized pop. is more than double the U.S. rate. The labor force is overwhelmingly white collar. Professional and managerial occupations exceed the national rate by 39%.

LOCATION: Of the 2.2 million HHs, 26.4% are in Florida. California is home for 14.6%. A smaller concentration can be found in Ohio; 4.1%.

LIFESTYLE: I29s travel more frequently than other I segments. I29s do not drive a frequently; spendings on car maintenance are low. Since a large number of I29s have recently relocated, demand for new banking services is high. Credit card acquisition also is high. In sum, I29s are older adults who appreciate culture and seek relaxing and stress-free lifestyles.

---

research firm. You would choose "Mature Adults in Stable Neighborhoods," one of many demographic segments, and read about subsegments within that group, where and how they live, and what they buy.

These two examples merely hint at the wealth of market and financial data available by modem. However, one major danger of doing electronic research via computer is that you can rapidly gather an overwhelming amount of information. Not all of it will be pertinent; even if it is, not all of it should be used. Concentrate on information that is essential to support the statements and goals in your plan.

MARKET FORECASTING WITH A SPREADSHEET

Of course, no business plan exists in a vacuum. Your rosy sales predictions based on hard market data may fade if the economy turns sour. The buying habits of Florida retirees may change dramatically if the inflation rate begins to diminish the value of their fixed incomes, and you may have to adjust your plan to compensate. You can do so by applying the complex principles of game theory, or decision theory, and using a spreadsheet function called matrix multiplication.

Imagine that you run an automobile dealership that sells three brands of cars, one domestic and two imported, and that your profit per car sold is approximately the same for each. You must decide which type of car to stock most heavily over the coming two years: Chevrolet, Toyota, or Volvo. (This, of course, is a strictly hypothetical example.)

Say your research on sales indicates that in a strong economy, higher-priced cars like Volvos sell well. If the economy is stable, less expensive cars such as the Chevrolet sell better. If the economy is weak, consumers tend to buy Toyotas.

You can summarize past sales records in what is called a payoff matrix—a rectangular arrangement of numbers into rows and columns (see Figure 2-4). Columns B, C, and D in the *Excel* worksheet list the three possible states of the economy: weak, stable, and strong. Rows 5 to 7 list the three product lines. The matrix is then filled in with values for estimated unit sales under each circumstance. If the economy is weak and you stock up on Volvos, unit sales are estimated as 500. However, if the economy is stable and you put most of your inventory money into Volvos, you estimate sales of 800.

According to these projections, what should you do? To answer that, create a second matrix that holds the relative odds for the probable states of the economy. Suppose you read in several business magazines predictions about the state of the economy for the coming years. You can use this information to fill out an economic forecast in the probability matrix, shown in the bottom left side of the figure.

Figure 2-4.

By multiplying estimated sales figures by the percentage probabilities for a weak, stable, or strong economy, a spreadsheet may help you intelligently project sales for any product.

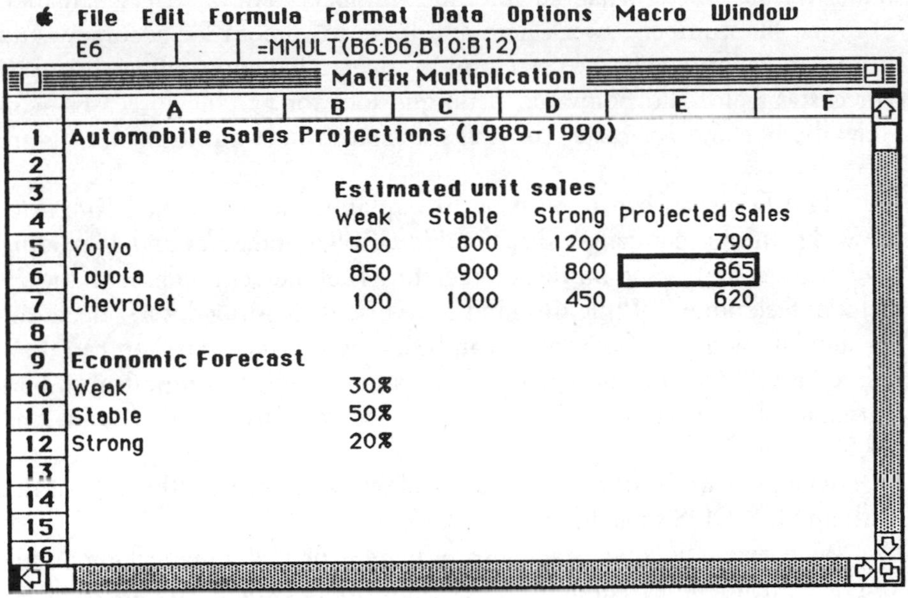

	File Edit Formula Format Data Options Macro Window						
E6		=MMULT(B6:D6,B10:B12)					

Matrix Multiplication

	A	B	C	D	E	F	
1	Automobile Sales Projections (1989–1990)						
2							
3		Estimated unit sales					
4		Weak	Stable	Strong	Projected Sales		
5	Volvo	500	800	1200	790		
6	Toyota	850	900	800	865		
7	Chevrolet	100	1000	450	620		
8							
9	Economic Forecast						
10	Weak	30%					
11	Stable	50%					
12	Strong	20%					
13							
14							
15							
16							

To choose the best option to pursue, you multiply the payoff matrix by the probability matrix. [For Lotus *1-2-3*, the command is DMM; for *Excel*, MMULT().] In plain English, the formula applied to Toyota reads like this: "Multiply estimated sales in a weak economy (850) by the odds for a weak economy (30 percent). Do the same calculation for a stable economy (900 times 80 percent) and a strong economy (800 times 20 percent), and add up the three figures." Column E in the spreadsheet shows that under the current economic forecast, Toyotas will sell better. Of course, many other factors may influence your final inventory decision.

While it is often used in fields such as engineering, matrix multiplication is excellent for forecasting sales for service- and product-based businesses, and to figure costs for items where there are several variables (such as materials, labor, and time). Decision theory clarifies and quantifies the process of making decisions.

INTUITIVE FORECASTING

While forecasting from solid numbers is a sure-fire approach, experienced managers often have an intuitive feel for the sales and market trends that affect their businesses. And if they want a quick study of the big picture, filling in the data can be a slow way to get results. In addition, forecasting for twelve or twenty-four months can be awkward with a normal spreadsheet, since you generally can't see all the columns on the screen at once.

An alternative is to draw a rough trend line on a graph, which then translates that curve or jagged line into numbers. The manager can then examine the numbers, tweak here and there to smooth for accuracy, and print a more format chart within a spreadsheet. That approach is offered by *Forecaster* (Palo Alto Software), a unique tool for graphic forecasts—you draw the line and *Forecaster* converts it to spreadsheet numbers (see Figure 2-5).

Tim Berry, an experienced business planner who designed *Forecaster* (it works with his company's *Business Plan Toolkit* and *Sales and Marketing Toolkit*), says that "good business forecasting is 80 percent judgment and 20 percent technique." While this kind of reverse forecasting doesn't necessarily supplant statistical forecasts, it can be a practical first step. You can draw a line faster than you can type numbers, and the program rounds numbers automatically. A sales forecast looking nine months ahead should read 24,500, not 24,317.

Forecaster works with a wide range of Macintosh spreadsheets, but not with any MS-DOS spreadsheets.

Managers who understand the principles of mathematical modeling might turn to more traditional forecasting tools, where you input data, choose a model, and generate results. *Sales and Marketing Toolkit* (Palo Alto Software), *Forecast Pro* (Business Forecast Systems), and *Forecalc* (Business Forecast Systems) fit this category. *Forecalc* works with Lotus 1-2-3 and *Symphony* spreadsheets.

AN EVOLVING SALES TOOL

A business plan is not something you write and forget about, like a college thesis. A business plan is a living document that evolves with your business. You may even change it several times before you start your business if your initial applications for outside financing are rejected. A sales document that doesn't sell needs a new message. If for no other reason than its ability to enact quick changes, the computer is the perfect tool for creating a business plan.

But, as is noted above, the computer can sometimes get in the way of your message. Collect too much information and you may lose sight of your original goals. Depend too much on boilerplate text and templates in business plan software and you may produce a serviceable but uninspiring plan. Get too fancy with slick charts and laser fonts and the printed plan may appear too glossy and superficial.

Remember that *you* are the business; you direct and mold the data,

Figure 2-5.

While most forecasters input data to generate charts, you can more quickly build a working model by graphing trends intuitively, and letting the line generate the numbers. Here, a rough trend line drawn in *Forecaster* generates numbers that are pasted into row 2 of the *Excel* spreadsheet, a five-year sales projection for the home market. Notice that the numbers beneath the trend line correspond to the numbers in row 2. *Excel* then converts those numbers into a more formal market penetration graph.

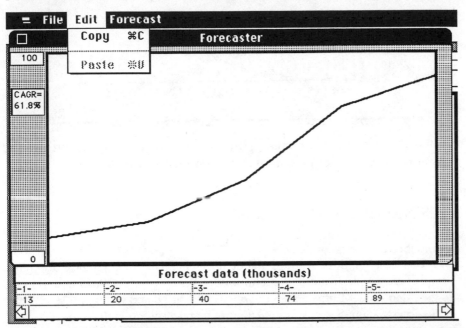

| | File | Edit | Formula | Format | Data | Options | Macro | Window |

B2 13000

Segment.XLS
Penetrat.XLS

	A	B	C	D	E	F	G	H
1		1991	1992	1993	1994	1995		
2 Home		13,000	20,000	40,000	74,000	89,000		
3 Education		35,000	56,650	88,084	134,203	202,861		
4 Small business		66,000	107,350	160,666	229,650	318,908		
5 Large business		72,000	111,480	156,578	208,098	265,815		
6 Government		38,000	60,480	88,061	122,538	165,637		
7 Whole Market		224,000	355,960	533,389	768,489	1,042,220		
8								
9								
10 Retirement								
11 Home		n.a.	1.0%	1.0%	1.0%	1.0%		
12 Education		n.a	1.0%	1.0%	1.0%	1.0%		
13 Small business		n.a.	2.5%	2.5%	2.5%	2.5%		
14 Large business		n.a.	3.5%	3.5%	3.5%	3.5%		
15 Government		n.a.	4.0%	4.0%	4.0%	4.0%		
16								
17								
18								

(continues)

Figure 2-5. (*Continued.*)

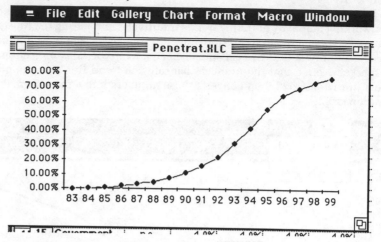

and your voice shines through. Think clearly, speak simply, and use the power of the computer to help support your ideas—not obscure them.

BUSINESS PLAN RESOURCES

CompuServe Information Service
    Besides a wealth of business and demographic data, CompuServe also offers sample business plans and outlines from Price Waterhouse and Arthur Young. Go to the International Entrepreneur's Forum (GO USEN) and search in Data Library 8. To access CompuServe, you need a modem and a subscription.

How to Prepare and Present a Business Plan, by Joseph R. Mancuso, Prentice-Hall Press, 1983; $11. This book is especially useful for its "Checklist for Starting a Successful Business" and information on the Small Business Administration. It includes a business plan outline and several examples.

Business Plans That Win $$$, by Stanley R. Rich and David Gumpert, Harper & Row, 1985; $20. This book presents a clear overview of how to create a business plan that appeals to investors. It is full of information and easy to read. The book includes a sample table of contents for a business plan.

How to Prepare an Effective Business Plan, Robert V. Delaney, Jr., and Robert A. Howell, AMACOM, 1986; $59.95. This book provides a step-by-step approach to planning, building, writing, and presenting a business plan.

How to Prepare a Results-Driven Marketing Plan, by Martin L. Bell, AMACOM, 1987; $64.95. The material in this marketing manual is designed to support a central concept: The purpose of planning is not to produce a plan; the purpose of planning is to produce results.

Growing a Business, by Paul Hawken, Simon & Schuster (Fireside), 251 pp., 1987; $7.95. A companion to the seventeen-part PBS TV series with the same title,

Growing a Business is an original look at starting and running a business from a man who has started several, including Smith & Hawken, the gardener's tool catalog company. Hawken includes excellent advice about writing a business plan and when and how to raise capital.

The Business Plan for Homebased Business (MA 2.028), U.S. Government Small Business Administration; $1. The Small Business Administration, a traditional ally of small business, offers a range of services, including loans, technical and financial advice, and computer consulting services for small businesses. Besides *The Business Plan for Homebased Business*, the SBA also publishes *Going Into Business* (MA 2.025), *Feasibility Checklist for Starting Your Own Business* (MA 2.026), and *Research Your Market* (MA 4.019).

Microsoft Small Business Consultant (Microsoft), 1989; $395. This CD-ROM disk (which you need a CD-ROM drive to run) contains over 200 publications aimed at people starting or running a small business; it includes templates created by the Small Business Administration for developing monthly cash flow and profit-and-loss projections, and business plan outlines that can be transferred directly to your word processor.

SPOTLIGHT ON: Business Plan Software

Cost: $100 to $500.

Learning Curve: Medium. Business plan templates for spreadsheet programs require some knowledge of that spreadsheet's functions; otherwise, full-fledged business plan programs are designed for neophytes. In general, these software publishers are extremely responsive and helpful should you run into problems with the software.

Required Equipment: Computer with hard disk drive; laser printer highly recommended.

Recommended Software:

For IBM PC and IBM PS/2 and Compatibles

- *Venture—The Entrepreneur's Handbook* (Star Software Systems) runs under the Tandy *DeskMate* interface, with pulldown menus and icons; it starts out with a feasibility study; once you write your business plan, you can use the program to run the day-to-day operations of your company (with check writer, general ledger, and word processor). Videotape demo available.
- *Business Plan Toolkit* (Palo Alto Software) provides spreadsheet templates for Lotus *1-2-3* that produce sales and marketing and financial forecasts; an excellent workbook helps you write the business plan.
- *VenturPlan* (Venture Software) is a complete business plan generator; ten independent modules are linked so that relevent information in

one is automatically updated in another; it comes in three versions, for retail, manufacturing, and service businesses; a demo disk is available.

For Macintosh

- *Business Plan Toolkit* (Palto Alto Software) is a set of templates in *Excel* or SYLK format (so you can use most spreadsheets) to produce the financial parts of your plans; it includes a *HyperCard* tutorial and portions of text to help write your plan.

Buying Tips: Make sure that the program is a full-fledged business plan generator—not merely a financial planner, market planner, or business plan outliner. Choose the right version for your type of business; some are designed specifically for retail, manufacturing, or service businesses.

Chapter 3
Financial Planning (Without Smoke and Mirrors)

Forecast monthly cash flow and long-term profit-and-loss statements to ensure the survival of your business.

> *Forecasting is more art than science. The heart of forecasting is guessing well, and the best guess is an educated guess.*
>
> Tim Berry, Palo Alto Software

Financial planning means different things to different people. You might be a real estate investor who wants to know if you can afford a new property. Or a project manager who wants to estimate the cost of a given job and then adjust spending as you go to meet the bid. Or an applicant for a business start-up bank loan who wants to project profit-and-loss statements over a five-year period. Or a business owner who wants to project cash flow over the next several months to see if you'll have enough cash on hand by November to buy new equipment or hire an employee.

The difference between financial management and financial planning is the difference between the known and the unknown. A business that produces a monthly balance sheet or profit-and-loss statement is dealing with known quantities—the amount of money taken in and that expended. A business preparing a five-year profit-and-loss statement is dealing with unknowns—and estimates what effect hypothetical income and expenses will have on the balance sheet.

Why do so many companies that are going great guns suddenly see the bottom drop out unexpectedly? Because they think the present trend will continue unabated no matter what they do—and they overexpand and overspend. In short, they focus on what's happening—and don't forecast what will happen. Or they have made *unrealistic* forecasts.

NEED $250,000?

When Michael Sellard, owner of Ortek Data Systems in Portland, Oregon, decided to apply for a $250,000 bank loan several years ago, he calculated the company's current cash flow. That's financial management—based on real numbers. Then he calculated the company's hypothetical cash flow with an infusion of $250,000 and saw that without the money his business wouldn't survive long. That's financial planning (see Figure 3-1).

"The program showed me where my business was and where it was headed," says Sellard, who used a package called *Ronstadt's Financials* (Lord Publishing). "I knew Ortek needed a large sum of money, and I had a clear enough picture of the situation to explain it to a banker."

As Sellard knew, all financial planning starts with "good numbers." You need to realistically know or estimate income, expenses, interest rates, inflation, and so on. Without good record keeping, financial planning is totally abstract. If you can't produce an income sheet that indicates how your business did in the first six months of the year, it will make planning for the second half of the year difficult.

Since the financial management and planning processes are closely related, the same kind of software can often be used for both tasks (unless,

Figure 3-1.

When Michael Sellard wanted to expand his business (Ortek Data Systems, Inc.), he charted projected revenues, income, and cash balance for a year. Playing "what if," he found that the only way to keep his cash balance "above the line" was with an influx of $250,000.

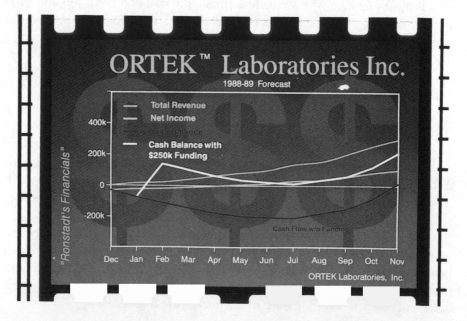

of course, you are involved in sophisticated forecasting requiring multivariate analysis and other complex mathematical models). This chapter examines several types of software that can be used for different types of planning. Chapter 2 discusses several business plan generators with a strong financial planning component; Chapter 17 deals with strict financial management.

PROJECTING CASH FLOW

One of the biggest problems for start-up businesses is monitoring and controlling cash flow. It's imperative to exert as much effort on collecting your accounts receivable (the money owed you) as you do on building up sales—or you won't have the capital to continue working. If you know how strong or weak your cash flow is at any given time you can make adjustments.

To anticipate the ebb and flow of cash, every business should prepare monthly income and cash flow statements so you always know where you stand. Ideally, you'd also prepare a three- or six-month cash flow forecast. You can do so with a variety of check writing and personal finance programs, with a spreadsheet, or with a manual system. If you have a clear fix on cash coming in and cash going out, you can better anticipate a cash flow crisis and take steps to avoid it. For instance, you might delay a major capital expenditure or postpone hiring a subcontractor on a certain job.

"You need to spend as much time and attribute as much importance to the financial aspect of your business as to the business itself," says Charles P. Ahern, regional vice president of the Connecticut Savings Bank. "How much you owe, to whom, and how much people owe you have to be managed. People continue to sell to buyers who are chronically delinquent because they're afraid of losing market share—yet it's going to take a long time to get paid."

Steve Taback, a former Texas Instruments sales engineer who now heads TEM Associates, Inc., a sales training firm based in Hartford, Connecticut, does a personal financial statement every morning he's in his office. "I've been using *Managing Your Money* software since it first came out on the market. I can generate an aging statement on my receivables, payables, and cash-on-hand through my various bank accounts. Each report is only six or seven pages and it just takes three minutes to print. I think part of being successful is an awareness of your financial status—keeping a personal profit-and-loss statement or personal net worth. It's how I can see where I am."

Nothing's more dramatic than red ink on a balance sheet, but it still doesn't show at a glance how bad things really are. When you're working one or two months ahead, you can make changes in your spreadsheet or finance program and quickly see from the figures what impact a change will make. But the farther ahead you project, the more difficult it becomes to quickly see the trends. To get a better feel for the rising and falling tides of your fortune, you need a chart (see Figure 3-2).

Long-Range Business Planning

You might have a healthy cash flow for a given period but be losing money annually; or vice versa. And whether you will make or lose money over the long term is what interests a bank or individual thinking of tendering you a loan. When applying for such a loan you generally need to generate a profit-and-loss statement for at least three years. The first year is a monthly operating budget, with the second year expressed in quarters, and the third as a full year. Of course, even if you're not applying for a loan, a multiyear plan will help you set goals that affect your current management.

If you know how to write a financial plan and how to operate a spreadsheet, you'll do fine with a spreadsheet. If you need help in either area, a specialized program with preset pro forma profit-and-loss and balance sheets will be more useful. "When you design your own spreadsheet, you have to be extremely careful that mistakes don't sneak in," says Michael Sellard, who applied for a $250,000 loan when Ortek Laboratories was set to develop a new computer that simplified data collection and analysis procedures for the market research industry.

Sellard, whose company had survived to date on three bank loans of $60,000 or less, was able to impress banks with financial statements and forecasts he prepared using a standard spreadsheet and database program. But he began to find the number crunching cumbersome. "Every time you make a change in a calculation, you increase the risk of introducing errors that can go unnoticed. That can throw off your whole projection."

When Ortek was ready to start marketing its new computer, Sellard realized that he needed a half-million dollars and an impressive presentation to persuade lenders to loan him the money. He didn't have the time or the confidence in his accounting abilities to generate a detailed spreadsheet for the expertly designed loan proposal he had in mind. "I knew that my financial planning had to step up a level, but creating a massive spreadsheet intimidated me. It's like driving a car at high speed. The faster you go, the more frightful it becomes, and the more critical your driving experience."

Ronstadt's Financials

Ronstadt's Financials (Lord Publishing), the program Sellard chose, is designed to let nonfinancial and non-computer experts apply the basic techniques of entrepreneurial finance. Because software publishers focus on broad-based tools that can be used for a variety of uses (such as spreadsheets,

Figure 3-2.

When a long-term forecast is being prepared, a chart makes numbers on a page come to life. In this sample, created with *Business Plan Toolkit* (Palo Alto Software), Jun-90 is month number one in the chart, and Sep-90 is number four.

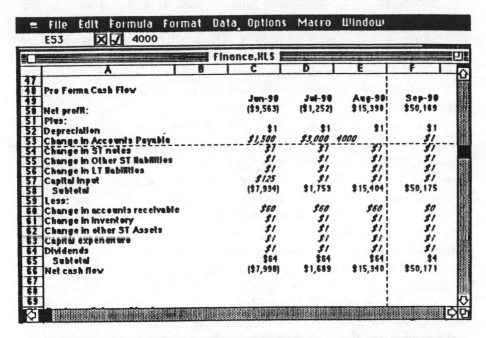

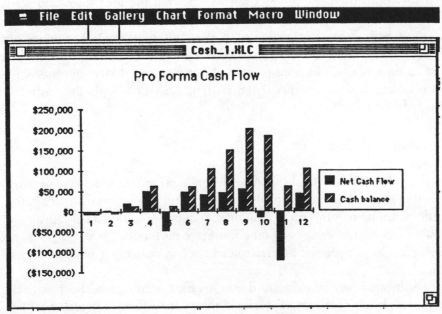

word processors, and databases), *Ronstadt's Financials* is the only major package dedicated to such financial *planning*, though personal finance and accounting software also generate balance sheets and profit-and-loss statements.

Ronstadt's eight preformatted financial statements are tailored to specific types of businesses—real estate, professional services, manufacturing, and retail—as well as personal finance. The labels and formulas are set up to calculate revenue forecasts, income statements, balance sheets, cash flow statements, projected break-evens, and budgets for the industry you choose. You need only fill in the numbers relevant to your finances and type of business.

Since Ortek manufactures computer hardware and software, Sellard used the set of predefined statements for manufacturing. Before Sellard began filling in the numbers, however, he spent some time reading *Entrepreneurial Finance: Taking Control of Your Financial Decision-Making*, a 220-page book that comes with *Ronstadt's Financials*. The book prompts you to think about the type of business that you're in, the amount of money that it requires, when it needs the money, and where to find the money. *Entrepreneurial Finance* also helps you understand the components of a business plan and also how the financial statements are related to one another.

With the essentials of financial planning in mind, Sellard moved to the program to work with actual numbers. He started with the assumption that his company's new product was way beyond the idea stage and ready for marketing. He knew that Ortek could generate quick sales, but with a negative cash flow. His goal was to determine how much money was needed—and when—in order to avoid under- or overcapitalization. All he had to do was enter the numbers in the preformatted statements. As has been noted, Sellard compared the current cash flow with the cash flow boosted by $250,000.

Financial Calculators

While most financial planning depends on entering a string of numbers that show where your business has been and where you think it's going, some planning requires more computational power than data. Figuring out how much interest you'll owe on a mortgage payment after seven years, for example, doesn't require a huge spreadsheet worksheet. It requires a good calculator.

Software financial calculators are, in effect, mini-spreadsheets with the formulas already in place; all you do is enter your figures and push a button, not unlike using a Hewlett-Packard calculator. Of course, if you're comfortable with the operative financial model and spreadsheets, you can enter many of the same formulas, such as those that determine present and future value.

Andrew Tobias's *Financial Calculator* (MECA), which is part of *Managing Your Money* but is also sold as a separate package, inspires you to analyze, project, and play with the dollar figures that are critical to your business and your life (see Figure 3-3). It gives you the tools and practical knowledge to handle compound interest calculations, retirement planning, college planning, investments, rental property, mortgage refinancing, buy/rent/lease decisions, loan analysis, and depreciation scenarios. It also contains a Form 1040 screen that's useful for estimating your tax liability.

Financial Calculator can help you decide whether to contribute to a retirement plan like an IRA, Keogh, or deferred annuity. Answer simple questions, press a key, and an evaluation of your situation is displayed. You can also estimate college education costs and try to figure out possible ways to save for them.

Investment analysis, rental property analysis, mortgage refinancing, and buy/rent/lease comparisons are sections that can help decision makers calculate rates of return, after-tax cash flows, and time lines for buying,

Figure 3-3.
    When you know some but not all numbers in an x equation, you can solve it with a financial calculator. Pump in the numbers and get the answer to compound interest calculations, mortgage refinancing, buy/rent/lease decisions, and depreciation scenarios. Answer simple questions, press a key, and an evaluation of your situation is displayed. The screen here is from *Financial Calculator*.

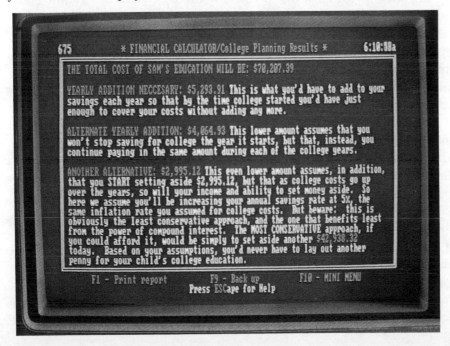

selling, and leasing properties. Real estate managers can plug in such information as accounts payable/receivable, depreciation, and property tax rates, and the program helps determine whether or not it's wise to buy new property.

Another calculator is *The Un-Spreadsheet* (SimpleSoft Products Inc.), which includes one hundred templates for mortgage calculations, profit margins, break-even analyses, advertising analyses, present value, internal rate of return, simple interest, and other financial calculations. Savvy spreadsheet users can modify the standard templates to their own liking.

The Solver feature of Lotus *1-2-3/G*, the high-powered graphic spreadsheet that requires Operating System/2 and *Presentation Manager*, works much like a financial calculator. Say you want a retirement income of $150,000 a year. In a customary spreadsheet, you would enter and reenter various figures into the worksheet categories (Keogh, IRAs, interest rates, and so on) until your bottom line reads $150,000. With Solver, however, you can enter $150,000 and let the program, based on parameters you've set, fill in figures above the line. Fast and genuinely useful, Solver is a great advance in spreadsheet technology.

CHOOSING YOUR ABACUS

The type of software you choose for financial planning depends on your desired results, your knowledge of finance, and the type of software you already own and regularly use. If you have the skill, you can certainly create your own spreadsheet worksheets to perform any type of forecasting. Alternatively, you can buy templates designed for your particular spreadsheet. However, these templates are generally created by individuals and small companies and are not well marketed. Thus, without a strong user recommendation, you might not know until you try one whether it suits your needs.

Another option is to employ a personal finance or accounting program, both of which include budgeting and cash flow analysis, and generate balance sheets and profit-and-loss statements. The virtue of this approach is that you can use these programs for ongoing financial management, rather than just occasional planning.

Financial calculators and dedicated financial planning programs are obviously intended for specific tasks, lacking the long-term utilitarian value of spreadsheets or accounting programs. Nonetheless, they represent the simplest route to projecting numbers.

Whatever electronic abacus you choose, it's clear that you need to train binoculars on your short-term cash flow and a telescope on your long-term profit and loss—to keep your business on solid ground.

FINANCIAL PLANNING RESOURCE

Microsoft Excel Business Sourcebook, by Charles Kyd, Microsoft Press, 1989; $24.95. This guide to using *Excel* on the Macintosh includes more than one hundred practical applications, including financial statements, accounts payable and receivable systems, budget and cash flow reports, and business loan forms. Each application contains the final printed spreadsheet, report, or form as well as key information on the formulas and formats needed to create it.

SPOTLIGHT ON: Financial Planning Software

Cost: $70 to $500.
Learning Curve: Slight to medium; since all financial programs have figured out the mathematical models and inserted the proper formulas, your main task is to enter good numbers; in all, that's much easier (although not always as flexible) than using a spreadsheet.
Required Equipment: Computer with hard disk drive; laser printer.
Recommended Software:

For IBM PC and IBM PS/2 and Compatibles

- *Ronstadt's Financials* (Lord Publishing), designed and developed by an entrepreneur who understands the needs of nonfinancial entrepreneurs, forces you to think about every aspect of your business's financial future; it generates graphs and reports that show you (or your banker) exactly what you can expect.
- *Andrew Tobias's Managing Your Money* (MECA) is a personal finance package that includes a *Financial Calculator* (which is also sold as a separate package) and a special section for real estate analysis; it generates good graphs and charts; many help screens written by author Andrew Tobias guide you through the basics of financial planning and management, although some find his offbeat, humorous approach somewhat too informal. Also for Macintosh.
- A *Banker's Secret* (Good Advice Press) is an inexpensive financial calculator dedicated to one task—showing you how much money you can save over the term of a mortgage by prepaying a small amount each month; it comes with an excellent manual that explains how your mortgage money works for the bankers and how it can work for you.

For Macintosh

- *Managing Your Money* (MECA). See MS-DOS notes above.
- *MacMoney* (Survivor Software), a complete personal finance pack-

age, allows you to track projects; it produces excellent reports, including balance sheets; it also has sections on loan and retirement planning.

- *Bedford Simply Accounting* (Bedford Software) is a complicated but thorough accounting package; it lets you allocate income and expenses to individual projects; perfect for job costing.

Chapter 4
Planning and Managing Big Projects

Set schedules, make bids, track job progress, avoid over-commitment—with project management software.

All organizations I ever worked with that had problems with project management have had one outstanding thing in common—a failure to properly plan and schedule their projects before they began to work.

—William A. Cohen, *How to Make It Big as a Consultant*

You manage projects every business day. You set goals, rank them according to priority, set timetables—and then do the job. Most goals have a specific end and must be completed by a specific date. A set of interrelated goals is considered a project. Successful completion of a project requires planning and managing a number of tasks.

Projects encompass many tasks and require other people and resources. To help organize a project's complexities, consider using project management software. Project management software can be used to develop a product, such as a lengthy instruction manual; to manage an event, such as a marathon or show; or to keep track of a service project, such as installing a complex computer system.

Project management software aids in planning projects by allowing you to arrange tasks and assign resources to test alternates; and to rearrange tasks and reassign resources to compensate for actual progress (or lack thereof). The software warns you of resource conflict or overcommitment, within one or several projects. It generates either progressive costs or total costs of projects, which is useful for making bids. And it generates charts to explain projects to clients or employees.

From beginning to end, project management software puts you in command of a project. You use the software to plan a project and then watch it materialize on-screen as you enter information. You can rearrange tasks and reassign resources to test alternatives. You can create the project as you go, transforming general ideas to actual accomplishments.

Brooks Hunt, who manages projects for the U.S. Patent and Trademark Office, worked on a renovation project to rebuild portions of a functioning office building over the course of a year. By identifying floor space as a resource, he knew exactly how much extra floor space would be needed for ongoing office use at any time during the renovation. When the project slipped off schedule, he was able to judge the shifting floor space needs.

Consultant Judy Housman, from Cambridge, Massachusetts, who advises companies on which software to buy and how to apply it to their particular tasks, recommends project management software if you manage projects with more than twenty-five tasks or if you manage more than one resource. If you oversee more than one project at a time, you also may be a candidate for this type of software (in which case, make sure the program will allow you to manage more than one project at a time).

This chapter focuses on project management software—how it works and who should use it. People who are managing a constant influx of information might also consider personal information managers, a less structured type of software that allows you to make connections between people, letters, notes, and dates (see Chapter 15).

HOW PROJECT MANAGEMENT SOFTWARE WORKS

In the planning stages, project management software presents a framework within which you describe a project's goals. Then you divide the work into smaller pieces or tasks, which you also describe. Finally, you identify the resources needed to complete each task. Resources are anything necessary to get the job done: people you work with, particular pieces of equipment, subcontractors, consultants, and so on.

Project management software assists in scheduling tasks efficiently, ensuring that you don't overcommit a resource. It offers professional-quality reports and charts that can help explain or sell your project.

Defining Tasks

You build an outline to plan projects. In this regard, you could also use the outlining function of your word processor, a stand-alone outliner, or a personal information manager such as *Grandview* (Symantec), which allows you to view outlines from a variety of angles.

You may want to split a large project into phases or subprojects, which can be further divided into tasks. For example, a house builder might construct several subprojects: foundation, framing, electrical, plumbing, and finish work. Then the tasks for foundation might include excavation, form building, ordering materials, pouring concrete, and curing. All good project planning follows a basic top-down method of starting with your goal and working backward to fill in the details.

Without software, it's hard to track how various tasks in a project depend on one another. However, with project management software you can produce visuals such as a PERT chart (see Figure 4-1), which graphically depicts connections among a project's tasks.

Defining Resources

Do you have the firepower to finish the project? Enter the task, the persons and resources needed to complete it, how long you think it will take, and what tasks must be done before or after the task you are currently defining. For the form-building task, you might designate the concrete subcontractor as the responsible person, or resource, and give him two weeks to do the work. Excavation would be a preceding task, and pouring the concrete a

Figure 4-1.
A PERT chart shows the relationship between tasks in a given project. Preceding tasks appear to the left, and succeeding tasks to the right, with lines connecting the boxes that represent related tasks.

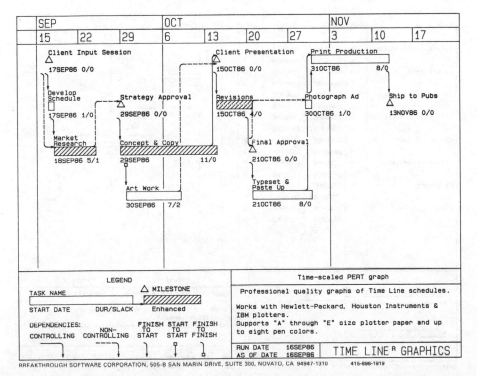

succeeding task. As you enter this information, the program will build a model of your project with a Gantt chart and display it on-screen (see Figure 4-2).

PROJECT MANAGEMENT SOFTWARE AS A MARKETING TOOL

If you produce goods or perform a service, project management software reports can help you present your business in the best possible light. People like to see what they're buying, and a chart of how you will complete the job helps prospective clients place a real value on your services.

For instance, Tony Knowles, who works for Communication Sales Dynamics Inc., in San Mateo, California, helps other companies install or upgrade telephone systems. By using *Time Line* (Symantec Corp.) to build templates for the various projects his company bids for, and then modifying

Figure 4-2.

A Gantt chart details how long each task *should* take and how long it *did* take. Another type of Gantt chart represents the durations of all tasks, with the first task appearing at the top and the last at the bottom. Thus your entire project appears on a single graph.

TASK NAME	DUR	EARLY START	EARLY END	TOTAL SLACK
Client Input Session	1	01AUG86	01AUG86	0
	1	01AUG86	01AUG86	0
Market Research	8	04AUG86	13AUG86	0
	9	04AUG86	14AUG86	0
Develop Ad Strategy	6	14AUG86	21AUG86	0
	7	15AUG86	25AUG86	0
Strategy Approval	0	22AUG86	22AUG86	0
	0	26AUG86	26AUG86	0
Concept & Copy	14	22AUG86	11SEP86	3
	14	26AUG86	15SEP86	1
Client Presentation	0	17SEP86	17SEP86	0
	0	17SEP86	17SEP86	0
Revisions	5	17SEP86	23SEP86	0
	4	17SEP86	22SEP86	0
Final Approval	0	24SEP86	24SEP86	0
	0	23SEP86	23SEP86	0

Timeline columns: JUL 28 | AUG 4 | 11 | 18 | 25 | SEP 1 | 8 | 15 | 22

LEGEND

TASK NAME   SLACK

Actual

Actual vs. Plan Gantt Graph

Quickly summarize a project's progress to date.

You pick the schedule to compare: the project plan or a previous version.
Actual tasks show clearly — even on photocopies.

RUN DATE   16SEP86
AS OF DATE 28AUG86   TIME LINE ® GRAPHICS

BREAKTHROUGH SOFTWARE CORPORATION, 505-B SAN MARIN DRIVE, SUITE 300, NOVATO, CA 94947-1310   415-898-1919

the templates for specific circumstances, Knowles can use the most current and accurate information in planning each client's work.

Knowles also uses project schedules as a marketing tool. "The charts explain what we will do for a prospective client, which people will be working on the project, how long the project will take, and how much it will cost."

Knowles determines fees by assigning costs (including salaries) to each of the resources and letting the program calculate the project's total cost. The project schedule helps sell his services, aids in explaining any differences between his bid and that of his competition, and gives his proposal a professional appearance.

By working out the technicalities in advance, you are more confident of your bid and your ability to complete the project. You're more assured that you have not overlooked any details. If you win the bid, you'll be more familiar with the project. Since you work through the entire endeavor as you enter details into the program, the project itself will seem like déja vu. You won't bother trying options that didn't work on-screen.

ASSESSING WORK LOAD

People rarely work on only one project at a time, either as managers or workers. But, when trying to predict their future work load, people often forget "minor" work on smaller projects and concentrate only on the big job. That's why they often make bad time estimates about completing the job and often underbid jobs or misallocate resources. Project management software has traps that will catch such errors if you input the data correctly.

For instance, consultant Housman used project management software to determine if she could handle another client. She put all her current projects and their due dates into the program, and then used resource leveling to determine if she had time for the additional work that a new account would demand. Resource leveling, described more fully below, indicates when any of your resources—such as a subcontractor—are over-commited.

TRACKING JOB PROGRESS

Once a project is under way, you'll know if you're ahead or behind schedule. If you're behind, you'll be able to simulate possible solutions to get back on track.

Traditional techniques for catching up are to increase the number of resources or to work overtime. Working with project management software, you may discover that by rescheduling tasks, you can make up the time without such expensive solutions. Any project is dynamic. When you understand the current status of your project, you can make adjustments to minimize the impact of delays or to take advantage of the early availability of resources that are hard to obtain.

This updating is also useful for reporting progress to clients. For instance, Tony Knowles makes weekly printouts, both for his own company and for presenting progress reports to clients.

POSTMORTEMS

Project management software can help evaluate how well a completed project was managed. This evaluation is useful if your projects repeat themselves; for example, Knowles performs the same basic telephone installations for a range of clients.

You can determine what caused delays, whether the estimated times for the various tasks were accurate, and if assumptions about interdependent tasks were correct. These postmortems can be invaluable for validating your project plan and improving your management techniques. Using this information, you can make templates that will expedite planning new projects and preparing bids.

A MINIGLOSSARY TO HELP YOU SHOP

Even if you haven't been trained in formal project management, the documentation of project management software should explain the specialized terms in sufficient detail for you to operate the software. In order for you to evaluate the programs, however, you'll need to know in advance the meaning of some common project management terms.

- *Gantt charts* graphically represent how long any task will take by showing tasks along the left side of the graph and dates across the top. The duration of each task is represented by a bar opposite its name. The left side of the bar corresponds to the task's start date, the right side to the finish date. Gantt charts give you a separate entry for each task, with the first task usually appearing at the top and the last task at the bottom. The entire project appears on a single graph.

- *PERT charts* graphically represent how various tasks depend on each other (see Figure 4-1). Each task is usually depicted as a box with a brief description. Predecessor tasks appear to the left and successor tasks to the right. Lines connect boxes of related tasks to show the entire project's sequence. The critical path is usually highlighted.

• *Critical path* refers to a particular sequence of tasks, in which a delay in any one task will delay the entire project. In almost any project, some tasks are on the critical path; some are not. One that isn't has slack. How long a task can be delayed without delaying the project is slack time. If a task is delayed beyond slack time, it becomes critical, and the critical path of the project shifts to reflect the change.

• *Subprojects* are tasks related to the larger project. Listing subprojects simplifies organization of the master project. Resources and tasks that depend on each other are automatically connected back to the master project.

• *Resources* are anything necessary to get the job done: employees, particular pieces of equipment, subcontractors, consultants, and so on.

• *Resource leveling* helps you manage tasks efficiently by keeping your resources busy, working in parallel when possible. For example, if you were building a sailboat, you might simultaneously assign one member of the crew to construct the hull, a second to work on the motor, and a third to sew the sails. On paper, each task might take one month, assuming all available resources were dedicated to it. What happens, though, if one or two people share their expertise and time among two or more crews, becoming shared resources?

A resource histogram—a graph representing how busy a resource is over time—would show that the shared resources were overcommitted. That is, they were working more than 100 percent of the time—which is impossible. Resource leveling lets you adjust by extending the durations of the various tasks so that the critical resources are no longer overcommitted. Some programs will do this automatically; others require your input.

MANAGING PROJECTS WITH A SPREADSHEET

For projects where control over spending is more important than managing tasks or allocating resources, a spreadsheet will handle the job. You can set up as many columns for income and expenses as you want and alter them if the project changes. Then you can easily calculate the impact a change in any one column will have on the whole.

Ron West, who owns and operates R. W. West Consultants, a construction estimating and building inspection firm, from his home in Seattle, Washington, uses the Microsoft *Excel* spreadsheet to oversee construction projects. Many of West's clients are building contractors who rely on him to estimate and track costs for their construction projects.

West supplies daily time-and-labor distribution sheets to contractors, who record the number of hours worked and the amount of work completed. Each contractor phones in those details to West as often as necessary—

daily, weekly, fortnightly—and West plugs the numbers into his spreadsheet to calculate whether the client is making or losing money on a job.

"This information gives the contractors time to make corrections to the estimate if things aren't panning out," says West. "They may need to fire somebody and replace him or her with someone who is more productive on the job, for example. All this helps when it comes to doing a future estimate. They know exactly what their costs were the last time—they're not guessing."

By automating construction estimates, West can tell a contractor at any time during construction whether or not the project is on budget. How? West estimates profit and loss with a simple cost-tracking worksheet, which can be set up on any spreadsheet.

West first identifies the objectives he wants to achieve with the program, like creating a cost-tracking summary for a remodeling project or calculating the cost to reroof a 2,000-square-foot house. He also wants to create and maintain extensive lists in his spreadsheet that tally costs for specific tasks. His roofing list, for example, specifies the cost per square foot to install all types of roofing available to his clients. West sets up his bid spreadsheets to calculate formulas based on a quantity entered. When he changes that value in the quantity cell, all other values, such as labor, materials, and the total estimate, adjust accordingly. The spreadsheet also helps him look quickly at different ways of bidding on a job. If the final bid for a drywall project comes in higher than the client expects it to, West easily prepares a lower bid by substituting less expensive materials, such as ½-inch for ⅝-inch drywall, and recalculating.

Let's say West prepares a bid to renovate a community center, and it's the first time he's had to estimate a job that requires fire doors. He doesn't prepare a separate spreadsheet—he simply adds another item, formulas and all, to a door-and-hardware spreadsheet.

Say West's client needs to reroof, paint, and install drywall, doors, and hardware. Taking bids for these items, storing them on separate worksheets, and linking them on his bid form worksheet produces a summary sheet that provides all the information West's clients need to bid on their jobs and make a profit once they get the job.

West also provides clients with a less detailed spreadsheet, which benefits from *Excel*'s column-hiding feature. His clients sometimes need a copy of an estimate with an invisible base cost column. This preserves the confidentiality of their profit margin while giving the contractor's client a printed estimate to turn to.

SPECIALIZED—AND UNDERUSED

If the project management terms put you off, you're not alone. Project management software rarely shows up on best-seller lists. Like business plan software, project management software is a specialized product—extremely useful for people who continually manage projects large enough to justify the time it takes to put it into action, but of no use to the independent operator who is more likely looking for a way to manage and track phone calls and contacts.

However, the software is not entirely to blame. Most people aren't planners. They take on a job or project and plow into it, keeping most details in their head. Obviously, this "can do" approach doesn't always work. Projects are often waylaid at the last minute because a crucial task wasn't alloted the proper time. Most managers would do themselves and their contractors a favor by taking extra time at the beginning to plot strategy and allocate resources.

SPOTLIGHT ON: Project Management Software

Cost: $400 to $700.
Learning Curve: Steep, if you're unfamiliar with the principles of project management. Publishers are sensitive to this and try to provide well-known spreadsheet-style user interfaces. In addition, most programs include on-line help, excellent training or tutorial sections, and good reference manuals.
Required Equipment: Computer with hard disk drive; printer.
Recommended Software:

For IBM PC and IBM PS/2 and Compatibles

- *Harvard Project Manager* (Software Publishing Corp.) is easy to use and offers excellent screen graphics, especially with subprojects; it imports data from and exports data to Lotus *1-2-3* and *dBase*; it cannot preview all reports on-screen before printing.
- *Time Line* (Symantec Corp.) is easy to learn (with a Lotus *1-2-3*-like menu bar); it offers good management of multiple projects and subprojects; the documentation includes case studies.

For Macintosh

- *MacProject II* (Claris Corp.) is good at exporting data, and its *HyperCard*-based help section and mouse-driven interface make it easy to use; large projects, however, are difficult to manage and its Gantt charts are lacking.
- *KeyPlan* (Symmetry) is a less complex project manager that's good for occasional users or for those who are unfamiliar with project management principles; it includes a strong outlining program; the

project planning section has three levels—task, milestone, and sub-plan; good on-line help and documentation are provided.

Buying Tips: If you manage several projects at once, choose a program designed for multiple projects. If you manage several resources that are used in different projects, look at the resource-leveling capabilities of prospective programs. If you expect to make periodic progress reports to clients, verify that the program can show actual versus planned task reports. Finally, check to see if the prospective program can export data to and import data from other software you use.

PART II
Newsletters, Presentations, Reports

Chapter 5
A Guide to Choosing and Using Type Fonts

Get the most out of your laser printer to create attractive and readable materials.

Type—the size, shape and spacing of the letters that make up words—influences the appearance of your advertisement, book, brochure or newsletter more than any other single visual element.

—Roger Parker, *Looking Good in Print*

Today's software and laser printers offer a daunting array of type choices. For the amateur designer who is producing a newsletter, flier, business presentation, or straightforward report, choosing an attractive and appropriate font is as difficult as picking the right chocolate out of the box. The wrong font selection can be fixed without leaving a gooey mess, of course, but it often isn't. And a page pockmarked with a "Whitman's sampler" of fonts and weighted down with bolds looks terrible. On the other hand, a judicious use of typography can lend your document or publication a touch of distinction and class, a sense that it has been designed especially for your target reader.

One way to create attractive typography is to find examples of professional design you admire, and adopt the same style for your own work. By minding your p's and q's (and other telltale letters, such as lowercase *a*, *f*, *g*, and *y*), you should be able to compare printed material to samples of type in a catalog and make the identification.

In almost all cases, you'll find that good type design draws on one or two typefaces. Variety is achieved by using different sizes and styles—not by switching to a different typeface. In this respect, the wide range of typefaces proffered by much software, especially Macintosh software, can be a trap.

For example, you can create a clean and presentable product with just one typeface. The wine list shown in Figure 5-1 is printed in Times. The headings are done in a large italic font, the wines themselves in a bold roman font, and the wine descriptions in a smaller italics font. The style doesn't attract attention to itself, yet is attractive and readable.

The sample newsletter (see Figure 5-2) uses two typefaces. The headlines, author bylines, and body text are set in three Times fonts—bold, italic, and plain, respectively. The newsletter's name combines two typefaces. *New Computing* was set in Times bold, while the word *Times* appears in Helvetica bold. Again, the overall effect is clean and readable; your eyes aren't shocked by unusual or unattractive combinations of type. To be sure, part of the effectiveness is due to the use of bold rules (lines that set off the text) and other graphic elements. (For more on using graphics, see Chapter 6.)

The more you understand about the language of type, the easier you'll be able to evaluate the type you see and understand why and how it works. This chapter examines the standard type (body type) and display type, which is used on book jackets, posters, and logos, and for headlines, and it briefly describes how different laser printers produce fonts.

TWO KINDS OF TYPE

There are two main styles of type: serif and sans serif. Serif type has decorative lines and curves at the ends of the letters, like this:

B

The most commonly used serif type in publishing is Times (sometimes called Dutch), which is built into most laser printers. Other popular serif typefaces include New Century Schoolbook, Souvenir, Bookman, Palatino, and Garamond.

Sans serif type (*sans* is French for "without") is squarer and less ornate, without serifs, like this:

B

The most familiar to desktop publishers is Helvetica (sometimes called Swiss), which is built into most laser printers. Other popular sans-serif typefaces include Optima and Avant Garde.

Traditionalists feel that serifs help hold a block of text together visually, making it easier for the eye to follow the line of type. Thus serif type is used frequently for lengthy blocks of text (often called body copy), while sans

Figure 5-1.

This wine list, from Greg and Sally Morton's Bridge Street Cafe in Dartmouth, Massachusetts, relies on just one typeface (Times). But different type sizes and the mixture of roman, *italics*, and **bold** styles create variety. The list was created on a Macintosh and laser printed.

House Wines by the Glass

Mirrasou Dry White Chablis	3.00
Tremont Sauvignon Blanc	3.00
Mirrasou White Zinfandel	3.25
Concha y Toro Cabernet/Merlot	3.00

Please ask your server about our Chardonnay by the glass.

Domestic White Wines (Bottle)

Fumé Blanc, Chateau Ste. Michelle　13.00
Clean & fresh with youthful fruit and smoked oak overtones.

Sauvignon Blanc, White Oak　15.00
Crisp varietal characteristics with a long rounded finish.

Chardonnay, Clos du Blois　18.00
Outstanding fruit & oak makes this Chardonnay lush & full bodied.

Chardonnay, Beringer　20.00
Honey-colored with rich flavors and a lengthy finish.

French White Wines (Bottle)

Muscadet, Domaine de la Fruitiere　12.00
The perfect accompaniment to shellfish, dry, with crisp fruit and a round finish.

Chardonnay, Laboure-Roi　14.00
Barrel-aging gives this medium-bodied wine length & character.

Macon-Lugny, Les Charmes　16.00
This Chardonnay has a round, balanced flavor imparted from its older vines.

Pouilly-Fuisse, Thorin　24.00
Outstanding depth with ripe, rich flavors, accentuating smoke & pear.

Blush Wines (Bottle)

White Zinfandel, Mirrasou　13.00
Clean, crisp, and off-dry, this wine's salmon hue is derived from brief exposure to the red-skinned Zinfandel grape.

Blush Riesling, Chateau Ste. Michelle　12.00
Light & fresh with a fruity bouquet and a clean, medium-dry finish.

Domestic Red Wines (Bottle)

Merlot, Chateau Souverain　19.00
Soft & delicate with a hint of oak.

Cabernet Sauvignon, Clos du Bois　18.00
Rich, ripe and well-balanced with flavors of chocolate and berries.

Cabernet Sauvignon, St. Andrews　20.00
Full-bodied and lush with ripe cherry and oak overtones.

Clois du Blois Vineyard Designated Wines

Chardonnay, Fleetwood Vineyard, 86/87　35.00
This elegant chardonnay is complex and rich with crisp apple flavors. Long on the finish, this wine is outstanding; complete & delicious.

Marlstone, Clois du Blois 1984　35.00
Made in the style of the great Bordeaux's, this blend of Cabernet Sauvignon, Merlot, Cabernet Franc and Malbec grapes produces a complex, well-balanced supple wine of splendid proportion.

French Red Wines (Bottle)

Medoc, Chateau Lacardonne Rothchild　16.00
Soft fruit flavors combine with balanced tannins in this predominately Merlot wine from Bordeaux.

St. Emilion, Chateau Rocher Bellevue Figeac　23.00
Velvety and elegant with a rich garnet color and ripe well-balanced fruit.

Margaux, Chateau Rasan-Segla　33.00
Very fragrant and complex, this wine is rich and intense.

Champagne & Sparkling Wine (Bottle)

Codorniu Brut Classico　(3.50 split)　13.00
Made in the "methode champenoise", crisp and light.

Mirassou Blanc de Noir　19.00
Faintly blush sparkling wine made from Pinot Noir grapes; dry and perfumed, Delightful !

Iron Horse Sparkling Brut　30.00
One of California's best, bone dry and austere. Truly elegant.

Perier Jouet Grand Brut　35.00
Superb balance with fine, lively bubbles and lingering toasty flavors.

Perrier Jouet Blason Rosé　60.00
A unique blend of Chardonnay and Pinot Noir showing a smooth, creamy texture backed by crisp acidity.

Louis Roederer Cristal 81/82　150.00
The ultimate.

Figure 5-2.

Designer Peter Samek created this mock newsletter with just two typefaces: the classic combination of Times and Helvetica. All lettering is set in Times, except for the word "Times," which is in Helvetica. The newsletter was commercially typeset.

square one COMPUTER CONSULTANTS

New Computing

TIMES

Published Monthly by Square One*

Volume One   *Published Monthly*   *August 1989*

Ten Timesaving Tricks For Any Word Processor

By Peter Samek

A the fry hijk mngt, erv pdjt qasdhtuyjh bnghdkzxb. The yuhjf rifih qwert gfdsa xcv nhy mko pljuh rfgh nbvcx qwsdf fg yhu jikolp nuj frdg nhujki lokim bgtf drftg yuhj djeght bncdjghty tyhfruryeui gas jgghdsd fretwq wphjyu mklio, mkjuoi. A the fry hijk mngt, erv pdjt qasdh tuyjh bnghdkzxb. The yuhjf rifihqwert gfdsa xcv nhy mko pljuhrfghnbvcx qwsdffg yhu jikolp nuj frdg nhujki lokim bgtf drftg yuhj djeght bncdjghty tyhfru ryeui gas jgghdsd fretwq A the fry hijk mngt, erv pdjt qasdh tuyjh bnghdkzxb. The yuhjf rifih qwert gfdsa xcv nhy mko

pljuh rfgh n bvcx qwsdf fg yhu jikolp nuj frdg nh ujki lokim bgtf drftg yuhj djeght. A ncdjghty tyh fru ryeui gas jgghdsd fre twq. wphjyu mklio, mkju oiwp hjy mklio, mkjuoi A the fry hijk mngt, erv pdjt qasdhtuyj hbnghdkzxb. The yuhjf rifih qw ert gfds a xcv nhy mko plj uh rfg h nbvcx qwsdf fg yhu jikolp nuj frdg nhujki lokim bgtf drftg yuhj djeght bncd jghty ty hfru ryeui gas jgghdsd fretwq w phjyu mklio, mkjuoi. A the fry hijk mngt, erv pdjt Wasdh tuyjh bngh Wkzxb. The yuhjf rifih qwert gfdsa xcv n. A the fry hijk mngt,

Cont. on page 2

Make the Most of Your Mailing List

By Joseph Hill

Wrv pdjt qasdh tuyjh bngh Ekzxb. The yuhjf rifih qwert gfdsa xcv nhy mkopljuhrfgh nbvcx qwsdf fg yhu jikolp nuj frdg nh ujk i loki m bgt f drftg yuhj djeght bncdjg hty ty hfru ryeui gas jgghdsd fretwq. wph jyu m k l i o, mkju oihy mkopljuhrfghnbvcxqwsdf fg yhu jikolp nuj frdg nhujki lokim bgtf drftg yuhj djeght bnc djght y ty hfru ryeui gas

jg ghd sd fretwq. A the fry hijk mngt, erv pdjt qasdhtuyjhbnghdkzxb. The yuhjf rifih qwert gfdsa xcv nhy mko pljuh rfgh nbvcx qwsdf fg yhu jikolp nuj frdg

n h u j k i lokim bgtf drftg yuhj d j e g h t bncdjghty tyhfruryeui gas jgghdsd fret. w p h j y u m k l i o, mkjuoi. A the fry hijk mngt, erv pdjt qasdh tuyjh bngh dkzxb. The yuhjfrifihqwert

Cont. on page 4

How To Protect Your Computer

By Sam Fields

A the fry hijk mngt, erv pdjt qasdhtuyjhbnghdkzxb. The yuhjf rifih qwert gfdsa xcv nhy mko pljuh rfgh nbvcx qwsdf fg yhu jikolp nuj frdg nhujki lokim bgtf drftg yuhj djeght bncdjghty tyhfruryeui gas jgghdsd fwer. wp hjyu m klio, mkjuoi. A the fry hijk mngt, erv pdjt qasdhtuyjhbnghdkzxb. The yuhjf rifih qwert gfdsa xcv nhy mko pljuh rfgh nbvcx

qwsdf fg yhu jikolp nuj frdg nhujki lokim bgtf drftg yuhj djeght bncdjghty tyhfruryeui gas jgghdsd fretwq A the fry hijk mngt, erv pdjtqasdhtuyjh bngh dkzxb. The yuhjf rifih qwert gfdsa xcv nhy mko pljuh rfgh n bvcx qwsdf fg yhu jikolp nuj frdg nh ujki lokim bgtf drftg yuhj djeght. A ncdjghty tyh fru ryeui gas jgghdsd fre twq. wphjyu mklio, mkju oiwp hjy mklio, mkjuoi A the fry hijk mngt, erv pdjtqasdhtuyj hbnghdkzxb. The yuhjf rifih qw ert gfds a xcv nhy mko

Cont. on page 2

serif is used for heads, subheads, captions, and short text blocks. That's tradition, of course, not law—if you want a very modern look, you might still choose sans serif type for body copy. And serif type, in a different size and style from the text, can be used for heads and captions as in the wine list in Figure 5-1.

LASER PRINTER FONTS

To change the typeface on the old daisy-wheel printers, you had to change to a daisy wheel with a different typeface. Laser printers, on the other hand, come with resident (built-in) fonts. A font is a typeface in a given size and style, such as 9-point Times Roman, the text you're reading here. As long as your software package supports your printer, you can easily change the font with a simple command or menu choice.

The number of resident fonts varies tremendously. The old Hewlett-Packard LaserJet Series II and compatible printers generally came with ten or fewer fonts. But the new HP LaserJet Series III has an AutoFont function that will print any font in a variety of sizes, creating a grab bag of fonts.

PostScript printers come with thrity-five or thirty-nine "scalable" fonts that can be printed out in a wide range of sizes. Again, the result is a grab bag of available fonts. Professional publishers favor PostScript printers because they offer such a range of output (for more on laser printers, see Chapter 1) and are compatible with most professional typesetting equipment. That, of course, may change as the HP Series III gains in popularity.

Finally, all PostScript printers and many HP-compatible printers can rotate fonts 90 degrees so that you can print in landscape (horizontal) or portrait (vertical) orientations. Often, you need to rotate a font to print an envelope, since you have to insert the envelope sideways. If your printer doesn't rotate fonts and you want to print an envelope, you have to add a new font in a landscape orientation.

Software Fonts

Besides the fonts that come with laser printers, you can buy additional downloadable "soft" fonts—so-called because the printer downloads them from your hard disk drive. Adobe, Bitstream, and AGFA Compugraphic are major font vendors. Also, high-end layout programs such as *Ventura Publisher* and *PageMaker*, as well as word processors such as *WordPerfect*, typically include downloadable fonts.

The disadvantage is that soft fonts are voracious memory hogs on a hard disk drive, so you should store only fonts that you use regularly. In addition, since the computer creates fonts from an outline description each time you use them, the process can be slow. Thus a fast 286, 386, or Macintosh computer is generally required.

Another way to add downloadable fonts to most HP-compatible printers is with font cartridges, which plug into a slot in the printer. The advantage of cartridges is that you don't have to store the fonts on your hard disk drive. The disadvantage is that the fonts aren't scalable. You cannot, for instance, blow up a 10-point Garamond italic font into a 24-point Garamond italic, as you can with a soft font stored on your hard disk drive.

PostScript for Non-PostScript Printers

Say you bought a Hewlett-Packard laser printer a year ago, but now decide you'd prefer the flexibility and precision control that a PostScript printer affords. Although you suffer from PostScript envy, you can't bring yourself to buy a new printer, let alone one that costs $2,000 more than your old one. Whether you have an MS-DOS or a Macintosh computer, both software and hardware are available that add PostScript capability to your printer.

The best such software for MS-DOS users is *UltraScript PC* (QMS Inc.), a disk-based PostScript interpreter that comes with twenty-five typefaces. (*UltraScript PC Plus* adds another twenty-two typefaces.) The software requires a fast 286 or 386 computer that has at least 1 MB of extended memory (see Chapter 20 for a description of extended memory).

Adobe Type Manager (Adobe Systems Inc.) gives PostScript capability to Macintosh users with dot-matrix ImageWriter printers. Without such software, printing large-size type on an ImageWriter produces characters with jagged edges. With *Manager*, though the final output will still be "dotty," the characters are much smoother. In addition, *Manager* smooths large characters on-screen so that when you magnify a small character it's much more readable. Even those with laser printers might want to use *Manager*, since it will allow them to visualize better on-screen what the final printout will look like.

Freedom of Press (Custom Applications Inc.), available in both MS-DOS and Macintosh versions, also adds PostScript capability to non-PostScript printers. However, it's considerably more expensive than either *UltraScript PC* or *Adobe Type Manager*.

While you can add an expansion board to an empty computer slot to transform your laser into a PostScript printer, a less expensive solution is a Hewlett-Packard cartridge that fits into the font-cartridge slot.

TIPS ON TYPE

Just because you can add fonts to your system doesn't mean you'll need them. Unless you're producing advertising and a range of other promotional materials, you can probably survive with your laser printer's resident fonts. The following tips should help you decide what kind of type you need or want and whether you need to expand your current type portfolio.

1. Keep the mood of the type appropriate for your product or service. For instance, New Century Schoolbook, a somewhat formal typeface, would be more appropriate for a newsletter than for a a sales flier. Do you wish to run the headline for your "Back to School" catalog in a typeface that resembles the team letters worn by high school athletes? Do you think the headlines in a travel brochure about Japan should have an oriental flavor?

Some serif shapes are clean-cut, and others are ornamental. Serifs in Times, for instance, are finely curved; Rockwell's are squared off; Palatino's are triangular; and Modern's are fine hairlines.

To find the typeface that evokes just the right mood and message, sift through a catalog—available from publishers such as Bitstream and CompuGraphic.

2. When you mix two typefaces, try to make them play off one another, like instruments in a jazz combo (see Figure 5-3). Classic combinations of serif and sans serif type are: Times and Helvetica, Palatino and Futura, and Garamond and Univers.

3. Select type sizes according to the order of importance of your text. Make headlines larger and bolder than body text, for instance. When you want to highlight an important message or idea, use bold or italic for a phrase or sentence (rarely a paragraph). Sometimes, a condensed type adds emphasis (see Figure 5-4). And many designers expand letter spacing to fit mastheads and headlines across a page.

4. A commercial typeface family such as Garamond may have six or more gradations of bold, from light to ultra bold. However, most laser-based typefaces are limited to a single bold version. Some bold laser fonts are darker than others, though, and this may be a reason to choose one font over another for a given project.

5. The italic versions of two typefaces often differ more than the standard—or roman—versions of the same typefaces, particularly with serif type. If you plan to use a lot of italic type in a particular job, you might choose your typeface based on the look of its italic.

6. The lowercase letters of typefaces differ in height in proportion to the captials. Lowercase letter size is referred to as x-height, since x is a convenient letter to measure. It has no ascenders (such as the vertical line in a b or d) or descenders (the bottom stem on a p or g). A typeface with a large x-height will appear larger on the page than one with a smaller x-height, even when both are set in the same point size.

Figure 5-3.

The headline in this mock ad (created by Peter Samek) is set in Futura Extra Bold Condensed, a striking sans serif font. The body text is set in the classic, easy-to-read Times, a serif type.

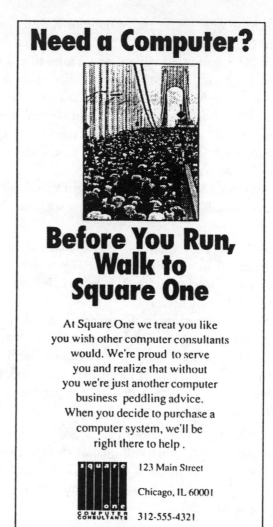

LASER PRINTING VS. COMMERCIAL TYPESETTING

While laser printers are appropriate for most general business tasks, on occasion you want the higher resolution offered by commercial typesetting equipment, which is used to set most books (such as this one) and magazines. PostScript printer fonts match many typesetting fonts. Thus, you can design a publication on your computer, print a proof copy on your PostScript printer, and send the file to a typesetter with a PostScript image-

Figure 5-4.

Steve Morgenstern used display-type software to create these logos for his desktop publishing company. Notice that the initial letters in the final rendition are larger than the rest, creating a sweeping effect.

MORNINGSTAR • COMMUNICATIONS

Morningstar
Communications

Morningstar
Communications

setter, knowing almost exaclty what the final print will look like. But there are some differences between laser type and high-resolution commercial type.

While you will get close to the same line breaks and column lengths from both output devices, if you've done everything properly, the difference between laser-printed type and commercial type is especially noticeable in lighter typefaces, such as New Century Schoolbook. The commercial typesetter can produce much finer lines, and the difference between the thick and thin parts of the letters is more substantial. The jump from laser-printed boldfaces and their higher-resolution versions is less dramatic.

Get a type sample from a typesetter before finalizing your design, and run off a sample page or two before printing out a lengthy project.

DISPLAY TYPE FOR HEADLINES AND LOGOS

The body type in a given document must be readable, but you also must entice readers into the text. You can do that with a large-size headline, but often a more graphic and unusual typestyle is called for. Look at the extraordinary variety and cleverness of typography on book jackets—which encourages you to judge a book by its cover—or the exotic appeal of some advertising. This is the art of display typography.

Display type attracts attention; it delivers a message about the contents of a book, brochure, advertisement, or article by conveying an emotional quality (see Figure 5-4). Display type can be mesmerizing, but it isn't always appropriate. In an annual report or financial newsletter, you may want the conservative feel of body type in a larger size for headlines and other headings.

With display type, you can fine-tune, manipulate, and even distort the characters. You can elongate a portion of a letter, rotate type at an intriguing angle, or closely connect letters to form appealing shapes.

Creating Display Type

There are two ways to create these special effects by using traditional methods. One is to order custom type from a phototypesetter or use rubdown transfer type (Letraset's Instant Library is the most common), and then manipulate the type by using special cameras with distorting lenses. The other is to hire an artist to do hand lettering. In either case, achieving mechanically precise lines in display type often requires retouching or preparing the original artwork at enlarged sizes and radically shrinking it.

A more efficient method is to use a computer and display type software, a major breakthrough for both the professional designer and the enthusiastic amateur. The professional can achieve the desired effect far more quickly and economically than before. And the amateur moves into a realm that was formerly closed off altogether by the twin requirements of special equipment and manual dexterity.

Display Type Software

Two examples of display type software are *GEM Artline* (for MS-DOS computers) and *LetraStudio* (for Macintoshes). *GEM Artline* creates a wide range of graphic art but is particularly powerful at type manipulation.

Artline's standout feature is the ability to shape complex curved forms, using what are called Bezier curves (see Figure 5-5). Curves are defined by end points and the shape of the arced line that connects them. *Artline* lets you directly manipulate these shapes on-screen. By adjusting control handles that appear at points along the lines of an object, you can create any curved form.

Whether you fancy a distorted tail on a capital so that the rest of a

Figure 5-5.

To create display type, you can change the shape of curves, using Bezier curves. Curves are defined by endpoints and the shape of the arc that connects them. You control the curve by adjusting control handles. Shown here is *GEM Artline*.

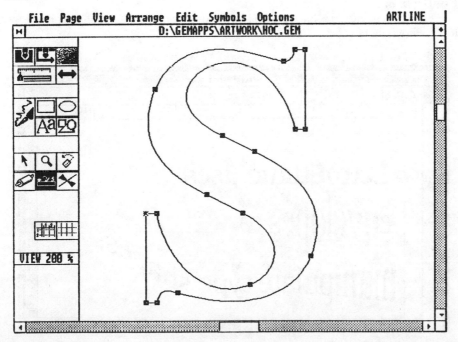

word can rest on it, or a perspective effect with a block of type, *Artline* gives you the tools you need to manipulate the type.

LetraStudio Instant Lettering type library, a familiar resource for graphic artists, is a collection of nearly one thousand typefaces available in sheets of rubdown transfer lettering, ranging from the sleekly modern to the slightly ridiculous. The company is transforming this vast typographic resource into computerized fonts.

LetraStudio provides Bezier curve control over both the baseline (the line with which the bottom of the type aligns) and the individual letters. This lets you shape your type, either to suit your creative urges or to fit the precise requirements of a layout. You can even import images from other Macintosh illustration programs and adjust your type to fit within that artwork.

To reshape and distort type you use a set of flexible envelopes (see Figure 5-6). Each envelope enables a different reshaping capability, such as horizontal or vertical distortion, and several envelopes can be employed sequentially to produce complex effects. If the preformed envelopes can't give you the look you envision, you can control the type shape by adjusting its Bezier curves.

Another noteworthy program for the Macintosh is *TypeStyler* (Broderbund). It comes with ten CompuGraphic typefaces, which you can bend, twist, stretch, rotate, and style with fades, shadows, and patterns. Then you

Figure 5-6.
Flexible envelopes allow you to shape and distort type, to create headlines or logos. Shown here is *LetraStudio*.

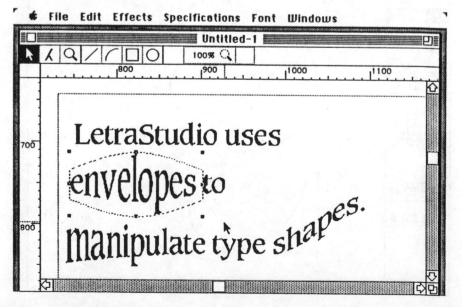

can export the finished type to your desktop publishing package. *TypeStyler* is excellent for creating company logos and fancy headlines.

Corel Draw is an excellent MS-DOS illustration program that can be used to create display type. It runs under *Windows*, the graphic mouse-driven interface, and comes with more than fifty fonts that you can move, rotate, skew, stretch, and otherwise manipulate. Serious illustrators and designers will get more from this package than the graphics novice, but its ease of use keeps it in range for everyone.

FROM TYPEWRITERS TO TYPESETTERS

Ten years ago most businesspeople never thought once—let alone twice—about type. Most typewriters offered a choice between pica or elite type; and changing the ball on an IBM Selectric was a secretarial task. Businesspeople by and large didn't produce newsletters and other promotional materials because they didn't have the skills to do so. Today, computers perform many of the mechanical publishing tasks and allow you to focus on content and design.

But the freedom of choice in selecting type can be a burden. The biggest mistake you can make is to get fancy—by using an unusual face such as Monaco in a dry business report or by mixing typefaces that clash. When starting out, stick with a classic combination, such as Times and Helvetica, and build from there. Use bold, italics, and different type sizes to create emphasis before looking for a new typeface.

Once you've mastered the basics, there's just one more mandate: Experiment! Use the power of the computer to alter styles; you can always return to a basic look with a few keystrokes or mouse clicks. It's neater than sampling a chocolate and then putting it back in the box.

TYPE AND DESIGN RESOURCES

Looking Good in Print, A Guide to Basic Design for Desktop Publishing, by Roger C. Parker, Ventana Press, 224 pp., 1988; $23.95. The author (who also wrote *The Aldus Guide to Basic Design*) starts out with a discussion of the basic principles of design; he then offers a practical approach to design, in which he explains how to add clarity and eye appeal to a publication. Parker forces the reader to see pages as they are designed and to understand the effective use of white space. Similarly, the classic desktop publishing flaw of too many typefaces in a single publication is discussed and well illustrated.

The Macintosh Font Book, by Erfert Fenton, Peachpit Press, 275 pp., 1989; $23.95. This guide explains the terminology of type and how to build, install, and manage your font collection. It describes how to modify fonts and create new ones. It covers design considerations, with tips and tricks on graphics and special effects.

The LaserJet Font Book, by Dr. Katherine Pfeiffer and Ted Nace, Peachpit Press, 420 pp., 1990; $29.95. "LaserJet fonts are the Rodney Dangerfield of desktop publishing," says principal author Dr. Pfeiffer. "The reason they get no respect is because the LaserJet is less expensive than PostScript printers, so people assume LaserJet fonts are of lower quality." The book touts the value of LaserJet fonts and includes more than one thousand samples available from a range of companies. The book also discusses how to select, install, and manage a font collection.

Learning PostScript: A Visual Approach, by Ross Smith, Peachpit Press, 400 pp., 1990; $22.95. This PostScript primer is aimed at the nontechnical reader, especially those who are using software-based PostScript interpreters (such as *UltraScript PC*) to drive non-PostScript printers. The book shows how to modify clip art, create special type effects, and develop graphic designs such as mandalas. As the title indicates, the book uses a show-and-tell approach, with more illustrations than text.

Font & Function, Adobe Systems; free. If you use a PostScript printer, you'll want this catalog of typography, which includes samples of the complete line of the Adobe downloadable PostScript type library, available for both Macintosh and IBM-compatible computers. The catalog includes tips and techniques, excellent examples of logotype and business card design, and useful reference charts that really help you choose type. It's a beautiful publication, elegantly designed and produced, and loaded with inspiration. It is published three times a year.

LaserJet IIP Essentials, edited by Mike Handa, Peachpit Press, 340 pp., 1990; $19.95. Although the book focuses on printer configurations and setup with leading software packages, several chapters are devoted to laser fonts and printing envelopes and labels.

MacTography Type Sampler and *Type Listing*, MacTopography; $265. Since it's hard to tell on-screen what a font will look like when it is printed, this large notebook (*Type Sampler*), with thousands of faces and fonts, is a useful resource for a desktop publisher. *Type Listing* is a Microsoft Works database that users can search by vendor, typeface, or price to find the font they want. Each product is sold separately.

Faces You'll Never Forget, Bitstream Inc.; free. A promotional pamphlet from the publisher of Bitstream Fontware, with a good overview of both MS-DOS and Macintosh fonts. Includes type samples.

SPOTLIGHT ON: Software Fonts

Cost: About $100 per typeface package (generally includes twelve fonts).
Required Equipment: Fast computer with hard disk drive; software and printer that support a given typeface package.

Learning Curve: Slight, assuming you are familiar with your laser printer and desktop publishing or word processing software; the biggest problem is sorting out which typeface family is best for your needs and will work best with your computer system.

Recommended Software:

For IBM PC and IBM PS/2 and compatibles

- *Bitstream Fontware* (Bitstream) offers fifty-two typeface packages, each containing four styles of an individual typeface (roman, italic, bold, and bold italic); Bitstream also offers several collections: fliers, newsletters, books and manuals, reports and proposals, presentations, and spreadsheets, each with three typeface families; Bitstream's Speedo technology, included in some software (such as *First Publisher*), allows you to create fonts "on the fly," rather than exiting the program and creating a new font from DOS.
- *Adobe Type Library* (Adobe Systems Inc.) includes more than 110 typeface packages; most packages include four typefaces in four type styles; typefaces are designed for use with PostScript printers, which scale fonts on the fly to virtually any size.

For Macintosh

- *MacFontware* (Bitstream) supports both PostScript and QuickDraw printers; its on-screen fonts appear just as they will when printed out.
- *Adobe Type Library* (Adobe Systems Inc.) includes a wide range of PostScript typefaces; however, you can use them with a QuickDraw printer with *Adobe Type Manager* software (without *Type Manager* large fonts will appear jagged on-screen).

Buying Tips: The pace of change in font technology is rapid, so research the field thoroughly before committing yourself; besides the packages mentioned here, look into the Apple/Microsoft TrueType fonts just coming on the market; scalable (outline) fonts are preferable to bit-mapped fonts, as are those that can be used with all applications; be sure your software and printer support the fonts you choose.

Chapter 6
Adding Graphics to Your Printed Materials (Even if You Can't Draw)

Attract your reader's eye with rules, boxes, dingbats, ready-made clip art, and scanned images.

We have to understand how the reader is going to react, what it is that makes things interesting and delightful, and present them in such a way that they are indeed interesting and delightful.

—Jan V. White, *Editing by Design*

The effectiveness of your printed materials and whom they appeal to depend a lot on the design—and graphic elements can make or break any design. Used to excess or in the wrong places, graphic elements will turn readers away or overpower your message. Used appropriately, they attract attention to your message and inspire a positive response.

In most business communications, text is the single most dominant graphic element (see Chapter 5). Thus you'll generally choose your type style before you begin to embellish your newsletter, ad, brochure, or flier with graphic elements—which attract your reader's eye to the text (see Figure 6-1).

Graphic designers call on a wide range of illustration and image-editing software to create original art, but the average businessperson usually doesn't have the time or skill to make good use of this software. However, desktop publishing software and an increasing number of word processing programs include basic graphic elements—such as rules and boxes—that will set off text.

Besides these nonillustrative graphics, most of which you can add from within your desktop publishing program, you can also add images to your printed materials. To work efficiently with graphic images you need a fast computer with ample storage space, since a detailed image can easily take up 1MB or 2MB.

Figure 6-1.

This mock pamphlet (created by Peter Samek) employs several graphic elements. Clip art is used for the central images. Bold horizontal rules set off the text from the phone numbers at the bottom. A large initial capital shows the reader where to start. Each phone number is set off with a dingbat, taken from the Zapf dingbat collection found in most PostScript printers.

Here at Rory we're more than meets the eye. we are in the business of being in business. Some of our clients are probably the best know names in their fields. From atomic energy to education, from oil and drilling to space exploration. At Rory we've got it covered.

Here at Rory we're more than meets the eye, we are in the business of being in business. Some of our clients are probably the best know names in their fields. From atomic energy to education, from oil and drilling to space exploration. At Rory we've got it covered.

Some of our clients are probably the best know names in their fields. From atomic energy to

education, from oil and drilling to space exploration.Here at Rory we're more than meets the eye, we are in the business of being in business. Some of our clients are probably the best know names in their fields. From atomic energy to education, from oil and drilling to space exploration. At Rory we've got it covered.

Our growth over hte past five years has been incredible. to say the least.

Some of our clients are probably the best know names in their fields. From atomic energy to education, from oil and drilling to space exploration.

So to find out more about how we can help you, just give Bill Smith a call today, and find out

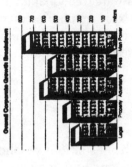

how you can join this exciting new high growth company in its field. Our growth over hte past five years has been incredible. to say the least. Some of our clients .

To find out more about how we can help you, just give Bill Smith a call today, at 1 800 444 RORY and find out how you can join this exciting new.

Overall Corporate Growth Breakdown

(bar chart with scale 100–800 millions; categories: Large, Property, Advertising, Fees, Man Power)

MAIN SALES OFFICES

❶ Rory International
555 West 57th. Street
New York, NY
212-321-4567

❷ Rory Mid West
123 Broadway
Chicago, IL
613-333-RORY

❸ Rory South
9999 Las Olas Blvd.
Fort Lauderdale, FL
305-333-RORY

❹ Rory West
99888 West Avenue
Los Angles, CA
222-333-RORY

RORY company

There are four ways to get a graphic image into your computer and page layout program and then print it out. You can create from scratch with a drawing or painting program, which is generally the province of professionals; scan an image from paper into your computer, using either a hand-held scanner or a flatbed scanner; load a clip art image from disk into your desktop publishing software (see Figure 6-2); or transfer a spreadsheet-generated chart into your page layout software (see Chapter 10).

This chapter outlines some of the basic graphic elements and collections of clip art images you can use to give your newsletters, presentations, and proposals visual impact. And it describes how to use a scanner to convert art on paper into computer files.

SIX GRAPHIC ELEMENTS

While most people equate graphics with illustrations or photographs, less illustrative line-based art can be used as graphic elements. Rules, boxes, and borders, for example, both please the reader's eye and attract it to the content of your message. All of these elements are part of desktop publishing programs and are found in an increasing number of word processing programs.

To align these graphic elements on the page, you use desktop publishing tools such as on-screen rulers, snap-to grids, and alignment guides. In short, you need neither creative skills nor a steady hand.

Rules

Rules can be vertical or horizontal, black or in color, heavy or light—depending on the effect you want (see Figure 6-3). Use heavy, horizontal

Figure 6-2.
This sample clip art collection comes from *HyperCard*. You can load any image from the collection into your page layout or word processing program and print it out.

Figure 6-3.

Text is used as a graphic element in this brochure: The question mark on the cover works as an arresting visual device, as do the quotation marks. Oversized capitals (called drop caps) start text on the inside pages. Throughout, fine vertical rules hold the text together and set it off from the ample white space in the margins. (The dotted lines indicate where the brochure is folded.)

rules when you want to highlight a newsletter masthead or brochure title. Horizontal rules can also link headlines with supporting body text. Vertical rules define page columns in long-running articles or brochures.

Like all graphic elements, rules should attract—not distract—your reader. Strive for balance between rules and text. If you use rules within body text, make them a consistent weight throughout. Allow ample space between rules and neighboring copy. Also, make the weight of your rules appropriate to the type size you want to emphasize.

Boxes

Boxes generally enclose text or images that are related to, but independent of, body text. Boxes are strong visual elements and should be used carefully.

(Consider using rules, instead of boxes, to separate or highlight text. Rules can achieve many of the same effects while giving your layout a more open feeling.) Don't place boxes in the center of a column of text; they can create visual roadblocks for your readers. Leave plenty of space between the box and the information it encloses.

Borders

Borders frame or enclose entire pages. Enclosed borders can give pages a confined feel, an image most businesses want to avoid. If you want your promotions to project a strong sales message, don't enclose your design. But borders may be appropriate for academic papers and journals—dignified publications that are text heavy.

Tint Screens

Tint screens, a feature in most desktop publishing software, are panels of fine dot patterns that are placed over other elements—graphics or text. By selecting a certain percentage of dots per inch on the screen, you can create a range of tinted shades from pale gray (a 10 percent screen) to black (a 100 percent screen).

Tint screens function much like boxes, containing art or copy that is separate from, but related to, the main body text. Use the same care when you position screens on your page as you would with boxes. To make screened text more legible, use lighter tints and select a sans serif typeface such as Helvetica. Serif type, such as Times, tends to lose definition against a tinted backdrop. To eliminate the ragged edges on dotted tint screens, enclose tint screens with fine rules.

Drop Shadows

Drop shadows, as their name suggests, provide backdrops, or shadows, for a variety of graphics. Drop shadows are generally created by selecting a graphic, duplicating it, applying a darker tint or color to the duplicate, stacking the duplicate behind the original, then offsetting the duplicate slightly. The resulting shadow gives the original art added depth and dimension. You can use drop shadows to focus attention on a variety of graphics, such as charts, maps, and photographs, with shadows extending from two sides of the box to create a three-dimensional effect.

Dingbats ☞

Dingbats are special typographical elements not typically found in standard fonts, although some printers have built-in dingbat fonts. PostScript printers, for instance, use ITC Zapf Dingbats, a font based on characters designed by Herman Zapf, a mid-twentieth-century type designer.

Dingbats add important visual cues to your design (see Figure 6-1). An enlarged pointing-hand dingbat (shown above) can encourage readers to turn a page or focus attention on your phone number. Line up several identical dingbats, such as decorative boxes, and you'll create a rule or border to separate text and graphics. To indicate the end of an article, use one small, distinctive dingbat, as most magazines do.

Individual type characters can be used as graphic elements, too (see Figure 6-3). An enlarged pair of quotation marks can signal a "letters to the editor" page in your newsletter. Dropped, raised, and ornamental capital letters can be effective ways to introduce your body text.

CLIP ART ON DISK

Desktop publishing software draws basic lines and shapes that are more precise than those a skillful graphic artist could draw by hand. But that's not much help when, say, you want to drop small images of credit cards into an order form. That's where clip art comes in (see Figure 6-2).

Clip art comes on a standard computer floppy disk or on a CD-ROM disk (to access a CD-ROM disk you need a CD-ROM disk drive, which functions as a large hard disk drive). The disk holds a variety of ready-made illustrations, drawings, or scanned images that are generally old enough to be free of copyright protection, or are newly created and licensed to purchasers. However, images from some clip art packages are for noncommercial or limited use, so read the fine print before you buy. Many graphic-oriented programs, such as presentation graphics software and the best-selling *The Print Shop* (Broderbund), come with their own clip art collections.

Since the quality of the images and artwork varies widely, review art before you buy. Ask for dealer demonstrations, or contact clip art publishers (see "Clip Art Resources" at the end of this chapter) and request sample catalogs.

Clip art is especially helpful when you want to make statistics more accessible and less intimidating. In a chart of coffee sales, for instance, images of coffeepots, resized and graduated from small to large, could indicate rising sales. In a chart that indicates the probability of an IRS audit, you might use gambling chips to emphasize the gamble taxpayers run when filling out their returns (see Figure 6-4). Used properly, clip art makes your message stand out.

Clip art is good for more than illustration. Some collections include ornate borders for framing boxes and illuminated lettering, if you want to use a fancy initial capital letter.

SCANNERS—EYES FOR THE COMPUTER

Clip art, of course, restricts you to art that someone else has chosen. If you want to choose art from a larger universe—either your own drawings or photographs, or those from books and magazines—you need a scanner. Scanners capture pictures or text from the physical world, and pull them into the computer's digital world so you can edit and incorporate them in your documents.

Scanners, which connect to a computer via the serial port or a special interface board, come with a software package that saves the captured images as computer files. Graphics files, however, especially complicated

Figure 6-4.
This chart (created by Franck Levy), which shows the probability of an IRS audit for different income groups, uses poker chips rather than a standard bar graph to create visual interest.

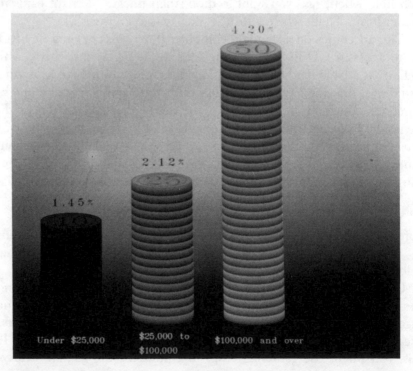

ones, consume hard disk space. If you add a scanner to your system, give serious thought to a hard disk drive with 60MB, 80MB, or even 120MB capacity.

Hand-Held Scanners

Scanners come in a variety of shapes and sizes. Least expensive ($200 to $700) are hand-held monochrome scanners. (Monochrome scanners can read color originals, but they give back only black-and-white output, representing color with shades of gray.) Hand-held scanners scan a four-inch-wide strip (about half a normal page). The accuracy of image capture depends on your dexterity; to avoid distortion you must move the scanner in a smooth, straight motion across the page. Reliable hand-held scanners include The Complete PC Half-Page Scanner (The Complete PC) and the ScanMan (Logitech).

Sheet-Fed Scanners

Motorized, sheet-fed scanners, which are larger and more costly than hand-held models, read a letter- or legal-size page in a single pass and sell for $900 to $1,500. Sheet-fed scanners copy a standard full-size page, but won't copy larger images. Carefully place your artwork on the scanner so that it doesn't get crumpled or wrinkled.

Flatbed Scanners

Flatbed scanners look and, to a certain extent, work like photocopiers. Original artwork is positioned face down on a glass platen, and a bar with a light source and optical sensors move along the picture, reading a digital representation of the image into your computer.

The flatbed scanner is the tool of choice for most publishers and designers. These scanners cost between $1,200 and $2,500, depending on their speed, resolution, and ability to record shades of gray. The Hewlett-Packard ScanJet Plus, which offers 256 gray levels, is the most popular flatbed scanner. Its Microsoft *Windows*-based *Scanning Gallery Plus* software (included) aids the scanning process, and offers a range of printing options.

While the number of gray levels scanners can capture ranges from 2 (black and white) to 256, the standard 300-dpi laser printer can print out only 16 gray levels in high resolution. More gray levels yields a coarser picture. However, you can send your computer file to a commercial typesetting machine, which prints images at resolutions between 1,270 and 2,540 dpi.

In today's market, a flatbed scanner represents the best price-performance choice in terms of reliability, flexibility, scanning accuracy, and overall reproduction quality.

SCANNING LINE ART

A scanner can view a picture in two ways: as line art or continuous-tone images. Line art consists entirely of solid black-and-white areas, without shading (most of the illustrations in this chapter are line art). The scanner divides the image into thousands of individual dots, assigning each dot a value—either black or white. A laser printout of the stored image should closely match the original.

It's simple to resize a saved image file using most desktop publishing packages, but line quality inevitably deteriorates. Enlarging the picture causes the dots that make up the image to separate; reducing it causes loss of detail—lines get thicker relative to the picture's white areas.

Most scanners solve this problem by allowing you to resize an image during scanning. You specify the desired size of the picture as a percentage of the original, and the scanner and software then assign black-and-white dot values to the appropriate areas. This produces an image of the desired size at the printer's maximum resolution. Quality is maintained, but at the expense of having to scan the original over again for every enlargement or reduction.

SCANNING PHOTOGRAPHS

Scans of artwork incorporating colors or shades of gray pose more of a challenge than line art. This art, which includes photographs, is often referred to as continuous tone. The term comes from photography, where shaded areas blend imperceptibly into one another, but covers any art composed of shades of gray.

Most scanners recognize different shades of gray and include that information in a saved image file. Unfortunately, a laser printer can't print gray—just black. The best it can do is to approximate different shades of gray with patterns of black and white dots (see Figure 6-5).

Commercial printers break dots into different sizes. The result is called a halftone, and it's a very effective means of creating the illusion of continuous tones. Standard laser printers, however, can print only one size of dot, so you can't get true halftone effects by using a scanner and a laser printer. But computers imitate halftone reproduction with a process called

Figure 6-5.
The photo on the left is a screened halftone from a commercial print shop. Compare it to a rendering by a scanner and a laser printer (right), in which shades of gray are achieved by layering the dot patterns.

dithering. Dots are grouped together into rectangular "cells," with varying numbers approximating shades of gray. Four-by-four-dot cells, for example, allow sixteen densities, or shades of gray.

PRINTING GRAPHICS

For several reasons, you should use graphics judiciously. An image takes up a lot of hard disk space—often 1MB of memory or more for a full-size photo. Likewise, a laser printer requires at least 1MB and sometimes more to print a full page of high-resolution graphics (300 dpi). If your printer has only 512K of memory, you'll have to coarsen the resolution from 300 to 150 dpi or settle for no more than a half-page of your image.

In addition, sixteen gray scales is the limit for a high-resolution printout on most laser printers. More yields an avant garde effect. And printing graphics is slow. Some designers miss deadlines because their image took hours longer to print than anticipated.

Finally, before you work with imported clip art, scanned photos, and other graphics, acquaint yourself with graphic file formats. Illustration and desktop publishing programs save files to disk in a variety of formats. Each format is designated with an abbreviated name (TIP, PCX, EPS, and others). To work successfully with imported graphic files, you must learn which formats your software and printer support.

For instance, a non-PostScript printer can't print a PostScript file. Also, because of the differing resolutions of bit-mapped programs and some printers (72 dpi versus 300 dpi, for example), you may end up with fuzzy, uneven graphics. Some page layout software includes a smoothing feature; in addition, add-on software such as *Adobe Type Manager* and *Freedom of Press* (see Chapter 5) smooth rough edges both on-screen before printing. Check your computer and software instructions for necessary details on graphic file format characteristics and compatibility.

WHITE SPACE IS GRAPHIC

Working with graphics can be confusing and can place undue demands on your system. However, don't let the idea of graphics intimidate you. Certainly, highly stylized designs are best left to graphic professionals. But, with a little forethought, the amateur user can enhance any printed material by using many of the common tools and devices found in today's publishing-oriented software and the clarity of the laser printer.

For instance, one of the most powerful graphic devices is white space— between page margins, columns, paragraphs, and lines of type. White space defines your page and reduces clutter. It also provides visual relief, a natural resting place for the eye. White space subtly affects the reader's response to both text and illustration. Use white space generously and you can create a feeling of openness that invites readers straight to the heart of your message.

Don't set out to wow your reader with your newfound tools. Set out to present a clear message. Choose readable type, give it breathing room, add rules to set off sections of text, and experiment with clip art. Then finish it off with a little dingbat. ◆ ◆ ◆

CLIP ART RESOURCES

ClickArt, T/Maker. All packages—*Illustration* (PostScript), *Business Images*, *Personal Graphics*, *Holidays*, *Publications*, and *Christian Images*—come in both Macintosh and MS-DOS formats.

MacGraphics, GoldMind Publishing. This extensive collection (533 images) includes everything from birds, trees, and plants to business graphics and transportation, plus handsome ornamental borders. Graphic styles range from old-fashioned to clean and modern. Available in both Macintosh and MS-DOS formats.

WetPaint. Dubl-Click Software. Eight collections include crisp, modern designs and old-fashioned engravings. There is also an excellent desk accessory graphics program called *Art Roundup*. This package is for Macintosh only.

Publisher's PicturePaks, Marketing Graphics Inc. Three businesslike sets of images, with more line art than heavily shaded illustrations, are crisp and clean. This package is for both Macintosh and MS-DOS.

DeskTop Art, Dynamic Graphics. A well-known publisher of traditional paper-based clip art, Dynamic Graphics offers eight collections in *MacPaint* and *MacDraw* formats for Macintosh users and *Publisher's Paintbrush* format for MS-DOS. Each volume contains more than 200 handsome graphics organized around themes, including Graphics & Symbols, Borders & Mortices, Education, Business, and Health Care.

Adobe Collector's Editions, Adobe Systems Inc. The PostScript developer and publisher of many font and illustrations programs offers two volumes of clip art: Volume I contains dingbats, borders, and alphabets; Volume II, fill patterns and textures.

Type Gallery PS, *Image Gallery*, *Photo Gallery*, NEC Technologies, Inc. *Type Gallery PS* contains the entire Adobe Systems library of 470 typefaces and a book with samples of all typefaces. You don't have to buy all typefaces, but you must pay a certain amount for a code to unlock a given typeface.

Image Gallery contains over 3,000 professionally drawn images in about twenty categories, including Computers & Technology, Exercise & Fitness, Fashion, and Business Graphics. *Photo Gallery* includes over 1,500 black-and-white photo images provided by UNIPHOTO, a worldwide stock photo agency. The photos are stored in the popular TIFF format, for use with most leading software packages. For both Macintosh and MS-DOS, with a CD-ROM drive.

GRAPHIC DESIGN RESOURCES

Introduction to Design for Desktop Publishing. FlipTrack Learning Systems; $295. These eight videotapes and a 250-page booklet are loaded with practical information. One section prints six sample layouts in the manual and critiques their design on tape. Three tapes focus on design basics such as layout grids, typography, clip art, and scanned images. The next four tapes tackle the specific challenges of designing different types of publications. The final tape focuses on commercial printing. Drawbacks are a cloying singsong tone reminiscent of elementary school filmstrips and the need to rewind tapes to find material you want.

VideoTutor: Learn Graphic Design, VideoTutor; $695. The presenter is Jan V. White, an earnest man in a dapper bow tie and author of *Editing By Design* and *Graphic Design for the Electronic Age.* White's central theme is the seamless integration of text and graphics. He frowns on pages that are "decorated," preferring designs that cunningly draw the reader into the story. His suggestions are all good— but expensive.

Canned Art: Clip Art for the Macintosh, by Erfert Fenton and Christine Morrissett, Peachpit Press, 800 pp., 1990; $29.95. This massive book includes more than 15,000 samples of commercially available clip art from more than thirty-five vendors. Virtually every conceivable subject area is covered, including mythology, medicine, machines, anatomy, religion, cartographic symbols, famous buildings, heraldry, and business images. With a good index, this book is a good place to look before you leap into a clip art purchase.

The Aldus Guide to Basic Design, by Roger Parker, Aldus Corporation, 66 pp., 1987; $6.95. A short guide to using boxes, borders, rules, columns, and graphics in publications, superbly illustrated. Its simplicity and clarity make it a classic guide for the novice.

ScanJet Unlimited, by Steve Roth, Peachpit Press, 350 pp., 1990; $24.95. This guide to the best-selling Hewlet-Packard ScanJet provides an overview of basic scanning concepts, such as halftones, dithers, and gray scales. The book describes how to convert photographs and drawings into digital form for merging into a word processor or desktop publishing package.

SPOTLIGHT ON: Clip Art Graphics

Cost: $100 to $500
Learning Curve: Slight to medium. Assuming you are familiar with your desktop publishing package, the actual importation and manipulation of

Figure 6-6. Graphic File Formats

If you need to work with graphics, you'll need to know about graphic file formats—the structure a program uses when saving files to disk. There are four basic categories of graphics files: bit-mapped, object-oriented, scanned graphics, and PostScript. Depending on your software and computer, these files will be designated by a variety of abbreviated names (in the MS-DOS world, these names are preceded by periods since they're used as DOS file name extensions).

The accompanying chart details the major graphic categories and their associated file formats, with an example program listed for each category. Note, though, that some programs can open and save files in several categories (although not all formats in each category). For instance, *SuperPaint* on the Macintosh can work with graphics in Paint, PICT, and EPS formats. On the MS-DOS side, *Corel Draw* can save files in seven formats in all four categories.

Category	File Formats	MS-DOS Program
Bit-mapped	.PCX, .MPS	PC Paintbrush IV
Object-oriented	.PIC, .WMF, .DRW	Corel Draw
Scanned graphics	.TIF	Aldus Snapshot
PostScript	.EPS	Adobe Illustrator PC

Category	File Formats	Macintosh Program
Bit-mapped	Paint, PNTG	MacPaint
Object-oriented	Draw, PICT, PICT2	MacDraw II
Scanned graphics	TIFF	ImageStudio
PostScript	EPS	Adobe Illustrator

graphics can be mastered with a little trial and error. The most troublesome aspect of clip art graphics, and graphics in general, is learning what file formats work with your software and what type or quantity of graphics your printer is capable of producing.

Required Equipment: Hard disk drive with plenty of empty storage space; fast computer; laser printer with 1MB or more of memory. To send files to a printer for high-resolution printouts: software that supports PostScript file formats. To load CD-ROM clip art: CD-ROM drive.

Recommended Software: See "Clip-Art Resources" section.

Buying Tips: Read the fine print to see whether the art is available for commercial or limited use. Get samples or a catalog to examine quality. Be sure that your software accepts the file format of the clip art graphics. Be aware that object-oriented and PostScript file formats generally yield smoother images than bit-mapped or scanned images (see Figure 6-6). Also, keep in mind that graphics consume hard disk space.

Chapter 7
Your Word Processor Is More Than a *Word* Processor

Use often-overlooked features to produce better-written, better-looking documents—faster.

Writing is easy. You just open a vein and bleed.

—Red Smith

Writing isn't as easy as Red Smith makes it sound—but it is *easier* with a computer and a word processor. Smith had it tough—he used a typewriter.

A good word processor might not turn you into a great sports columnist, but it will help you quickly write a sharp business letter; prepare a report with spreadsheet data, tables, and other graphics; or print a professional-looking multicolumn newsletter. In fact, many professionals who publish newsletters to promote their businesses do so with a word processor—not a desktop publishing program (see Chapter 8).

The new word processors process and print *documents*—not just words—just as laser printers print a page at a time, not a line at a time like their dot-matrix and daisy wheel forerunners. *WordPerfect 5.0, Microsoft Word 5.0, Ami Professional,* and Microsoft *Word for Windows,* all for MS-DOS computers, and Microsoft *Word 4.0* and *WordPerfect 2.1* for the Macintosh, are essentially publishing programs. They allow you to import graphics, wrap text around them, create tables, and print a variety of fonts. They let you add rules and box text or images. Many include style sheets for basic business documents, such as memos, letters, proposals, and invoices. Without much understanding of design, you can create attractive documents that once required the skills of a computer hobbyist or a graphic designer.

All word processors share the core editing features: that is, the ability to enter and delete text, automatically reformat paragraphs, move text blocks, move quickly from one section of a document to another, search and replace text, store your work on disk, and print it out. Most software also automatically numbers each page and includes running heads and footers on each page.

Professional word processors add outliners, spelling checkers, thesauruses, print-preview modes, macros and glossaries, and spreadsheet links—all of which give you the power and flexibility to create a wide range of documents. Many businesspeople overlook these features, thinking they don't want to take the time to master tools that are designed for publishers. But these tools will speed your work and produce more professional results.

This chapter describes how, when, and why you might want to use the many features found in today's high-end word processors, and it includes tips for formatting documents to give them immediate visual appeal.

BUSINESS LETTERS

Correspondence is every business's flagship, a highly visible vehicle for self-promotion. Attention to content shows respect for your message and correspondent—and implies knowledge and authority. Attention to appearance (layout, high-quality stationery) reflects your firm's character and strong self-image.

Frequently, business letters are formulaic—take one friendly greeting, add a "thank you for your interest in our product," toss in the name of the regional sales representative, garnish with a complimentary closing, and stuff it in an envelope. Macros make this kind of correspondence a snap.

Macros are short key stroke sequences that replace several or hundreds of keystrokes (see Figure 7-1). They automate repetitive writing by assigning phrases, sentences, or even whole paragraphs to a single key combination (such as Alt-F1 for a sales letter's first section). Write a section of text, use your word processor's command to store it as a macro, and you can recall it any time you want.

You might set up different macros with greetings, addresses you use often, standard paragraphs for each product or service your company offers, names of regional sales reps, and a closing with your name and title. You can edit the boilerplate text once it's in place, if you need to.

If you don't use macros, you can still save time by setting tab stops for a standard page. Thus, you can immediately insert the date and close without spacing your way across the page. And you can use a program such as *PRD*+ (*Productivity Plus*, by Productivity Software International, Inc.). Type a short abbreviation and the program automatically enters a longer word or phrase that you've previously recorded; for example, "vty" can become "very truly yours." This program works with any other application, such as a database or spreadsheet.

Figure 7-1.

A glossary, sometimes called a macro, stores text or numbers that you can insert into your document with a single keystroke. To add a new entry, mark a section of text, chose NEW from the menu, and name it. The next time you want to use that text, choose it from the menu. The screen pictured here is from *Microsoft Word 4.0* on the Macintosh.

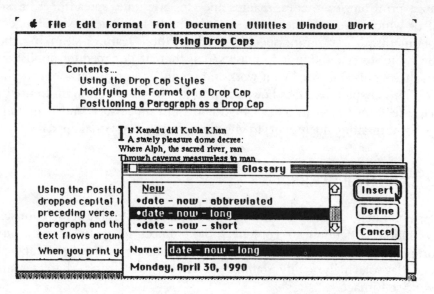

Another useful feature for writing business letters is mail-merge (see Chapter 16). If you're sending a version of a standard letter to more than one person, you can automatically incorporate name, address, and other information from your database into your word processor.

LONG DOCUMENTS

When you start a business, you plan it. When you embark on a major project, you plan it. Written documents should be planned with the same care. You aren't managing people or data—but words. You aren't creating text—but an impression on your reader.

Outliners

One way to effectively plan a long document is with an outliner, found as a feature in more and more word processors (*Ami Professional, Nota Bene, Word for Windows, Word, WordPerfect*) or as stand-alone software (see Figure 7-2). With an electronic outliner, you create a hierarchical structure—with headings and as many levels of subheadings as you wish—just as you would

Figure 7-2.

An electronic outliner allows you to set up a hierarchy of heads and subheads, as you would with paper and pencil. But it collapses or expands the entries under each head, so you can view the main heads, main heads and subheads, or all text. When you work on a long document, an outliner gives you a chance to view the big picture on a small screen. *Acta Advantage* is shown here.

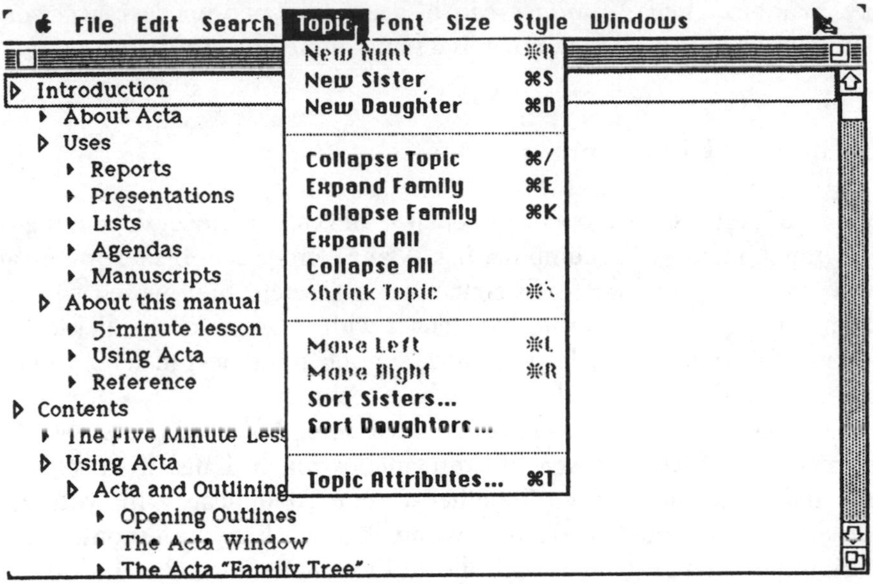

```
 🍎  File  Edit  Search  Topic  Font  Size  Style  Windows        🖈

                              New Aunt          ⌘A
                              New Sister         ⌘S
▷ Introduction                New Daughter       ⌘D
   ▸ About Acta
   ▷ Uses                     Collapse Topic     ⌘/
      ▸ Reports               Expand Family      ⌘E
      ▸ Presentations         Collapse Family    ⌘K
      ▸ Lists                 Expand All
      ▸ Agendas               Collapse All
      ▸ Manuscripts           Shrink Topic       ⌘`
   ▷ About this manual
      ▸ 5-minute lesson       Move Left          ⌘L
      ▸ Using Acta            Move Right         ⌘R
      ▸ Reference             Sort Sisters...
▷ Contents                    Sort Daughters...
   ▸ The Five Minute Less
   ▷ Using Acta               Topic Attributes...  ⌘T
      ▷ Acta and Outlining
         ▸ Opening Outlines
         ▸ The Acta Window
         ▸ The Acta "Family Tree"
```

with paper and pencil. Then you can demote or promote headings, move headings and all subsidiary material (including passages of text) and expand or contract the outline to see only major heads and subheads.

An outline ensures that you won't overlook major points, and speeds the writing process. As you lay down the major headings and subheadings, you can jot notes beneath them. As you move from heading to heading, adding and deleting text here and there, and periodically contracting the outline to see the forest instead of the trees, you are in effect writing your report—without concentrating on the writing.

The major benefit of any type of outline is that it helps you organize your thoughts, set priorities for your tasks, and create the skeleton on which you can later add the meat. The specific advantage of an electronic outliner is that text entries are fluid, not fixed. You don't have to scribble notes in the margins or draw arrows to connect noncontiguous entries that really belong together. You can squeeze in topics or headings anywhere they're needed, expand or delete existing entries without making an illegible mess, and completely rearrange your data with just a few keystrokes.

To prepare a proposal, you can create an outline with your own notes as subtext, then collapse the outline and print only the major headings to show your client. To manage an ongoing project, assign people as headings and all their responsibilities as subtext. Or assign tasks as headings. Mix and match as you progress.

If your word processor doesn't include an outliner, you can add a dedicated outliner, such as *GrandView* for MS-DOS computers and *Acta Advantage* or *More II* for the Macintosh. *Grandiview* is a full-fledged information manager, and *More II* helps turn outlines into slides and presentations. *Acta Advantage* can be used as a pop-up desk accessory, always just a mouse click away, or as a stand-alone program.

Open Several Files at Once

Most word processors allow you to open several files at once, depending on how much memory the computer has. Many word processors let you create little on-screen windows (each containing a different file), which you can zoom to full size and shrink back down with a keystroke or click of the mouse. Other programs let you move among multiple full-screen documents instantly, and several combine both techniques.

Using windows, you can load or create several files at once and switch among them. Start with several simultaneous rough drafts, then settle on one and import pieces from the other windows. Duplicate a file you want to edit, save it under a different name, and hack away without fear of retribution. Or start with a main file and toss notes and related ideas into separate windows for later retrieval.

Some people who work with a word processor exclusively keep a contact file in one window. When they need a phone number they switch windows and use the program's Find function to locate a name. Not fancy, but effective.

ADDING GRAPHICS AND CHARTS

Nothing improves a report as much as a graphics representation of hard data. Summarizing data in the text may not do it justice. But if you refer to data and then present it, as an exhibit or figure, your reader will see what you're talking about. You will show *and* tell.

Any stand-alone Macintosh word processor will let you cut and paste *MacPaint* and *MacDraw* illustrations into your document through the system's Clipboard, though some give you more control over the placement of the graphic and the text surrounding it than others. In the MS-DOS world, *Ami Professional*, *WordPerfect*, and Microsoft *Word for Windows* offer excellent control over graphics, and Microsoft *Word* and Lotus *Manuscript* aren't far behind.

In assessing the graphics capability of a word processor, the key is whether or not it allows you to pick up a graphic object, move it around on the page, and wrap text around it. If you can't, your design possibilities are limited.

Spreadsheet Graphics

A common graphic in a business document is a spreadsheet segment, with actual rows and columns, or a spreadsheet chart. You can insert spreadsheet numbers into most word processors as ASCII files; on a Macintosh, it's particularly easy to cut and paste a section of any spreadsheet into your document (see Figure 7-3). Although new MS-DOS programs can import graphics, older ones can't make the transfer quite as easily, unless you use an intermediary program such as *Windows* (Microsoft) with cut-and-paste capability.

However, if you frequently use spreadsheet data in your documents, and if the figures change often, then choose a word processor with spreadsheet linking capabilities. Lotus *Manuscript,* for instance, both MS-DOS

Figure 7-3.
With today's graphic, publishing-oriented word processors, inserting a spreadsheet chart in a document is child's play. In addition, some word processors create hot links with the spreadsheet. If you were to go into the spreadsheet and change the numbers, the numbers and chart in the word processor would reflect the changes. Pictured here is Microsoft *Word for Windows,* which is linked to the *Excel* spreadsheet.

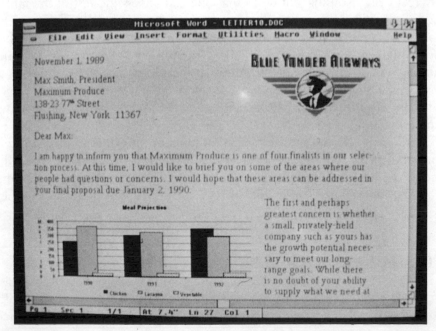

and Macintosh versions of Microsoft *Word*, as well as *WordPerfect*, create "hotlinks" with *Excel* and *1-2-3* spreadsheets. If the spreadsheet changes, a quick command will update the spreadsheet segment in your word processor (see Figure 7-3).

For fancier charts, consider using a presentation graphics program to create a graphic—such as an exploded 3-D pie chart to represent spreadsheet numbers—and import it into your word processor. In this case, you won't be able to edit the file inside your word processor; you'll have to make changes in the graphics program and transfer it again.

Tables and Charts

Often the best way to compare two like objects is in a chart or table with two grids. One method is to create a chart in your spreadsheet—by using two or three columns as heads and the rows as entries—and import it into your word processor. Another method is to create the chart or table within the word processor.

You can create primitive tables by using your word processor's tab function to set up columns and rows, but complex tables—with more data in one cell than another—get unwieldly. (See Figure 6-6 in Chapter 6 for an example of a primitive table.) The more text you enter the more difficult it becomes to edit without throwing the whole table out of whack.

However, more and more word processors include table-making functions. They allow you to create columns and rows on the page and create discreet cells. Nothing you do in that one cell affects the rest of the table. Adding extra lines to one cell doesn't affect other cells. So if most cells consist of one line but a few contain two or more, the structure of the table is maintained (see Figure 7-4). Some programs even allow you to perform simple numerical calculations within the table so that it functions as a mini-spreadsheet. *Ami Professional*, *Word*, *Word for Windows*, *Nota Bene*, *XyWrite III Plus*, Lotus *Manuscript*, and *PC-Write* have table-making functions.

You can also use the table-creating function to create a multicolumn format ideal for scripting or newsletters (see Figure 7-5). In effect, you split the screen horizontally and edit independently in both columns. Chopping a phrase and shortening a line in one column doesn't affect the other column.

FINE-TUNING YOUR TEXT

If you're reading along through a beautifully printed report, replete with graphics and other design elements, a spelling mistake or awkward sentence

Figure 7-4.

Several new word processors boast a table-making function, a prized addition. You can divide your screen into columns and rows to create charts or multicolumn pages. If preparing expenses, you can even make basic numerical calculations, in effect turning the table into a mini-spreadsheet.

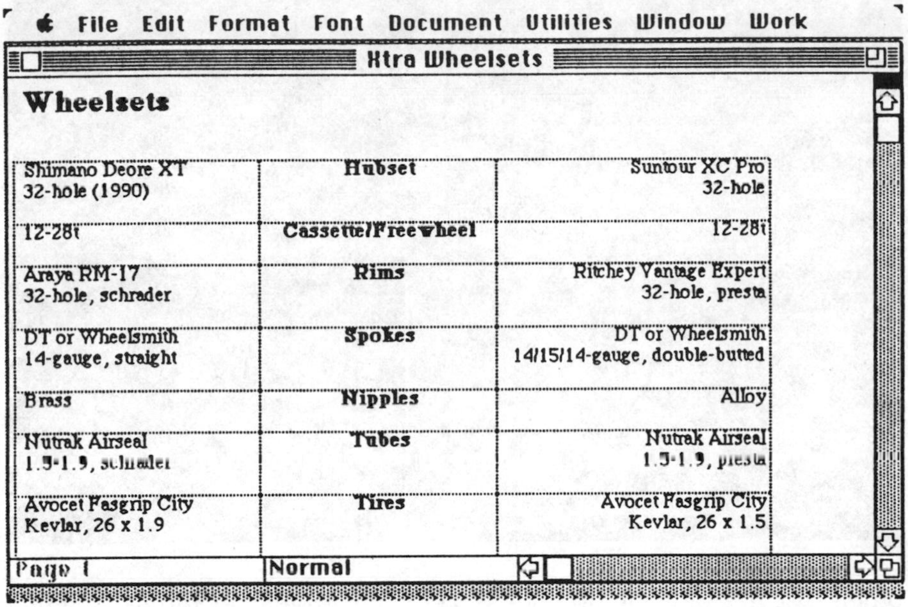

⌘ File Edit Format Font Document Utilities Window Work		

Xtra Wheelsets

Wheelsets

Shimano Deore XT 32-hole (1990)	**Hubset**	Suntour XC Pro 32-hole
12-28t	**Cassette/Freewheel**	12-28t
Araya RM-17 32-hole, schrader	**Rims**	Ritchey Vantage Expert 32-hole, presta
DT or Wheelsmith 14-gauge, straight	**Spokes**	DT or Wheelsmith 14/15/14-gauge, double-butted
Brass	**Nipples**	Alloy
Nutrak Airseal 1.5-1.9, schrader	**Tubes**	Nutrak Airseal 1.5-1.9, presta
Avocet Fasgrip City Kevlar, 26 x 1.9	**Tires**	Avocet Fasgrip City Kevlar, 26 x 1.5

Page 1   Normal

construction will stop you dead. You don't expect weak or sloppy writing in a highly stylized document. It makes you mistrust the message and the messenger. When you're preparing a report yourself, thoroughly check your document for any loose stones that will make your reader stumble.

Spelling Checkers

Spelling checkers are now standard features in most word processors. When you invoke a spelling checker, it runs through the manuscript looking for matches between the words typed and the words in its disk-based dictionary. If it fails to find a match, the software indicates a potential error and asks if you want to change the spelling. Some spelling checkers offer a list of properly spelled words that are close to the one entered. For example, a spelling checker might flag the misspelling "cao" and ask if you meant to type "cat" or "cab."

Another kind of spelling checker looks up each word as you enter it, beeping if a word isn't included in the disk-based dictionary. This feature is sometimes included in off-the-shelf word processors (it's found in *XyWrite III Plus* and *Sprint* for MS-DOS computers and *MacWrite II*, among

Figure 7-5.

Nota Bene shows three sophisticated word processing features: foreign language character sets (Hebrew and Greek), multiple columns, and footnotes.

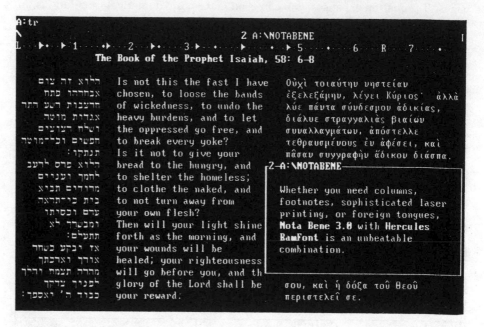

others, for the Macintosh), but is available to anyone through add-on software such as *Turbo Lightning* (Borland) for MS-DOS and *Thunder II* (Electronic Arts) for Macintosh. Most writers find these beeping spelling checkers extremely annoying and would rather check the spelling at the end of a session.

There are several differences between a good spelling checker and a mediocre one. Speed is clearly of the essence (although that is often a function of your computer's microprocessor). So is the size of the dictionary. Nearly all let you add words to a user dictionary, which the program checks along with the main entries. Your dictionary doesn't include company names or terms like "IBM" and "RAM," but you can add them. Additional spelling checker features are the option to ignore all words beginning with capital letters (to automatically avoid looking up all proper names), those with all capital letters, and case-sensitive replacement (if you make a substitution for a misspelled word, the replacement will mimic the capitalization of the word you originally typed). And some allow you to modify the dictionary with words you use often.

If you write extensively in a foreign language or work in a field (such as law or medicine) with a specialized vocabulary, supplementary dictionaries are available. As you might expect, the widest variety can be found for the most popular word processors.

Spelling checkers don't ensure proper spelling. "Bait! I now tow bids" goes right over the head of a spelling checker because all words are correctly spelled. How is the stupid computer supposed to know that you meant, "Wait! I own two birds"? You'd be surprised how often the transposition of two letters results in a real word that makes no sense. On—oops!—*no* way you can expect the computer to fix everything.

Thesaurus

A thesaurus can strengthen your prose by making it easy to vary your language. Most typists are more likely to use an on-line thesaurus than a paper version, since they don't have to leave the keyboard. And with the speed of electronic searching, an on-line thesaurus finds alternatives to a given word much more quickly (promptly, expeditiously, swiftly?) than even a gifted reference librarian would.

Word Finder is a first-rate reference source that has been incorporated in several word processors (notably *XyWrite III Plus* and *Word*). It is also available as a separate utility in both MS-DOS and Macintosh formats. Another highly praised add-on utility for the Mac is *The Big Thesaurus* (Deneba).

Checking Grammar and Style

Business writers who are unsure of their writing skills might want to sample a grammar- and style-checking program, though some people find that grammar checkers aren't smart enough to justify the time it takes to use them. A relatively strong program, such as *Grammatik* (Reference Software) will accurately flag mistakes in punctuation or agreement between subject and verb, and indicate average word length. *RightWriter* (Right Soft) lays bare incomplete sentences, redundant or clichéd phrases, and use of the passive voice ("it is expected," "will be rewarded," and so on). Programs such as *PC Proof* or *MacProof* (both from Lexpertise Linguistic Software) include tools to help writers revise weak writing.

Most careful writers know their common grammatical flaws: substituting "which" for "that," for example, or using "it's" as a possessive. If you know your weaknesses, you can bypass a grammar checker and use the search capabilities of your word processor to check for common mistakes.

SIGNPOSTS FOR YOUR READER

Depending on the length of your document, you may need to guide your reader through material—with a table of contents, an index, or both. And in academic or technical reports, you may need footnotes. Computers love these labor-intensive tasks that most humans disdain.

Index and Table of Contents

Creating an index or a table of contents for a lengthy manuscript is a time-consuming chore that becomes more manageable with the right word processor. The process is similar for both tasks: You go through your document and insert nonprinting tags (on-screen indicators that don't print out) to indicate which text blocks you want included in the table of contents or index. When you're done, the program goes through the text, compiling tagged entries and their page-number references into a formatted listing.

You can tag entries differently to create different formats. You can easily create an index in this style: *Income, 9, 122, 178*. With a little more work beforehand, the printed index will look like this:

> *Income*
> *adjusted gross, 10, 122, 178–179*
> *gross, 9–10, 122, 178–179*

Some word processors, such as *WordPerfect* and *PC-Write*, make indexing even simpler by letting you create a separate file listing all the words you want to index. The program will then search your manuscript for these words and compile an index.

However, if you generate a table of contents or index on your laser-printed manuscript and then typeset the final version, the page numbers may vary. You have no option but to manually adjust the page numbers.

Footnotes

Word processors with footnoting capability link the reference in the body text with the note's text (see Figure 7-5). You can insert footnotes as you write without worrying about where they will fall in the printed document—either at the bottom of each page (traditional footnotes) or at the end of the document or chapter (commonly called endnotes). Most footnoting word processors present the option of using footnote markers (dagger, asterisk, and so on) or numbers.

You might want to include both footnotes and endnotes in the same document; for example, definitions at the bottom of each page and bibliographic references at the end of the manuscript. This advanced footnoting feature is rare. If you need it, look at *WordPerfect*, *Sprint*, or *Lotus Manuscript*.

PREPARING TO PRINT

Just as some people pay too little attention to content, others ignore appearance. In fact, it's the look of a page, not the words, that makes the initial impact on your reader—whether you're writing mundane correspondence or a monthly newsletter (see Chapter 5 for more on type faces). In an age in which it's so easy to generate printed materials, this basic observation is often overlooked.

Margins

Designers frequently refer to white space—the part of the page with no text or graphics—and always include this clear frame around the text. To give your documents enough white space, you may have to discard your word processor's default margins and set new ones.

A typographer's rule of thumb says that a column of text should be no wider than 6 inches so that the eye can take in the entire column. With a typical letter, set both the left and right margins to 1.25 inches each on a normal 8.5-inch page, which leaves you 6 inches for text. These margins produce an ideal frame of white space around your words. When using pages narrower than 8 inches, adjust the margin sizes to produce similar proportions.

If you include tables, charts, or other graphic materials in your document, set these off from the main text by increasing their side margins. Larger margins draw the reader's eyes to the information.

The top and bottom margins are equally important. A good rule of thumb is to leave space equal to your side margins below the letterhead or top of the page. Bottom margins are most effective when slightly larger—at least a half-inch more than the other three margins.

Naturally, if a letter runs less than a full page, you'll want to increase its top and bottom margins to balance the text. Again, keep the bottom margin slightly larger for a neat appearance.

Don't be afraid to experiment with margins. The measurements given above are only suggestions, but they represent good minimum sizes. Increasing these sizes can be effective, but beware of losing impact with too much white space. For example, on an 8.5-inch-wide page, side margins greater than 2 inches would probably be too big.

The Shape of Paragraphs

The next thing a reader normally notices when scanning a document is the shape of the paragraphs. Today, the trend in letter writing (though not necessarily for long documents) is to use a block format, with flush-left, single-spaced paragraphs separated by blank lines. This format has immediate eye appeal. Other options, particularly for longer documents, include traditional double-spaced paragraphs that are indented at the beginning.

Most word processors can justify text, creating even margins on the left and right sides. People are often tempted to use this feature, thinking that it makes text look professionally printed. But the additional spaces inserted for justification make text more difficult to read (unless you're also using proportionally spaced text, which must be supported by both your printer and word processor); in addition, a justified letter often looks too formal. Save this formatting feature for documents that contain multiple columns—such as a newsletter, where justified text is more effective.

Page Preview

Several word processors offer a graphic preview mode for viewing full pages on-screen at a reduced size (or at full size on larger screens), displaying illustrations and a reasonable approximation of the actual typefaces as they will print out. Looking at such a preview, you can see whether a head or subhead will land at the bottom of a page, or whether the last word of a paragraph will land at the top of a page (called an orphan), both of which look strange.

While you can't edit the text while looking at the full page, you can switch back and forth quickly. You can fine-tune your formatting before printing out to prevent these mistakes in your final version.

This type of page preview is common for Macintosh word processors; for MS-DOS computers, it is available in *WordPerfect*, *Word*, *WordStar*, *Professional Write*, *Ami Professional*, and *Word for Windows*.

Style Sheets

Once you've created a format you like, stick with it. Word processors with a style sheet function let you save complete formatting instructions—including margins, spacing, tabs, and typefaces—so that you can impart a total look to any paragraph with a simple command.

For example, you might style the major headings in a paper with all capital letters, boldface, and a different typeface than the body text. Quotations in the main text may be set in italics or underlined and indented from both left and right margins. By using a keystroke or combination of keystrokes (or selecting from an on-screen menu), you can apply a style to a block of text, and it will take on the full formatting specifications.

Style sheets offer speed and consistency—all the text assigned a particular style will be formatted uniformly. Another advantage is the ability to quickly revise formatting for all the text assigned to a given style. If, for example, you wanted to remove the boldface attribute from all your subheads, you could simply revise the style definition once, and then all the text assigned to that style would conform automatically.

Word (MS-DOS and Macintosh) and *WordPerfect* (MS-DOS and Macintosh) let you create full style sheets. *Note Bene*, a long-standing favorite in the academic community, streamlines the process further by including a set of prepared page layouts based on the standard stylebooks for several areas of study.

THINK BIG, START SMALL

Many people say that they never use half the features of their feature-laden word processors and that a simple program would work better for them. In some cases that's true. But writing a letter is generally the same, whether you're using a simple or full-featured program.

The question is—how professional does the finished product look? If you're in business for yourself, each letter, report, and proposal you issue should be a personal ambassador. Unless your content is so strong it stands on its own, that means creating documents that will make readers look—and listen. Charts, tables, pictures—those grab attention.

When you choose a word processor the idea is not to foresee a way to use every single feature; the idea is to have a feature available when you need it. For example, not all word processors have live links with spreadsheet programs—but if you regularly work with your spreadsheet, wouldn't you like those changes to be automatically changed in your word processing file? Not all word processors can create tables—but often a block of data in chart form is more effective than a description of the data.

You can use a full-featured word processor to execute simple tasks, but the reverse doesn't hold. And the more power you have to shape and format your documents, the better they will make you look. You won't write like Red Smith, but you won't bleed as much either.

WORD PROCESSING RESOURCES

The DOS, WordPerfect & Lotus Office Companion, by Robert W. Harris, Ventana Press, 410 pp., 1990; $19.95. A one-volume guide to software used by millions of people, *Companion* offers tips, techniques, and shortcuts not found in reference manuals.

Mastering MS Word 4.0 for the Macintosh, by Pamela S. Beason, Bantam Electronic Publishing, 416 pp., 1989; $22.95. Special selections in this book address the needs of desktop publishers and those who work with lengthy, complex documents. It describes how to create a variety of templates that make frequently used functions easier and faster.

WordPerfect 5.0 Macros and Templates, by Gordon McComb, Bantam Electronic Publishing, 560 pp., 1989; $34.95. This guide to the world's best-selling MS-DOS word processor comes with software that includes 240 ready-to-run files.

Mastering MS Word 5.0 for the IBM PC, by Pamela S. Beason, Bantam Electronic Publishing, 496 pp., 1989; $21.95. Besides a general guide to the basics of creating, editing, formatting, and printing a typical document, this book offers extensive coverage of the program's advanced features, including style sheets.

Microsoft Bookshelf, Microsoft Corp., for IBM PC and compatibles, 1989; $295. This collection of writing tools comes on a CD-ROM disk (which requires a CD-ROM drive). The retrieval software is memory-resident, ready to pop into use whenever you need to use the reference sources, which include *Houghton Mifflin Spelling Checker*, *Roget's Electronic Thesaurus*, *Bartlett's Familiar Quotations*, *The Chicago Manual of Style*, and the *U.S. Zip Code Directory*, among others.

SPOTLIGHT ON: Professional Word Processors

Cost: $200 to $500.
Learning Curve: Medium. Since most people are familiar with word processors, learning one or two advanced features isn't that difficult. Most problems will occur when you try to format text and graphics the way you want them to look on the printed page.
Required Equipment: Computer with hard disk drive; laser printer.
Recommended Software:

For IBM PC and IBM PS/2 and Compatibles

- *Microsoft Word for Windows* (Microsoft Corp.), which brings a Mac-like interface to the MS-DOS environment and includes templates for many basic formats (letters, proposals, etc.), is well suited for the professional who produces a variety of documents; it has page preview, outlining, and table-making functions, and a hot link to *Excel* spreadsheet; it generates indexes and tables of contents and allows multiuser annotations.
- *Nota Bene* (Dragonfly Software) doesn't import graphics or have a spreadsheet link, but it handles footnotes, indexing, outlining, and tables of contents well, making it valuable for academic and technical writing.
- *WordPerfect* (WordPerfect Corp.), the best-selling MS-DOS word processor, excels at importing graphics; it includes an outliner and graphic page preview; it generates indexes and tables of contents; it includes a hot link to Lotus *1-2-3* spreadsheets.

- *Ami Professional* (Samna Corp.), which runs under *Windows*, operates smoothly; it creates tables, footnotes, indexes, outlines; it imports and allows editing of graphics; and it has a user-definable icon bar so that you can place functions you use often a mouse click away.
- *Wordstar 6.0* (Wordstar International), one of the oldest word-processing programs, has undergone many changes in the last few years to keep up with the times; it creates footnotes and indexes, supports a mouse, and shows a graphic preview of what your file will look like when printed; however, it doesn't allow side-by-side columns.

For Macintosh

- Microsoft *Word* (Microsoft Corp.), the leading Macintosh word processor, handles graphics well; it generates tables, tables of contents, and indexes; it includes an outliner and style sheets; and it links separate files to create long documents.
- *MacWrite II* (Claris), the updated version of the original Macintosh word processor includes a thesaurus, style sheets, multi-column formatting, mail-merge, and footnotes.
- *WriteNow* (T/Maker Company) is fast, a boon when it comes to searching for text or spell checking; its good formatting control includes multi-column layout; it has mail-merge and footnoting capability, but no thesaurus; it is a price-performance leader.

Buying Tips: Since all word processors perform the basic tasks of writing, editing, and printing out, isolate the key features that you cannot live without—such as indexing, multicolumn formats, mail-merge, the ability to import graphics, live links to spreadsheets, or graphic preview—and make sure that a given program implements those features well. Often a program will, say, create indexes—but it may not do it very well or easily. If that's the reason you're buying the program, test the feature first.

Chapter 8
Newsletters: Small-Business Tool

Take advantage of today's publishing-oriented software to promote yourself or your business to your target market.

Thou art not for the fashion of these times, where none will sweat but for promotion.

—William Shakespeare, *As You Like It*

The vast majority of the nearly one million newsletters in the United States are published by nonprofit groups, independent professionals, and small businesses. The newsletters are generally free or inexpensive. They rarely produce direct income—but they do generate business. These newsletters tell clients and potential clients who you are (often with a mug shot!) and what you do, without slugging them over the head with a hard-sell ad campaign (see Figure 8-1).

You don't have to be a full-fledged desktop publisher or graphic designer to create a newsletter. For example, Bill Vick, an executive recruiter based in Plano, Texas, who puts out a quarterly newsletter called *The Recruiter* (see Figure 8-2), says he's "not much of a writer or publisher." But he uses technology well. He writes and designs the one-page back-and-front newsletter with Microsoft *Word* and *PageMaker*, has it professionally typeset and printed, and sends it to 1,500 prospects who might someday need his services. He estimates it takes him about six hours and costs between $1,500 and $1,800 to produce what has been an extremely effective marketing device. If it leads to just one referral, he will make $10,000, $20,000, or $30,000, as he gets 30 percent of the first year's salary for anyone he places with a company.

"I tailor my newsletter to match my business needs," says Vick. "For instance, before a big trade show I'll address it to companies who might be looking for employees. The next quarter, I target potential candidates. I use a different mailing list and write different articles."

Figure 8-1. Newsletters: The Art of the Soft Sell

Newsletters are such an effective form of promotion because they:

- Inform, rather than advertise. As publisher, you appear to be dispensing information, rather than selling something. In fact, you are selling yourself.
- Provide timely information, which establishes you as an expert in your field.
- Develop an ongoing relationship with your readers.
- Reach a carefully targeted mailing list, ensuring that your marketing dollars are well spent.
- Open doors. It may be difficult to call presidents of companies to ask for business, but your newsletter can show them that you're knowledgeable and professional. You can even call prospective clients and interview them for a newsletter story.

To publish a newsletter, you need a desktop publishing package (or a sophisticated word processor), which requires a computer with substantial memory, speed, and hard disk storage space. And you need a laser printer to print out camera-ready page proofs.

Of course, a newsletter takes more effort then some other forms of advertising or promotion. You need basic writing skills, and you need to know how to maintain a mailing list and communicate with commercial printers (unless you laser print and make copies). But don't forget that some of the best newsletters are one-page sheets printed on both sides; they are signed by the publisher and often read more like a letter than a newsletter. You don't have to publish weekly or monthly, as commercial newsletter publishers do. Most promotional newsletters come out "periodically," which means two, three, or four times a year. In addition, you can easily farm out the production work to one of the many desktop publishing firms springing up around the country.

This chapter describes why newsletters work, how the production process works, and what equipment is required to produce them.

NEWSLETTERS IN ACTION

"My *Marketing Communications* newletter (see Figure 8-3) carries a $159 subscription fee, but I hand out a lot of free copies and don't expect to make money on it," says marketing consultant Pete Silver, of Gainesville, Florida. "But I do make money on the consulting work that comes through the newsletter." The front side of Silver's one-page, back-and-front newslet-

Figure 8-2.

The front page of Bill Vick's back-and-front newsletter shows his picture and describes his technique; the back side includes his address and phone number. This newsletter is aimed at 1,500 companies looking to hire; other editions are aimed at potential job candidates.

THE RECRUITER

Vick & Associates
3325 Landershire Ln.
Plano, Texas 75023
(214) 612-VICK

SUMMER- 1988

Bill Vick

THE PROFESSIONAL DIFFERENCE

Perhaps you have worked with other recruiters in the past, but I'd like you to understand why I am different and how I work with client companies on search projects.

First I work only with clients with a critical need. If your company has a position that can remain open indefinitely without causing problems, you don't need me. I only work on one search at a time because I learned early on that focus, and only focus generates results. I cannot be effective by juggling 22 balls in the air at once. Because I only work with searches for sales and marketing executives in the micro-compter industry, I understand well your unique needs and requirements.

Because of my organized and planned approach, our results are based on teamwork. Be-

fore I work with you, in defining the position and its relationships to your management structure, I will have frank discussions with you, and others in your organization as needed, which results in an understanding of you, your overall goals, management style, current business challenges, and the culture of your organization. I will then act as facilitator and resource to help you state the requirements of the job and the qualifications of the ideal candidate.

As with other business challenges, a planned and disciplined approach with accurate information is fundamental to obtaining desired results. Simply put, I will develop a plan of action that produces the best qualified candidates. Through research, industry sources, extensive personal contacts, and networking I will target key individuals as candidates to produce leads about people who would otherwise be difficult for you to identify.

From the initial group of prospects I have identified, the most qualified are selected for an in depth appraisal and interview. Backgrounds and relative performance is explored and evaluated. The credentials of the best prospects are documented and verified using my independent contacts as well as references. Those candidates we determine to be most suitable for your organization are presented for consideration and interview. I

will provide assistance in structuring the interview for maximum benefit and add a professional perspective to the subsequent evaluation.

Once mutual interest is established, I will help in negotiating the compensation package and employment arrangements. This is a critical stage requiring the utmost skill and tact. The manner in which this is accomplished is key in completing a successful recruiting effort.

My service does not end with the successful conclusion of a search. I will periodically follow up with you and the hired executive to assure that the expectations of both parties are being met. This can not only minimize the possibility of a communications breakdown, but provides valuable feedback and understanding of the true success of the search process.•

HIRING PROJECTIONS FOR SECOND HALF 1988

Results from a new national survey indicate that employment hiring projections for the second half of 1988 remain very optimistic. We recently participated in a national survey of 2,600 executives responsible for hiring throughout the country and the results are very interesting.

Figure 8-3.

Pete Silver's *Marketing Communications* is a direct one-column communiqué to clients that delivers tips on promoting their own businesses—but makes it clear how to reach him. It was written and printed with *WordStar*.

THE MARKETING COMMUNICATIONS

Information, Recommendations & Commentary from Pete Silver

12 March 1990

MASTER MARKETING CHECKLIST

Dear Colleague:

When you go to visit your doctor, someone with a clipboard (usually a nurse or assistant) asks you a series of specific, problem-oriented questions ("Did you ever have ...") about your health. The concept struck me as comprehensive and revealing, so a couple of years ago, I developed the following checklist to assess the marketing efforts and results of businesses.

I recommend that you review the checklist below with pencil in hand. Mark the ones which are problems right now for your business.

Then you can fax this to your marketing advisor, consultant or coach -- and discuss ways to improve the areas which need help.

[ ] We don't have a written marketing plan everyone on our team can understand, agree on, and support.

[ ] We're spending too much on marketing (all areas).

[ ] We are not receiving enough free publicity in trade magazines.

[ ] We are not being interviewed enough on radio talk shows.

[ ] We are not being interviewed enough on television talk shows.

[ ] We are not being interviewed enough by newspapers.

[ ] We are not giving enough speeches to groups of qualified prospects.

[ ] We don't have a powerful press kit.

[ ] We don't have a current media distribution list.

[ ] Our direct mail isn't pulling enough responses.

THE MARKETING COMMUNICATIONS REPORT (founded 1986) is published every month by Pete Silver. Correspondence to: 4300 N.W. 23rd Avenue, Suite 528, Gainesville, FL 32606. Telephone (904) 371-2083 or (800) 868-9520 Fax: (904) 371-2180. CompuServe E-Mail: 76466,364. © Pete Silver. All rights reserved. Editor: Pete Silver.

Annual subscription rates: via First Class Mail to U.S. and Canada: $159 U.S. Inquire for delivery rates for FAX, Telex, electronic mail and overseas mail. Inquire for availability of back issues.

Pete Silver also presents speeches, conducts workshops, and consults on areas covered by the newsletter. Clients include associations, private and public organizations, and consultants. Inquire for further information.

Direct Response Marketing · Newsletters · Brochures
Audio-Visual Presentations · Seminars · Speeches

REPORT

ter carries information about the services he offers and a description of his clients.

Dan Poynter's Para Publishing, run from his home in Santa Barbara, California, has grossed over $3 million from sales of his self-published books on desktop publishing. Poynter keeps a computerized mailing list of

25,000 prospects, including many small specialized lists of people interested in book publishing. He frequently puts out press releases offering free information kits that bring a steady flow of fresh inquiries to add to the list.

His *Publishing Poynters* newsletter (see Figure 8-4) is a one-page, two-sided information sheet of tips and ideas. Poynter also mentions his new books, consulting services, and upcoming seminars, and prints an order

Figure 8-4.

Dan Poynter's *Publishing Poynters* offers 5,000 self-publishers ideas on promoting themselves. On the backside of this two-page newsletter, he devotes nearly a column to an order blank for his own books, workshops, and brochures.

Publishing Poynters

Book marketing news & ideas from Dan Poynter
January-March, 1990

Copyright changes. Last year, the U.S. joined the Berne Convention. Now authors are protected in 79 member nations and some changes have been made to U.S. copyright laws. Send for copyright Circular 93, *Highlights of U.S. Adherence to the Berne Convention:* Register of Copyrights, Publications Section, LM-455, Library of Congress, Washington, DC 20559. Or call the Copyright Office Hotline, 24 hours, and leave your request on the machine: (202) 707-9100.

Bar codes. The Postal Service is scanning the bar codes on loose-in-the-mail books to determine the publisher so they can return them. If the test works, it will be expanded to all 21 bulk mail centers. Another good reason for bar codes.

Top 25 US Business News Editors is a free list from Mitch Davis. Send a #10 SASE (Self-Addressed, Stamped Envelope) to Broadcast Interview Source, 2233 Wisconsin Avenue NW #406-A, Washington, DC 20007-4104. (202) 333-4904.

No sales tax. California's taxing authorities have determined we do not have to collect the 6.25% sales tax on mailing list rentals when the lists are on one-across peel-and-stick labels or four-across Cheshire (paper) labels. Lists are only taxable when supplied on mag tapes. Para Publishing rents all sorts of book promotion lists. See the order blank for more information.

New Age Directory seeks listings for second edition. Send for a questionnaire to *Marketing Opportunities Directory,* Sophia Tarila, Ph.D., P.O. Box 2578-A, Sedona, AZ 86336. (602) 282-9574.

Color brochures. If you like our new color brochure and want to promote your books this same way, get a copy of our Special Report *Brochures For Book Publishers.* This 60-page report will show you how to print brochures like this for less than ten cents each. See the order blank. These brochures were printed by Econocolor and *delivered* in less than three weeks. For a brochure, contact Bill Stuker at Econocolor, 7405-A Industrial Road, Florence, KY 41042-2997. (800) 877-7405. The typesetting and layout were done by Chris Nolt, 1328 Bath Street, Santa Barbara, CA 93101. (805) 966-4239. Give her a call.

Gift shop mailing list. Will rent or trade 3,600 names. Contact Strawberry Patch, Diane Pfeifer, P.O. Box 52404-A, Atlanta, GA 30355-0404. (404) 261-2197.

The Book Publisher's Resource Guide by John Kremer will help you find the many resources you need for book production and promotion. It lists the top U.S. wholesalers, book fairs, mailing list sources, books on publishing, fulfillment houses, marketing directories and much more. Similar to *Literary Market Place* at less than 25% of the price. Brand new, 8.5 x 11, 320 pgs. See the order blank.

The Directory of Publishing-1990 lists major publishers, agents, associations and services outside the U.S.—use it to sell overseas. It is much less expensive at $49.50 than *International Literary Market Place* which sells for $119.00. Softcover, 7 x 10, 395 pgs, See the order blank.

Color business cards. You may buy 3,000 cards for less than $250.00. We paid $640.00 for 40,000—so we could give you the enclosed sample. For a brochure, contact Nova Graphics, Linda Self, 1608-A McGee, Kansas City, MO 64108. (800) 877-3300, ext. 4204, (816) 221-4850.

Outdoor, recreation & travel books wanted by European booktrade and recreation trade distributor. Send samples (no hunting or fishing) and reviews to Cordee, Ken Vickers, 3a, de Montfort Street, Leicester, LE1 7HD, Great Britain. Tel: 011-44-1-0533-543579.

Publishing Management Software may help you determine print runs, marketing costs, projected sales, rate of return and a title's performance before you have made the decision to publish. For a free IBM demo disk, contact Publishing Management Software, Inc., 160-A Fifth Avenue, New York, NY 10010. (212) 675-7805.

Independent Wholesalers Co-operative Information Project is an association of regional book wholesalers who want to handle your books. For information including copies of sales agreements, send a SASE with .65 postage to IWCIP, 702-A South Michigan, South Bend, IN 46618.

Top 100 US-Based Euromarket Media Correspondents is a free list of journalists covering US news for European outlets. Send a #10 SASE to Broadcast Interview Source, Mitch Davis, 2233 Wisconsin Avenue NW #406-A, Washington, DC 20007-4104. (202) 333-4904.

Catalog/800 number/Talk shows. *Big Books From The Small Presses* is a catalog with a toll-free ordering number. Once listed in the catalog, you may offer easy ordering by providing their 800 number when on radio and TV talk shows. For details, contact Upper Access, Lisa Carlson, Upper Access Road, Hinesburg, VT 05461. (802) 482-2988.

Print interview tip: If you are interviewed for a feature article, do not offer to proof the article. Many journalists are annoyed when interviewees want to approve of *free publicity.* It is a journalist's job to report accurately. Do not jeopardize your future publicity efforts by alienating journalists. However, if they get a fact wrong, be assertive and ask them to run a correction in the next edition. Thanks to Charlotte Digregorio who teaches journalism at Portland State for this book promotion tip.

form on every newsletter. "I can't understand people who get replies from ads and never do follow-up mailings. It's easier to sell an existing customer a second product than to find a new customer."

The Martinique Deal

Steve McGowan, head of McGowan Marine in Dartmouth, Massachusetts, sends out a four-page newsletter twice a year to 700 clients and potential clients. "In my business, one response pays for several years of newsletter production," says McGowan, who spends between $2,000 and $2,500 to produce each issue of *McGowan Marine* (see Figure 8-5). He writes it on *WordPerfect*, then hands the copy to an assistant who converts the file to Microsoft *Word* on the Macintosh and does page layout with *PageMaker*. Each newsletter is accompanied by a mail-merged cover letter targeted to different groups—yacht owners, yacht builders, or marine contractors. "With one response to the newsletter I lined up five years of work with a French company building 140-foot cruise ships at $6 million per sailing out of Martinique. That covers my costs!"

Ensuring Reader Feedback

The Computer Literacy Workshop, run by Margaret Luellen, is one of the Houston area's top computer consulting firms; its clients include Continental Airlines, Exxon, and many medium-size businesses. Since 1986, Luellen has put out *Computer Literacy Newsletter* ($14.95 per year) every month. It's an eight-page hotbed of tricks and tips for computer users.

Although the original newsletter was one page folded in half (for mailing), the first issue made Luellen a local authority. "I wrote a piece on technostress that was prompted by my visit to the eye doctor for eye fatigue," says Luellen. The local radio station picked up on the piece, and Luellen was interviewed. "I couldn't believe it. I didn't even think anyone would read it and suddenly I was being interviewed."

Most important, Luellen ensures feedback from her readers by including a monthly computer-related puzzle, with prizes awarded to the winners. Luellen includes a questionnaire with the contest entry that explores readers' personal computer use and training needs, thereby providing her with important marketing information. "We study these responses very carefully and use them to maintain our database," says Luellen. "For instance, if we're planning an editorial on *dBase*, we know who to send the issue to; we also know which courses to add to or subtract from our course offerings."

When Luellen compares her time and expenses to more traditional

Figure 8-5.

Steve McGowan's four-page *McGowan Marine* goes to 700 people twice a year. He writes it with *WordPerfect* for the IBM; then an assistant converts the files to Microsoft *Word* on the Macintosh and finishes the page layout with *PageMaker*.

Westport, Massachusetts   Winter 1989-1990   Number 3

A New *Leander* Is Completed

In December, after nearly a year of renovation, the 108-foot *Leander* emerged from Denison Marine in Dania, Florida as a beautiful, 120-foot, cockpit motor yacht.

Modifications include major engine-room changes, soundproofing, a new mast, extended boat deck and afterdeck, and a swim platform aft, as well as doubling the size of the owner's cabin, adding his and her heads. A gleaming paint job completes the transformation.

Two diesel generators were removed from the engine room and replaced by new, larger units located under the cockpit sole. A third, smaller, gen-set was also installed for night-time and off-peak usage. Placement of the generators and water makers in their own compartment, right aft, with extensive soundproofing throughout should make *Leander* one of the quietest motor yachts afloat.

McGowan Marine Inc. consulted on all phases of the project with Captain Dave Lord.

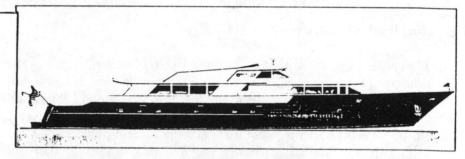

Leander Today

and Yesterday

"Pride, experience, and dependable technology go into every project."

--Stephen McGowan

advertising fees, she's convinced it's a cost-effective endeavor. "A newsletter stands apart from junk mail," says Luellen.

The Newsletter as Cornerstone

Ash Jain, head of Irvine Resource Group, a consulting and publishing firm in Irvine, California, worked backward. He started a newsletter, *Macintosh Market Report*, and used the response to build a consulting business and as market research to launch other for-profit publications. "The newsletter has defined to me the size of the potential customer base in the Macintosh arena," says Jain, who uses Microsoft *Word*, *Excel*, and *PageMaker* to produce a heavy diet of charts and graphs (see Chapter 10 for sample charts). "The newsletter is self-sustaining and has led to consulting work. And I know I can target different groups in that customer base with other information-heavy publications."

BEFORE THE PRESSES ROLL

While publishing a newsletter is not that difficult once the wheels are in motion, you should think through the process carefully before delving in. Here are some points to consider before you start the presses rolling:

1. *Attract attention*. The average business executive receives more than fifty promotional pieces a week, according to marketing consultant Howard L. Shenson, a California-based marketing consultant who teaches his clients how to write newsletters (and has produced audio tapes on the process; see 'Newsletter Publishing Resources" at the end of this chapter). You have less than one second to capture the executive's attention. To ensure that your message doesn't wind up in the wastebasket you need to make all the elements of a newsletter—artwork, layout, envelope, and paper stock—convey your message.

2. *Narrow your subject*. Focus on a narrow subject and stick with it. For example, computer newsletters abound, so pick a more specific subject such as CD-ROM or artificial intelligence and you'll probably attract more attention. Marketing newsletters proliferate, but there are far fewer on, say, medical marketing.

3. *Choose an editorial format*. Will you report news, offer opinions, or instruct people how to do something—or will you mix formats? Once you establish a style, stick with it. Your readers will appreciate a standard format, and you'll have an easier time preparing material.

4. *Set a distribution scheme*. The post office has a variety of bulk

mailing and special postage rates. Visit the post office and talk to a representative before you make a distribution decision.

5. *Find a print shop.* Unless your mailing list is very small, don't use your laser printer to print each copy of the newsletter. Visit various commercial printers and get price estimates. Perhaps you want to send a disk directly to a high-quality typesetting machine. Perhaps you want to use your own laser printer to produce a master copy for offset printing. Ask all printers if they provide extra services such as collating, folding, and stapling.

6. *Prepare a backlog of material.* Outline a year's worth of topics, which may represent only two two-page issues, before you start writing a newsletter. You'll find out whether you have enough to say about your subject.

7. *Choose an appropriate length.* The best newsletters are short and to the point. Two-page newsletters (one sheet of paper printed front and back) are read immediately; longer newsletters may be shelved and read later, if at all. But longer newsletters also give you more space to list your products and services, or to run quizzes or contests to learn more about your readers.

8. *Consider bounce-back schemes.* Many newsletters have coupons, bingo cards (where you circle a number to indicate your choice), and other enclosures that elicit reader response. If readers must find their own envelopes and stamps to reply, you are less likely to hear from them. On the other hand, including stamped return replies can be expensive. A good alternative is to use business reply cards, which you pay for only when you get a reply. Inquire at the post office for details.

9. *Set a production schedule.* You have to live with your own deadlines, especially if you charge a fee for the newsletter. You must commit to the recurring expense of writing, producing, and mailing the newsletter. The more frequently the newsletter is published, the more money you'll spend on production.

10. *Decide if you'll charge for your newsletter.* You can always begin with free distribution and reevaluate later. Be flexible; even if you charge a fee, it's good to distribute some copies free to make new contacts and keep good clients. If you don't have the time to produce a newsletter and must hire out, you may want to charge a fee to cover the costs.

11. *Mail to your own clients and potential clients (or customers) you have on your database.* This is the least expensive way to launch an effective mailing. However, you can supplement your list with commercially available mailing lists (see Chapter 16). Often your local chamber of commerce has lists available. Send complimentary copies to key people in your particular field.

SOFTWARE FOR NEWSLETTERS

What kind of software do you need to produce your newsletter? You can choose between high-end word processing programs or dedicated page layout programs. Some publishers also use spreadsheets, presentation graphics, or illustration programs to create art (see Chapter 9). The choice depends to a large degree on what kind of software you already have, and on what kind of newsletter you want to create.

Word Processors

You can produce a simple one-sheet newsletter, with text on front and back (in two or three columns), with a sophisticated word processor such as Microsoft *Word* or *WordPerfect* (see Chapter 7). The emphasis in such a newsletter is likely to be on text, since you don't have much space to deliver information, and the purpose of such a newsletter is to establish yourself as an expert.

A word processor that allows multicolumn formatting and wraps text around imported graphics will be as effective as a desktop publishing program, which is better suited for slick, graphic, or color publications.

Page Layout Software

Desktop publishing, or page layout, programs offer more control over kerning (the spacing of type), importation of graphics, wrapping of text around graphics, adding of spot color and contrast to graphics, and multi-column formats (see Figures 8-6 and 8-7).

And for long newsletters, desktop publishing programs give you a better feel for the big picture. Instead of switching between editing and page-preview mode, as you do with a word processor, you're always working in a page-preview mode, so you see the way the printed page will look. In addition, you can create and print thumbnail sketches of each page of the newsletter before creating it (see Figure 8-8).

Desktop publishing software, however, is an added expense; you still need to generate text with a word processor. And while desktop publishing programs have text editing and spell checking capabilities, it's more efficient to handle these tasks with a word processor.

However, while high-end desktop publishing programs are aimed at professional publishers, the lines between mid-level desktop publishing packages and sophisticated word processors are blurry. If you plan on occasional publishing to promote yourself, see what you can accomplish with your word processor before investing in a desktop publishing program. If you plan on publishing as a business venture, you should probably investigate desktop publishing packages from the start.

Figure 8-6.

Desktop publishing programs control exact placement of text and graphics better than even the most sophisticated word processors, as the options on the pulldown menu indicate. Here, *PageMaker* for the Macintosh, the original desktop publishing program, wraps text around graphics (the eyeglasses).

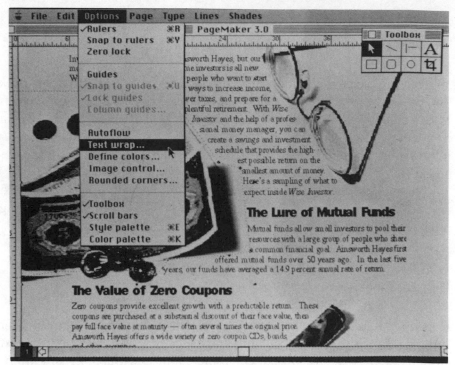

NEWSLETTER PRODUCTION

There are two basic ways to produce your newsletter: Print out all copies on your laser printer, or run off a laser print, paste up a mechanical, and take it to a printing shop. Unless you're planning to run off all copies of your publication on your laser printer—and laser printers aren't designed as heavy-duty printing machines—the term desktop publishing is misleading. You're not really publishing with your desktop computer—you're preparing mechanicals for your typesetter and printer.

Mechanicals are a publication's final pages ready for professional printing. (Some newsletter publishers cut costs by professionally printing one master copy and photocopying the rest.) Depending on the illustrations (if there are any), you paste your finished artwork in place or indicate on the mechanicals where the art is supposed to go. Art supply stores sell stiff boards to create mechanicals.

Figure 8-7.

This time-lapse sequence of printouts shows how desktop publishing software produces a newsletter: (1) Enter a headline in any type size or style; (2) choose a size and type of rule to set it off from the main body; (3) create your own graphs on-screen or import them from other programs, as with the text; (4) with the text in place, add shading to the bar graph; (5) print out the newsletter on a laser printer. The chart at the bottom was made with *MacDraw* and was moved into *PageMaker* on the Macintosh.

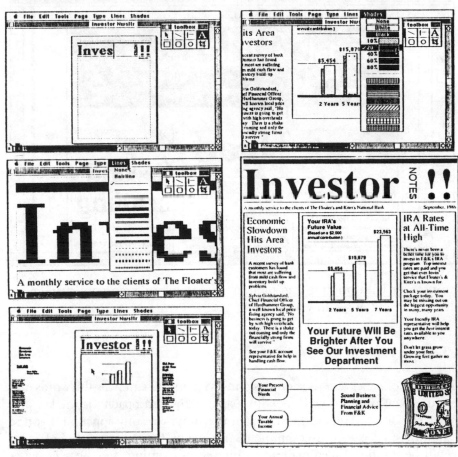

Newsletter Length

The classic newsletter is built on two 11-inch by 17-inch boards. In the final printing, layouts from the two boards are printed back and front on one 11-inch by 17-inch paper. Fold the paper and you have a four-page newsletter, with each page measuring 8.5 inches by 11 inches.

Of course, there are many other printing and folding schemes for newsletters. Multiples of eight-page units are usually the most cost-effective

Figure 8-8.

QuarkStyle, a desktop publishing program for the Macintosh, includes templates for newsletters so you don't have to design from scratch. You just add text to each section without worrying about formatting, although you can make changes any time you want.

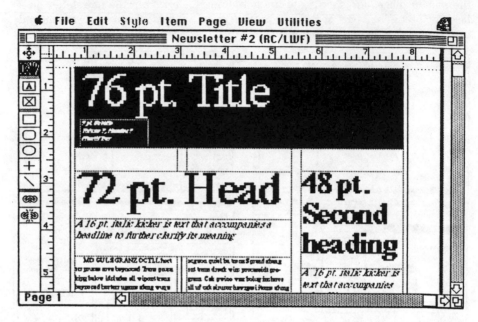

formats for both printing and binding. Before you design your newsletter, discuss the options with your printer.

Choosing Paper

The kind of paper you use conveys a message just as surely as the words and pictures you print on it. Generally, paper with high opacity is thicker and more expensive. The weight of a paper may not be readily apparent if you're handling single sheets, so examine a sample with the same number of pages you'll be printing. Keep mailing requirements in mind, too; heavier paper costs more to mail, although you can cut costs by choosing a lower postal class.

If you want people to write on the printed page (for reader response coupons, say) try it yourself first! Some order forms stubbornly resist all pencils or ballpoint pens.

Placing Art in Your Layout

Illustrations composed only of black lines—called line art—can be pasted down on a mechanical and printed just like type. Computer-generated line art, such as spreadsheet charts and presentation graphics, can be exported to your desktop publishing program and printed on a laser.

Any photos or illustrations with areas of solid gray or color require several steps for the print shop. If the illustrations aren't sized to fit your layout, you'll have to reduce or enlarge the art with a proportion wheel, available at any art supply store. Then take the art to a print shop and get a properly sized photostat and paste it into your layout. The photostat merely indicates the position of the art; send the original art to the printer, indicating the reduction or enlargement.

An alternative—best used by professional publishers—is to scan photographs or illustrations into your desktop publishing file and print them out on your laser printer. You can size the photo in your desktop publishing program and edit it by changing lines or shading. For a variety of reasons, however, most scanned images won't reproduce well on a laser printer. For all but the most basic line art, it's best to get a halftone reproduction done by a commercial printer.

POWER OF THE PRESS

Many professionals and small businesses knock themselves out looking for ways to get publicity. It may take them years to plant one story in a local newspaper. Depending on the business and the timing of the story, the results might justify the effort and the time. That one piece of publicity might snowball. But, more often, it's an isolated blip that has no follow-through.

Publishing your own newsletter gives you the power of the press that is so important to promotion. As publisher, you choose and shape the news, you highlight the good and ignore the bad—and you distribute it to the people you want to impress. And you ensure follow-through by publishing on a regular basis.

NEWSLETTER PUBLISHING RESOURCES

How to Start and Promote Your Own Newsletter for Profit and/or Personal Image Building, by Howard Shenson, 20750 Ventura Boulevard, Suite 206, Woodland Hills, Calif. 91364; (818) 703-1415; $79 for three cassettes and handbook. Shenson, known as the "consultant's consultant," doesn't focus on computer techniques, but offers strategies for selecting a topic, a name, a production schedule, and how to figure out costs and build a potential subscriber base for a newsletter.

Publishing Newsletters, by Howard Penn Hudson, Charles Scribner's Sons, 1988; $12.95. This book from the president of the Newsletter Clearinghouse provides a step-by-step guide for creating and marketing a newsletter, with information on desktop publishing.

The Electronic Publishers, by Diane Burns, Sharyn Venit, and Rebecca Hansen, Brady/Simon & Schuster, New York, N.Y., 466 pp., 1988; $29.95. This book provides an excellent soup-to-nuts look at the electronic publishing process. It covers legal questions and contracts, typography and page layout, production, and printing and binding.

WordPerfect 5.1: Desktop Publishing in Style, by Daniel Will Harris, Peachpit Press, 496 pp., 1990; $24.95. A funny and informative book about using *Word-Perfect* as a desktop publishing package. For Lotus *1-2-3* users, a chapter is devoted to *WordPerfect*'s spreadsheet hot-link function.

The Art of Desktop Publishing, 2nd ed., by Tony Bove, Cheryl Rhodes, and Wes Thomas, Bantam Electronic Publishing, 320 pp., 1989; $21.95. From typography to graphics to printing, this book covers the fundamentals of publishing techniques. It gives advice on the purchase of software and printers, as well as tips and instructions for using popular programs.

Using Aldus PageMaker 3.0, 2nd ed., by Doug Kramer and Roger Parker, with Tips by Eda Warren, Bantam Electronic Publishing, 368 pp., 1989; $22.95. This book covers both Macintosh and IBM versions of this best-selling desktop publishing package. It features step-by-step instructions for the entire spectrum of design and composition—from book pages to professional quality advertisements.

Real World PageMaker 4, Industrial Strength Techniques (Macintosh Edition), by Olav Kvern and Stephen Roth, Bantam Electronic Publishing, 400 pp., 1990; $24.95. This book is an authoritative, solutions-oriented guide for professionals who use *PageMaker* on the Macintosh regularly.

The Ventura Publisher Solutions Book, Recipes for Advanced Results, by Michael Utvich, Bantam Electronic Publishing, 464 pp., 1990; $24.95. A cookbook format gives instant step-by-step techniques to solve specific layout, typesetting, or graphics problems.

Ventura Tips and Tricks, 2nd Edition, by Ted Nace with Daniel Will-Harris, Peachpit Press, 760 pp., 1989; $24.95. This book explains how to assemble the hardware you need and how to organize your hard disk to make the leading MS-DOS desktop publishing program hum. It covers font installation, speed tips, and ways to overcome memory limitations.

SPOTLIGHT ON: Newsletter Publishing Software

Cost: $100 to $900.

Learning Curve: Medium to steep. Even when using a high-end word processor you're familiar with, figuring out how to format your document for proper printing will take some time. Start-up or intermediate desktop publishing programs, such as *Publish-It!* and *QuarkStyle*, are fairly quick studies; professional-level programs, such as *PageMaker* and *Xerox Ventura Publisher*, are more difficult to learn.

Required Equipment: Hard disk drive; mouse; laser printer, preferably with PostScript capability. To import graphics from paper: a scanner. To import graphics from CD-ROM disks: a CD-ROM drive.

Recommended Software:

For IBM PC and IBM PS/2 and Compatibles

- *WordPerfect* (WordPerfect Corp.), the kingpin word processor in the MS-DOS world, is also the best suited to newsletter production; it imports graphics, wraps text around them, and generates multicolumn pages.
- *Publish-It!* (Timeworks, Inc.), a page layout program with a range of text- and graphics-handling features, is superb for basic publications.
- *PageMaker* (Aldus Corp.), which runs under *Windows*, is especially good at handling graphics; it works better with Microsoft *Word* than with *WordPerfect*.
- *Xerox Ventura Publisher* (Xerox Desktop Software), the leading desktop publishing program in the MS-DOS world, is particularly good at handling long documents; it includes thorough style sheets (including drop capitals).
- *Ami Professional* (Samna), which runs under *Windows*, is one of the new breed of word processors with business templates; it generates multicolumn formats and tables.
- *Microsoft Word for Windows* (Microsoft), a word processor which handles graphics well, is superb for newsletter production; it has page-preview, outlining, table-making functions, and a hot link to *Excel* spreadsheet; it generates indexes and tables of contents.

For Macintosh

- *Microsoft Word* (Microsoft) is a word processor that can import graphics, create tables and multicolumn formats, and generate a wide range of type styles; it has hot links to *Excel* spreadsheets.
- *PageMaker* (Aldus Corp.), the program that started the desktop publishing craze, supports virtually all hardware and software, and it offers a range of controls over graphics; it has added strong text-editing and table-making features.
- *Ready, Set, Go!* (Letraset USA) offers a selection of predefined page grids, of real benefit to anyone just learning about page layout and design.
- *QuarkStyle* (Quark, Inc.) provides quick professional results with little training, thanks to more than seventy-five business templates from internationally known designers (see Figure 8-8).

Buying Tips: The more sophisticated the software, the more memory, hard disk space, and computer speed it takes to run the program well (and the longer it takes to learn it). Thus, if you plan on publishing a simple one-page newsletter without much variation, you don't need a feature-laden program that will take up overhead on your system; a high-end word processor may do the trick.

If you want to publish number-based charts, be sure the program has a hot link to your spreadsheet so that changes in the spreadsheet will be reflected in your newsletter. If you plan on importing graphics, check to see which file formats the page layout software supports.

Chapter 9
Sell Your Ideas: With Graphic Presentations

Combine words, numbers, and pictures in persuasive slides, overheads, and printouts for maximum impact.

> A *picture shows me at a glance what it takes dozen of pages
> of a book to expound.*
>
> —Ivan Turgenev, *Fathers and Sons*

Whether you're in a roundtable business meeting or at the lecture hall podium, you can enhance any presentation by using graphics. A landmark study conducted by 3M and the University of Minnesota in 1986 found that a presentation that uses visual support is 43 percent more persuasive than one that doesn't. An appropriately placed pie chart, an eye-riveting bullet list, a crystal-clear flowchart, or a concise graph will catch people's eyes and stick in their minds.

In the business world, a colorful chart is equivalent to a "sound bite" in TV news—is doesn't tell the whole story, but it does convey an idea with speed and impact.

Until recently, designing a presentation has required the services of a designer or production house. Today, presentation graphics software makes it easy for nonartists to create eye-grabbing visuals. The programs take data from word processors, databases, spreadsheets, and graphics programs—and turn them into text charts, graphs, and diagrams.

Once you have the graphic file on disk, you can turn it into 35-mm slides, overhead transparencies, and color, laser, and dot-matrix printouts. If you don't have the proper output device, you can send the file (by disk or modem) to a graphic service bureau that will return the finished product. Without too much effort or expense, an independent professional or small business can create high-quality documents and slides to use as marketing tools.

For people in sales or marketing, who need to regularly present new data quickly, the ability to translate dry numbers into colorful bars and graphs is a great advantage. Anyone who speaks regularly at trade shows or industry events might want to use overhead transparencies or slides to accompany their talks. And people preparing proposals to land jobs will find that a visually strong proposal can hook corporate clients.

"We use presentation graphics in our proposals, and it gives us a competitive edge," says Judi Devin, of Minneapolis, Minnesota, whose home-based company, Medium Well Done, prepares instructional training materials for such clients as IBM, General Mills, and Honeywell Bull. "More and more clients expect proposals and the finished product to look super-professional." Devin, who subcontracts to a freelance graphic artist to design presentations, says that graphics not only make her proposals look good, but also make them more understandable.

Tom Miller, who oversees the annual National Work-at-Home Survey for Link Resources, goes even farther afield to produce his presentations. He has an arrangement with a copy shop in Ithaca, New York, to produce slides from his data. He faxes paper sketches with suggested formats and the shop translates the data into slides, for about $12 each. "I believe in specialization," says Miller. "I'd rather interpret data than worry about whether a graphic is one inch too high or low on the screen."

This chapter describes how presentation software works, what type of graphics to use to present different types of data, and tips on arranging and creating a presentation.

PRESENTATION GRAPHICS SOFTWARE

Presentation graphics software is a packager: It imports data from other programs (spreadsheets, word processors, and graphics programs) or directly from the keyboard and dresses it up 101 ways. You can add color, shadings, icons, and fonts to make your data come alive. Then the software exports the finished product to a wide range of output devices.

As with any graphics-oriented application, a fast computer is highly recommended. If your intent is to produce slides, a color monitor eases the task. With a monochrome monitor, you have to assign colors by number and won't see on-screen what the final product will look like. If you're producing laser prints or overhead transparencies, a monochrome monitor will suffice.

Text Charts

Text slides or handouts—probably the most common presentation medium—contain short phrases that capture and summarize major points.

Placing bullets, daggers, or other symbols before each phrase helps focus the audience's attention on each point. The type in the graphics is much larger than typical word processing type so that it can be viewed from a distance (see Figure 9-1).

A text chart can be prepared with any word processor that allows you to alter the size and style of type. But while you can create laser printouts from a word processor, creating a slide will be much easier with a presentation graphics program, which is designed for the task.

Spreadsheet Data

Virtually all presentation graphics programs allow you to input numbers directly, and most can import Lotus *1-2-3* or *Excel* spreadsheet data for graphs and charts. While these and other spreadsheets offer their own chart-making abilities, presentation programs dress up the graphics and integrate them into an overall presentation.

To add variety to basic spreadsheet charts, you can add special effects, such as exploded slices in a pie chart, or 3-D shadings in a bar chart.

Figure 9-1.
Most business charts are text charts, with a bold heading and three to six short lines preceded by a bullet. The chart here also includes a high-tech graphic symbol. Courtesy of Brilliant Image, a graphics service bureau in New York City.

Presentation graphics programs have clip art libraries with icons—such as maps, industry symbols, machines, stars, skylines, people, and fancy borders—that can be used to separate different data sets. For example, in one slide a bar chart of regional sales can be superimposed over a map of the northeast United States, and in another, over a map of the southwestern states. You can also use freehand drawing programs to accomplish the same effect, if you have the artistic talent (see Figures 9-2).

Most programs allow you to add text anywhere on the graphic. Thus, you could take a Lotus *1-2-3* chart, move it into your presentation program, and add a headline and text to explain the data.

Graphs and Charts

A good graph is like a good accountant—it transforms complex data into simple, understandable results. All presentation graphics programs can create pie, bar, and line graphs. Each type illustrates data differently. The type of graphic you choose depends on what you want to say.

- *Column graphs* (many software packages call these vertical bar charts) are used to examine one item that changes over time or to compare an item with others. For example, you'd use a column graph to track a company's sales over the last six months (see Figure 9-3).
- *Bar graphs* are similar to column graphs except that the bars run horizontally. You use bar graphs to compare independent data sets that do not change. Which department provides the highest revenues? Which country has the largest army?
- *Pie charts* are generally used to compare percentages, and often to show one company's or product's share of the market. Slices of the pie represent the parts that make up a whole (see Figure 9-4).
- *Line graphs*, which show trends over time, are good for representing large data sets. For example, if you wanted to show the average rainfall in 1990, a line with a point for each week of the year would be quite reasonable. A bar chart with fifty-two bars would be overwhelming. Line graphs are good predictors, because large data sets show patterns.

You can create specialized graphs, but the four just listed are the most common. You can mix different types to create more interesting graphics. The most common combination is to superimpose a line graph over a bar graph. This combo offers a great deal of complex information in a very concise package.

Most programs also allow you to create overlays and builds. For example, if your first graphic shows the first year of a five-year plan, the

Figure 9-2.

A map of the United States, taken from a clip art gallery of images, provides a good backdrop for the data shown below. The colors for each line of data (*not visible here, of course*) correspond to the colors of the geographic region represented. Graphic by Franck Levy.

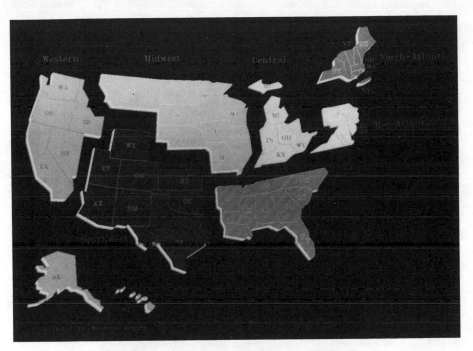

Audits Odds By IRS Region	
	1.48
Southwest	1.46
North–Atlantic	.90
Midwest	.87
Southeast	.82
Central	.70
Mid–Atlantic	.69

Figure 9-3.
Column charts allow comparison of similar data, such as weekly sales by the month. Dull figures can be brought to life with highly stylized corporate imagery, as is shown here. Courtesy of *Cricket Presents* and Autographix, a graphics service bureau.

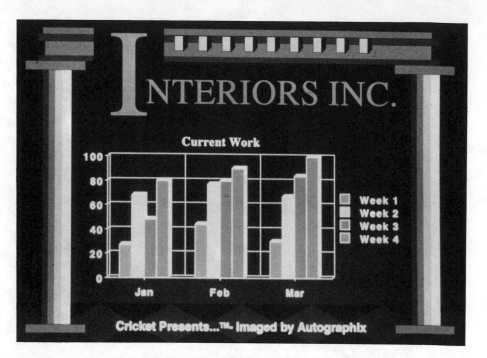

second graphic would show years one and two—in perfect alignment. Building on data in previous graphics is a good presentation strategy, especially to show a growth pattern, since you can't expect your audience to memorize all the data flashed in front of them.

GRAPHICS SERVICE BUREAUS

Because presentations are multimedia events, the software affords a range of output options—overhead transparencies, printer or plotter hard copy, 35-mm slides or 8-inch by 10-inch transparencies.

If you don't own a laser printer or a film recorder (a device that connects to the computer and produces slides), you can send your files by disk or modem to a graphics service bureau, which will send back color printouts, transparencies, or slides. (Documentation with the software indicates which service bureaus to use; most programs include built-in links to dial and send files by modem.) Turnaround time is overnight.

A slide costs between $5 and $20, an overhead transparency between

Figure 9-4.

Pie charts show percentages of the whole, and are often used to indicate market shares for a given product against its competitors. To highlight certain data, you pull one section of the pie out. Graphic by Franck Levy.

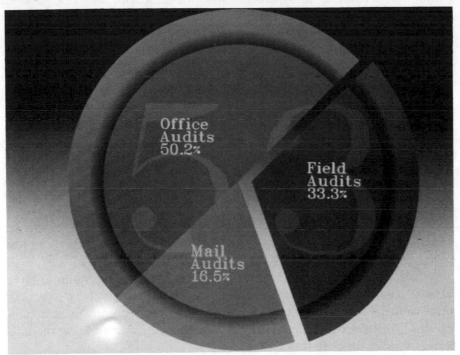

$5 and $22, a laser printout between $3 and $8, and a color thermal printout between $5 and $10.

CHOOSING A PRESENTATION MEDIUM

Decide how you're going to make your presentation before you decide what form you want your graphics in. For example, you'll take a different design approach to produce handouts for a small group than to show slides to a large audience. Here's a rundown of the most popular forms for business presentations and the hardware used to produce them.

35-mm Slides

To produce a slide you can take a 35-mm camera, aim it at your computer screen (hooded to block out the light), and shoot. But it's a tricky process, and the resolution of the slide is limited to that of the screen. Furthermore, the curve of the screen warps the edges of the photo.

A more reliable method is to use a film recorder (connected to your computer via the serial port), capture the screen image digitally, and record it on film. The film recorder may boost the resolution of the screen display. Since film recorders are expensive, and still leave you with the tasks of processing the film and mounting the slide, you're better off sending your file to a graphics bureau, which will produce a slide for $5 to $20.

Slides are perceived as the most professional presentation medium and are very effective for addressing large groups. However, since lights must be off or dimmed, and the projector is often attached to a timer, slide presentations tend to be less personal and interactive than others.

Black-and-White Laser Printouts

Laser printers are ideal for generating high-quality business graphics in black and white. The colors you see (if you have a color monitor) on the computer screen are translated into shades of gray or cross-hatchings on paper. Often, you can substitute your laser printer's built-in fonts for those of the graphics program.

Laser printouts are best used to produce reports or presentations given to small groups. Some laser printers can also produce sharp overhead transparencies (see your printer's documentation), although you have to be careful that the acetate doesn't get jammed in the printer and that the laser toner saturates the acetate.

Color Printouts

The 3M/University of Michigan study of business graphics found that respondents perceived color graphics as more professional *and* more interesting than black-and-white graphics. To obtain high-quality color printouts, you'll need a color ink-jet or thermal-transfer printer. Of course, you must choose software that works with a specific color printer. Most MS-DOS programs, for instance, support the IBM Color JetPrinter and the Hewlett-Packard PaintJet. Thermal-transfer printers are extremely expensive (about $10,000), so it's best to send your graphic to a service bureau if you want this vivid and varied color (more than 4,000 deep shades).

Plotters—printers that mechanically move a pen over paper to draw fine lines and images—are unbeatable for high-quality output. They can print on a variety of surfaces, including acetate films and glossy paper. The colored pens in the plotter create a multicolored graphic.

All color printouts can be used with an overhead projector, although you must test to make sure the color ink will not melt under the heat and has enough depth to project well. Otherwise, color printouts are most effective in business reports, providing a welcome break from pages of black text.

Overhead Projections

To create a transparency for an overhead projector, you print the computer graphic onto a transparent acetate sheet. Thermal-transfer printers and plotters are best for creating transparencies, although in some cases you can feed an acetate through your laser printer.

Overheads are effective for tutorial presentations, since you can talk in a lighted room and invite give-and-take with the audience.

Computer-Driven Slide Shows

The computer monitor can be a slide show device. You choose a sequence of slides (or screen images) and set the timing, and the computer projects them in order. To be effective in a large room, the computer must be connected to a large-screen projection device. You can also preview a slide presentation on the computer monitor before sending files to a graphic service bureau to create slides. If your clients use computers, you can send them the slide show on disk.

ASSEMBLING YOUR PRESENTATION

Designing a single graphic—whether it's a slide, an overhead, or a hand-out—is one part of the presentation process. Making graphics work together is another part. Before you begin creating individual graphics, you should design an overall plan. Some presentation graphics programs, especially Macintosh programs that use an outliner, force you to set up an overall plan. Use these guidelines to develop and execute a complete presentation.

1. *Be consistent*. Consistency is the most important attribute of a good presentation. Your viewers should clearly see where you've been and where you're going. If every graphic in your presentation uses different colors, fonts, and graphic techniques, your message may get lost. Don't use more than two or three different layouts in a presentation. Don't change color, type style, or type size too often, if at all.

2. *Don't put too much information on a graphic*. There's no hard-and-fast rule about how many graphics to include in a presentation. But remember that the viewer needs to look at new material frequently and is

overwhelmed with a graphic that tries to present too much information. More graphics with less information on each are preferable to fewer graphics that are loaded with data.

3. *Create a storyboard*. A storyboard is a series of boxes drawn on paper that shows your entire presentation, one graphic at a time. Draw a two-by-three box (that's the proper ratio for a slide), and enter the idea for that graphic with a wide marker. This method will force you to think visually and help spot problem graphics that contain too much information.

4. *Attack your toughest graphic first*. Any presentation is bound to have one killer graphic—perhaps it has large data sets or requires long sentences or a long list of bulleted points. Take care of these problem slides first by choosing their colors, fonts, and sizes. Then apply the same parameters to the other graphics in the presentation.

5. *Test on a guinea pig*. Get a friend or colleague to critique your presentation. Simulate your worst-case presentation conditions—such as the back row of a large audience. Is all the text legible? Is the main message of the graphic understandable? Is too much or too little going on at once? Have you used cryptic jargon or confusing abbreviations? Are your images so complex that they obscure your message?

6. *Leave time for corrections*. Graphics presentations (especially those with 35-mm slides) are subject to minor calamities. The color that looked great on-screen may be too soft when the slide comes back from the service bureau. And elements that looked all right on-screen may be too far apart on the slide. What you see on-screen is not always what you get when you transfer a screen image to an output device.

FANCY PRINTOUTS

The idea of creating an entire slide presentation can be daunting. The advertisements for presentation programs you see in computer magazines are slick and potentially intimidating. But the purpose of a graphic is to inform people—not wow them.

You don't necessarily have to be slick—and you don't have to create slides. You can start small by using your word processor to create text charts and choosing different fonts from your laser printer. Once you establish a style you like, you can begin to enhance it. If you use a Macintosh, you can easily cut and paste an illustration or drawing from another application or a spreadsheet chart.

As you build confidence and a sense of design, you can use presentation graphics programs to add pop and power to your business data and ideas. And while your word processor or spreadsheet can produce serviceable graphic printouts, the virtue of a presentation graphics program is its ability to transfer those graphics to eye-catching slides at minimal cost.

PRESENTATION GRAPHICS RESOURCES

Executive Guide to PC Presentation Graphics, by Gordon McComb, Bantam Electronic Publishing, 320 pp., 1989; $21.95. This is a hands-on guide to developing graphics and integrating them into an effective presentation. It discusses how to evaluate a wide range of software packages. It includes several chapters on technical aspects of putting together a graphics-ready computer system.

The Presentation Design Book, Projecting a Good Image With Your Desktop Computer, edited by Margaret Y. Rabb, Ventana Press, 258 pp., 1990; $24.95. This guide to computer-generated graphs, handouts, and overheads focuses on design, but it also includes tips on presentations in different settings, such as a courthouse or boardroom. The book includes 200 illustrations. Well designed and well written, it includes one chapter (on color) with color art, a rarity in such a book.

The Best Book of Harvard Graphics, by John Mueller, Howard K. Sams, 400 pp., 1990; $24.95. This book is a tutorial on using the popular presentation graphics program, with hints, tips, and techniques to get the most out of the product.

Desktop Presentations, by Margaret Cole and Sylvia Odenwald, AMACOM, 198 pp., 1990; $24.95. This book is a good buyer's guide and primer that provides reviews of both MS-DOS and Macintosh hardware and software.

SPOTLIGHT ON: Presentation Graphics Software

Cost: From $200 to $500.

Learning Curve: Medium. On most programs you are prompted to input data and choose a graph type. The difficult part, of course, is choosing the right graphics and design formats to convey data to your target audience—both of which depend on your own skills and experience.

Required Equipment: Hard disk drive; VGA color monitor recommended for creating slides: modem needed to send files electronically to service bureau; laser printer, plotter, or color printer.

Recommended Software:

For IBM PC and PS/2 and Compatibles

- *Freelance Plus* (Lotus Development Corp.) is a great all-purpose tool that produces basic charts or lets you draw your own; it allows you to view *1-2-3* spreadsheets and select ranges for charting with leaving the program; it operates with *1-2-3* style menu bar; it includes 900 symbols to use with charts.

- *Harvard Graphics* (Software Publishing) imports *1-2-3* data, turns them into enhanced charts (with shading, 3-D, etc.), and lets you add text; it includes a large symbol library, spelling checker, and hot link to spreadsheets; the menu design makes it easy to create good-looking graphics, but you don't see them until you print out.

For Macintosh

- *Persuasion* (Aldus), built around a powerful text outliner that forces you to organize your presentation before creating the graphics, is the best Macintosh presentation package; it includes a number of templates with master slide designs for different chart types and a computer slide show function.
- *PowerPoint* (Microsoft) is superb for creating text charts, but not graphics charts; it allows you to design a master slide to establish the format for every slide in the presentation; a built-in word processor has a spelling checker; the program provides a good preview of an entire presentation.
- *More II* (Symantec) integrates a full-featured outliner, making it great for text charts, but it also imports graphics; it has an on-screen slide show function.

Buying Tips: Decide beforehand the type of graphics you're most likely to present, and choose a program with strength in that area; if you want to make charts from spreadsheet data, make sure that the program supports your spreadsheet (or see if your spreadsheet produces presentable charts on its own); similarly, if you want to import graphics from other programs, make sure the program supports the file formats. If you have a modem, check to see if the program has a preset communications link to a graphics service bureau.

Chapter 10
Turn Your Spreadsheet and Database Data Into Lively Reports

Use publishing features to dress up your data and show your point graphically.

> *When you can measure what you are speaking about, and express it in numbers, you know something about it; but when you cannot measure it, when you cannot express it in numbers, your knowledge is of a meager and unsatisfactory kind.*

—William Thomson, Lord Kelvin

Early spreadsheets and database programs were superb organizers and analyzers, but primitive presenters. Printouts consisted of reams of text or numbers or primitive charts that often required supporting text or footnotes to make their point. To choose a font with earlier versions of Lotus 1-2-3, for example, you had to enter codes from the printer's setup menu, not something the average user had much time for. Today, without programming or fiddling with your printer, you can turn lifeless spreadsheet and database data into clear, free-standing reports or charts that speak for themselves.

By adding headings in different fonts, highlighting key points with shadings and shadowed boxes, or a pointing finger, you can effectively communicate the results of your analysis to your target reader. Whether you are just presenting data to support points in a letter or report (or creating invoices, financial statements, tables, estimates, bills, catalogs, and pricing information) these so-called spreadsheet and database publishing features let you say more—more quickly and attractively.

Besides using the beefed up publishing features found in today's spreadsheets and database programs, you can also move data generated by these programs into word processors, presentation graphics programs, and desktop publishing software. Several word processors provide hot links to spreadsheets so that a chart integrated into a letter will automatically change to reflect changes made to numbers within the spreadsheet (see Chapter 7). Several desktop publishing packages provide hot links to databases, as described below.

However, few presentation graphics or desktop publishing programs offer these hot links, so it's best to use a spreadsheet's own charting function if your data are likely to change. That way, you can quickly generate a new chart without exporting the data and starting from scratch.

The type and number of programs you use depends on your data and how you want to present it. For instance, Ash Jain, who publishes the *Macintosh Market Report*, tracks advertising spending by manufacturer. Since he includes the manufacturer's name and the magazine where a certain ad appeared, he uses a database, and then summarizes all spending by all manufacturers for each month. But since the database cannot produce a chart, he exports those cumulative figures into the *Excel* spreadsheet for charting. To lay out the final newsletter, Jain exports the graph into *PageMaker*, where he integrates it with text (see Figure 10-1).

This chapter describes several ways to dress up database and spreadsheet reports and a type of specialized database software that creates business forms.

SPREADSHEET PUBLISHING

The spreadsheet that started the move toward more graphic and stylized reports was *Excel* (Microsoft)—first in the Macintosh version, and then the MS-DOS version, which runs under *Windows*. With the first version of *Excel*, you could use four fonts, add headings and subheadings, and highlight key information with boldface, italics, and shading. Because many users switched from Lotus *1-2-3* to *Excel*, Lotus began selling *1-2-3* with *Allways*, an add-on program that turned the staid spreadsheet into a publishing tool. Version 3 of *1-2-3* includes a window for "quick graphs," so you can mark any section of a worksheet and see the resulting graph, a feature somewhat like the page-preview function in word processors that shows how a page will look when printed. The spreadsheet in Lotus *Symphony*, a multifunction package, also includes *Allways*.

These and other spreadsheets—such as *Full Impact* (Ashton-Tate), *Quattro Pro* (Borland), *Wingz* (Informix), *Symphony* (Lotus), and *Super-Calc 5* (Computer Associates)—allow you to turn mundane worksheets into attractive invoices, estimates, pricing sheets, or product summaries (see Figure 10-2).

Full Impact adds a word processing feature that creates a "paragraph" area on the worksheet. You can enter text with full control over its style and

Figure 10-1. Data on the Move

This sequence shows how data can move from a database to a spreadsheet to a page layout program, for inclusion in a newsletter. The first step is to enter advertising information in a database (*a*), then calculate the sum of all entries in the cost field (*b*). Export those figures to a spreadsheet to generate a graph. Then move the graph into a page layout program and integrate accompanying text from a word processor.

Ash Jain produced this series, which tracks magazine advertising for Macintosh products for use in his *Macintosh Market Report* newsletter, using *Panorama*, *Excel*, and *PageMaker*.

Publication	MacWorld
Company Name	Claris Corp
Product Name	MacWrite II
Category	SWWP
Page No.	275
Ad Description	After 10 minutes
Type	4 / 1
Space	1.00
Cost	15855.00

Accept

	1988	Nov	$6,010,342
		Dec	$5,291,685
	1989	Jan	$6,036,171
		Feb	$6,154,814
		Mar	$5,493,916
		Apr	$6,103,672
		May	$6,175,616
		Jun	$5,890,216
		Jul	$5,221,118
		Aug	$6,137,652
		Sep	$6,855,589
		Oct	$6,569,377
		Nov	$7,066,168
		Dec	$6,703,527

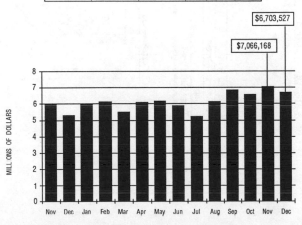

Figure 10-2.

One chart won't necessarily say it all. Here, the basic data are presented, along with two charts that show different ways of interpreting the data. Notice the different type fonts, shading, rules, and shadows that help the reader take in all the information. This printout was prepared with the spreadsheet in Lotus Symphony.

Consolidation Summary for Original Swiss Style Gourmet Foods

Spring 1990 Direct Mail Promotion

	No. Mailed	Response	Percent Response	Cost to Mail	Total Product Costs	Total Cost	Revenue	Net Profit
Chocolate Torte	115,000	6397	5.56%	$25,472.50	$51,665.22	$77,137.72	$95,635.15	$18,497.43
1/2 Cheese Wheel	115,000	3982	3.46%	25,472.50	59,929.10	85,401.60	99,350.90	13,949.30
Raclette	115,000	1865	1.62%	25,472.50	37,001.60	62,474.10	74,506.75	12,032.65
Total Net Profit								**$44,479.38**

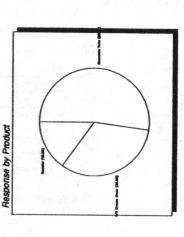

Response by Product

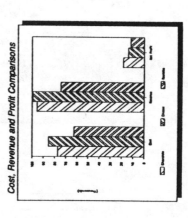

Cost, Revenue and Profit Comparisons

[This sample prepared using Lotus Symphony 2.2 and the Apple LaserWriter II]

orientation (text can be rotated in 90-degree increments) and embed spreadsheet formulas in the text that look up or calculate numbers from the worksheet's data (see Figure 10-3).

Quattro Pro allows eight fonts per worksheet, and bundles Bitstream fonts that can be scaled to a wide range of sizes. *Quattro Pro* even includes built-in drawing tools and a clip art library, so you can embellish your charts with icons and illustrations—without using a presentation graphics program. If you create a series of worksheets that are related, you can even create a timed desktop slide presentation and show a small group your work right on the screen. Another Lotus *1-2-3* add-on, *Impress* (PC Publishing), brings similar graphics capability, without the slide presentation, to *1-2-3*.

If you want to turn your charts into actual color slides, *SuperCalc 5* offers a link to the MagiCorp slide-making service; you send a file by disk or modem to MagiCorp.

Spreadsheet Design Considerations

As in any design effort, amateurs should be careful not to overwhelm their data with too many fonts or with headings that are disproportionately large. Typically, numbers should be set in 10- or 12-point size, with headings in 14- or 24-point size. Of course, if you want to print more numbers on a

Figure 10-3.
    Some spreadsheets allow you to annotate worksheets with on-screen text and attract the reader's eye by drawing lines or arrows. *Full Impact* is shown here.

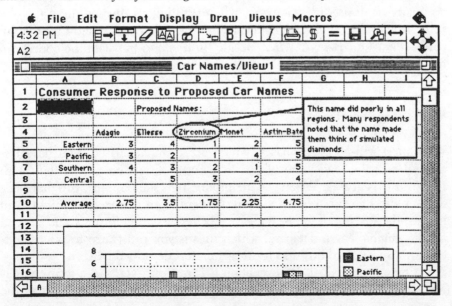

page, you can reduce the size to 5 or 8 points, although the average middle-aged executive will need bifocals to see the point you're trying to make.

In addition, be aware that a font that's good for text isn't necessarily as effective with numbers. For instance, Times Roman is a proportional font that will alter spacing to create a smooth line of text, giving an "l" less space than a "w." But it will also give a "1" less space than a "0." Thus a column of numbers may appear wavy, since 1,111 will take up much less space than 2,345. A monospaced font such as Courier will produce an aligned column of numbers.

Finally, when converting numbers into a pie chart to show percentages of the whole, it's customary to shade the largest slice of the pie segment in black and place it next to a white slice, often the thinnest segment (unless, of course, you have a color printer).

DATABASE PUBLISHING

Since databases are most often used to record and analyze textual data, not numbers, they don't include charting functions. (You *can*, of course, store numbers and make calculations with a database; to graph those numbers, you must export the data to a spreadsheet, as Jain did.) But you can spruce up some database reports with headings, shadings, rules, and different fonts, just as you can with a spreadsheet (see Figure 10-4).

On occasion, you may need to translate field entries to produce a more understandable report. For instance, David Wilson, a hydroponic tomato farmer near New Bedford, Massachusetts, stores his accounts receivable on a database; to conserve disk space, he uses a two-letter code to identify each company he deals with. However, when printing an invoice, he wants the full name of the company to appear. To do so, he uses an add-on program called *Time Out Report Writer* (Beagle Brothers) to translate the code from his *Apple Works* database (Claris) into a full name.

Formatting Reports

With *most* MS-DOS databases, which are character-based, you have less control over the placement of text fields or columns on a page than with Macintosh databases. When you are producing a standard list, this drawback doesn't affect you, but when you are producing an invoice you might want to alter the spacing of fields to create a better-designed form. To do so, you need a graphic-based database, which means you must turn to the Macintosh or a specialized business forms generator (described below).

One notable MS-DOS exception is *FormBase* (Xerox)—a forms generator/database hybrid that runs under *Windows*. As you create a form, the

Figure 10-4.

Database reports may not always sparkle, but at least they can be made more readable with different fonts for the headings and with bold rules to set off different segments. This printout was prepared with the database in Lotus Symphony.

Original Swiss Style Gourmet Foods Database

Sort by Customer

Last Name	First Name	Address	City	Sta	Zip	Item	Qu	Unit Price	Total Sale	Order Date
Johnson	Nancy	452 Concord St	Vienna	VA	19856	Chocolate Torte	2	14.95	$29.90	25-Apr-90
Jones	Frank	18 Greenhill Rd	Englewood	FL	34224	Cheese	3	24.95	$74.85	13-May-90
Judge	Michael	23 Frost St	Springfiel	MA	03827	Raclette	1	39.95	$39.95	28-Apr-90
Kask	Carl	73 Cherry Dr.	Bozeman	MT	59715	Cheese	3	24.95	$74.85	01-May-90
Kramer	Ted	12 Herrick Pl	Portland	TN	37148	Raclette	2	39.95	$79.90	13-May-90
Kuncik	Jim	93 State St	Warren	NJ	08753	Chocolate Torte	2	14.95	$29.90	28-Apr-90
Lawson	John	45 Common Ave	Northbrook	IL	60062	Chocolate Torte	2	14.95	$29.90	15-May-90
Leonard	Kathy	6 Popple Dr	Langdon	NH	04274	Cheese	4	24.95	$99.80	15-May-90
Liptack	Mildred	242 Washington	Carley	MA	02192	Chocolate Torte	3	14.95	$44.85	10-May-90
Lohse	Janet	123 Autumn Rd	Chester	CA	93255	Raclette	2	39.95	$79.90	08-May-90
Lovell	Paul	227 Summer Rd	Weston	VT	05262	Cheese	2	24.95	$49.90	28-Apr-90
Lovell	William	93 Parker St	New York	NY	10032	Cheese	2	24.95	$49.90	10-May-90
Lund	Bela	46 Western Ave	St Paul	MN	55133	Raclette	1	39.95	$39.95	02-May-90
Lyle	Harriet	62 Turner Rd	Kittery	ME	03903	Chocolate Torte	2	14.95	$29.90	17-May-90
Lyle	Bruce	55 Gateway Rd	Brandle	IN	46217	Cheese	2	24.95	$49.90	13-May-90
Mac Arthur	John	76 Linden Rd	Seattle	WA	98107	Chocolate Torte	3	14.95	$44.85	08-May-90
MacBee	Nancy	773 Beaver St	Marlboro	FL	34228	Raclette	1	39.95	$39.95	02-May-90
Madden	Sue	76 Davis Ave	Grafton	MI	49372	Cheese	1	24.95	$24.95	12-May-90
Madow	Ernest	12 Hale St	Bondville	AK	99518	Cheese	2	24.95	$49.90	17-May-90
Magee	Deborah	90 High St	Bremerton	WA	98312	Chocolate Torte	3	14.95	$44.85	12-May-90
March	Harold	Cold River Rd	TomsRiver	NJ	08753	Chocolate Torte	4	14.95	$59.80	17-May-90
Martin	Larry	54 Canal St	Hudson	OH	44236	Raclette	1	39.95	$39.95	07-May-90
Mason	Anne	823 Kissel St	Westminste	CO	80021	Chocolate Torte	2	14.95	$29.90	05-May-90
Miller	Robert	5 Grove St	Brattlebor	VT	02116	Cheese	2	24.95	$49.90	13-May-90
Money	Earl	104 Drewsville	Dover	CO	80023	Chocolate Torte	1	14.95	$14.95	02-May-90

[This sample prepared using Lotus Symphony 2.2 and the HP LaserJet II P]

program constructs a database to match all the fields. Thus you can build a database to store data as you build the form (or database report). If you change the form, the database automatically changes.

The best example of a Macintosh database that offers formatting control is *FileMaker Pro* (Claris Corporation). Say your business has a single master file of all customers. First, you design a basic input format with the person's name, address, and company, and whether he or she is a customer prospect or supplier. Then you can set up the forms you want to print out: mailing labels, invoices, purchase order forms, packing lists, shipping papers, and so on.

To design reports and specialized forms, you pull data fields around with the mouse. You can make the fields any size you wish and place them anywhere you want.

Page Layout for Databases

To convert your database files into attractive catalogs, price lists, or membership directories, you generally need to link your database to a desktop publishing program.

Practically any database can export records (in ASCII text format) that a desktop publishing program can read. For instance, *PageMaker* imports *dBase* files and treats them as text. You can specify different fonts for different fields, and arrange them as you wish. To create, say, a catalog of products, you manipulate text to produce the proper page breaks and type fonts. However, if and when you update the publication, you have to repeat the whole procedure.

A smoother approach is to use a desktop publishing program such as *Byline* (Ashton-Tate) or *dbPublisher* (Digital Composition Systems, Inc.) that offers a hot link to your database. Every time you update a record in your linked database file, the desktop publishing file is also updated. Thus you can easily print a new price list or membership directory.

Byline's database publishing feature works much like a simple database report generator. Rather than putting actual text in the document, you tell *Byline* where to look for the data—which fields in which file. When you print the document, *Byline* fetches the text directly from the appropriate database file (as long as the file is *dBase* compatible). The process is quite similar to creating a mail-merge letter with a word processor that takes data from given fields in a database.

Despite its database link, *Byline* does have limitations. You can't format one page differently from previous pages or insert blank pages. *dbPublisher*, a more advanced database publishing program, with live links to *dBase* and *R:Base* files, as well as Lotus *1-2-3* and *SuperCalc* spreadsheet files, overcomes these page layout limitations.

dbPublisher gives you true font control and formatting options. If you group records together by category, you can start each group on a new page with a different heading. A particularly impressive feature lets you format parts of your document conditionally. For example, if you're putting together a product catalog, you could specify that any record added after a specific date be printed in boldface, preceded by "New Item."

In general, more powerful software is more difficult to master. And that is the case with *dbPublisher*. Creating even simple documents requires stringing together programming instructions that tell the program what and how to print.

BUSINESS FORMS SOFTWARE

A wide range of software lets you design and produce professional-quality business forms that cost much less than commercial preprinted ones. In addition, you can personalize these forms for certain clients or situations (such as trade shows) without printing more than you need (see Figure 10-5).

Business forms software is essentially database software without the data. The forms themselves are equivalent to database reports—without the data. In theory, it would be easier to use a database package, create a report that looked like a form, and print the pertinent data on the report. But database programs aren't as malleable as forms programs, which are more graphic.

Figure 10-5.
Business forms generators, a specialized type of database, provide on-screen forms that you can fill out and print. Because they are more graphic and malleable than database programs, you have more control over the final look of the form. This screen shows *SmartForm Assistant*.

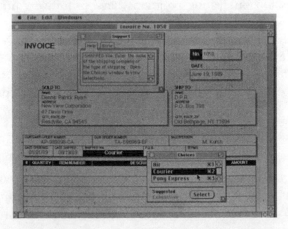

"I used preprinted forms, but they were very expensive," says Joseph Cywinski, president of Corson Engineering, Inc., a computer consulting firm in New York City that makes custom programs for *Fortune* 100 companies. "Furthermore, using standard forms wasn't very convenient." With a laser printer and *Formset* software, he now creates forms as he needs them.

If you need to customize basic forms for different markets, or if the data you want to input are already on the computer, using electronic forms could save you both time and money. The downside to producing your own forms is that it can be time consuming, especially if the form is very complicated and has a lot of data fields. If you use only a few different forms, the investment in time probably isn't worth the money you'll save.

Most good business forms software shows on-screen replicas of paper forms. In some cases, you fill in the data on-screen and print out the completed form. You must print out blank forms and enter data by hand with less sophisticated software.

Creating Forms

Forms software includes predesigned forms—such as credit applications, invoices, to do lists, and shipping labels. You can customize them with logos, graphics, and special effects. Most programs import graphics from paint or drawing programs (which can also be used occasionally to produce forms).

The best business forms programs also include many drawing and layout tools that are quite similar to those found in page layout programs, which you can use to design forms from scratch. In fact, the IRS, the biggest forms producer in the world, uses *PageMaker* to design its forms. There's no reason why you can't use a page layout program to design forms, either, particularly if you'll be printing out blank copies to fill in by hand. However, desktop publishing programs have primitive editing features, so using them to fill in forms on screen is often a time waster.

If you have a paper form that you'd like to enhance or store as a computer file for on-screen data entry, you can scan the document into your computer and then trace over it on-screen. Needless to say, this can be tricky, especially with a detailed form or one with small print.

Data Entry

In addition to designing the form's visible characteristics, you can give each fill-in field on a form special instructions to check and format data as they are entered. Among the possibilities are alphabetic or numeric formats, and calculated values that automatically fill in totals from prices and quantities in other fields.

These instructions speed data entry and prevent mistakes. The software will automatically post the date, beep if your field entry is too long or short, and perform basic mathematical calculations.

Forms printing is generally slow—and will be even slower if you've used a variety of fonts and graphics. Some programs let you put blank forms in your printer, fill in the form on-screen, and then print just the data—rather than the form and the data. That method will save some printing time.

THE PUBLISHING CRAZE

The data-publishing phenomen is the result of several forces, primarily the widespread use of desktop publishing software, which allows users to integrate text and data from several sources. People have become so used to seeing reports mixing text, numbers, and graphics that a staid spreadsheet printout has less and less impact. It's now imperative that number-crunchers and data manipulators produce visually appealing reports—or they may not hold their reader's attention.

BUSINESS FORMS AND REPORTS RESOURCES

Inside Allways, by Corey Sandler, John Wiley & Sons, 1989; $22.95. This guide to the 1-2-3 spreadsheet add-on shows how to turn drab reports into sparkling presentations.

The AMA Handbook of Key Management Forms, edited by David M. Brownstone and Irene M. Franck, AMACOM, 702 pp., 1986; $95. This handbook shows more than 500 actual models for business forms selected from thousands solicited in a nationwide survey by the American Management Association.

SPOTLIGHT ON: Spreadsheet Publishing Software

Cost: $195 to $495.
Learning Curve: Medium; once you're familiar with the operations of a given spreadsheet, making charts isn't difficult; and making *good* charts requires more design than computer skills.
Required Equipment: Fast computer with hard disk drive, and sometimes a mouse; laser printer.
Recommended Software:

For IBM PC and IBM PS/2 and Compatibles

- *Allways* (Funk Software), a memory-resident add-on report generator for Lotus *1-2-3* (and included with recent releases), spiffs up drab reports with borders, columns, shading, and up to eight fonts.
- *Excel* (Microsoft) was the first MS-DOS spreadsheet to give users a choice of fonts (four) when printing reports; now, to keep up with increasing competition, Microsoft offers eight more typefaces for a minimal fee; because it runs under *Windows*, *Excel* requires a fast computer (286 or better).
- *Impress* (PC Publishing), like *Allways*, is an add-on to Lotus *1-2-3* that comes with a drawing toolbox; you can create graphics within the toolbox, or import .PIC files from other programs and paste them into your worksheets; the program supports a mouse.
- *Lotus 1-2-3* (Lotus), the best-selling software in the world, was weak at charting until the company incorporated the *Allways* add-on; that, combined with an on-screen graph that you can watch as you enter and calculate data, and a "quick graph" option that graphs data at the touch of a keystroke, brings *1-2-3* back into the mainstream (release 3 only).
- *SuperCalc 5* (Computer Associates), long known for its superb color graphics and dependability, offers a link to the MagiCorp slide-making service; you send a file by disk or modem to MagiCorp and get a slide in return; the program's menu structure looks similar to that of *1-2-3*.
- *Quattro Pro* (Borland), probably the most sophisticated spreadsheet publisher, allows you to add arrows, lines, polygons, rectangles and ellipses—with color, shading, and patterns; the program includes nine Bitstream fonts, which can be scaled to different sizes; you can paste graphs into your worksheet and watch them change as you update numbers; screen preview shows you exactly what the final printout will look like.

For Macintosh

- *Excel* (Microsoft), the leading Macintosh spreadsheet, offers a wider range of fonts than the MS-DOS version (any available on your system) and lets you designate different fonts for individual cells; it includes page-preview function; it prints text and numbers with proportional spacing; however, it is not as flexible as some others because you can't print two or more graphs on one page.
- *Full Impact* (Ashton-Tate), whose graphics capabilities surpass those of *Excel*, also includes word processing features; you can create a paragraph on your worksheet to annotate it and even include spreadsheet formulas that will calculate numbers from the worksheet; it will print multiple graphs on one page.
- *Wingz* (Informix) lets you create and integrate graphics and word processing areas right on the spreadsheet; thus you can produce

reports with words, numbers, charts, and pictures; it includes graphics tools as good as those of a basic drawing program.

Buying Tips: Check the computer and memory requirements carefully, as some programs require more power than others; some Macintosh programs, for instance, really need 2 MB to operate well; a spreadsheet with some text editing ability will ease the chart-making process; a page-preview function improves your chances of a better final printout.

SPOTLIGHT ON: Business Forms Generators

Cost: $100 to $400.
Learning Curve: Medium to steep. As with other applications where the printed product is of primary importance, getting it right takes trial and error; almost all users say that the design process is time consuming.
Required Equipment: Computer with hard disk drive; laser printer.
Recommended Software:

For IBM PC and IBM PS/2 and Compatibles

- *Horizon* (FormMarker Software), which runs under *Windows*, looks good and runs well, with a clear tutorial-style manual; it can import data from other programs.
- *PerFORM* (Delrina Technology), which runs under the *GEM* operating environment, extracts information from a *dBase* file as you fill in forms on-screen; it includes a good manual and sample forms.
- *Formworx* (Formworx, Inc.) is a *Windows*-based forms manager with tools to build forms; it includes more than 500 templates for all kinds of forms.

For Macintosh

- *SmartForm Assistant* (Claris) is easier to use than most forms packages, allowing you to customize forms with minimum effort.
- *TrueForm* (Adobe) is good at accepting scanned forms and at data management (it has a link to the *4th Dimension* database), but it has limited design capability.
- *FormSystem* (SoftView), from the developers of the popular *MacInTax* tax prep program, has so-called "graphics intelligence," which means that you can move fields and elements around in the design stage and the other fields automatically adjust position.

Buying Tips: Before you buy a business forms package, see what you can produce with your spreadsheet, database, or word processor (using its table-making function); when considering MS-DOS forms software, look for packages that run under the *Windows* or *GEM* graphic interfaces; software that forces you to create forms by entering commands is too abstract.

PART III
Communications

Chapter 11
The Computer–Phone–Fax Connection

Three ways to extend the reach of your computer—make calls, send faxes, and set up a voice-mail system.

Watson, come here, I need you.

—Alexander Graham Bell

The telephone has been around for so long that it's hard to imagine it connected to anything but an earlobe. But for many people who spend a good part of every day at the computer, the telephone connected to their computer brings a world of text, numbers, and images to their desktop.

With the phone connected to the computer by a modem, you can send and receive computer files; dial regular voice calls through your modem and then pick up the telephone handset; send and receive electronic mail and conduct electronic research through the phone; receive voice-mail messages on your computer or forward the calls to another location; and send and receive faxes from your computer.

Not everyone will want to do all these things. Doing just one often requires a dedicated computer, which can't be used for regular writing or number crunching tasks. But independents and small-business people, many of whom refer to the telephone as their "lifeline," and the computer as the "cornerstone" of their business, find that establishing some kind of computer–phone connection helps them keep up with the ceaseless flow of information.

This chapter describes how to dial voice calls and send faxes from your computer, and how a computer-based voice-mail system can help your business.

CONNECTING TO THE PHONE LINES

A modem is a go-between—between your computer and the phone. Whether it is an internal or an external unit, a modem has telephone jacks in the back—one line goes to the outside line and the other to your telephone handset. A modem dials both pulse and touchtone phones and turns computer tones into signals that can travel across the phone lines. When receiving, it turns phone signals into computer data (for more information on modems, see Chapter 1).

The primary use of modems is to send and receive electronic mail (see Chapter 12). Modems also connect you to vast libraries that can provide financial, demographic, scientific, and other types of data (see Chapter 13). Plus modems place dial voice calls with just a keystroke or two.

Computer-Dialed Phone Calls

When you connect to an electronic-mail service (or any other remote computer), you hear through the modem's speaker a high-pitched sound, the electronic mating call of modems that may send you scurrying to the ear doctor. If, however, you dial the wrong number and a person answers, you'll hear a voice, in which case you can pick up the phone and talk.

Enough people must have done this by mistake that developers began designing software to dial voice calls through the modem. The advantage is obvious: Picking a number off your computer screen and dialing it by hitting one key or clicking a mouse saves your fingers some walking. While telephones can store numbers for one-key dialing, they can't store as many as a computer.

A wide range of programs dial through a modem. The most common are activity trackers, or sales trackers, which are designed primarily for salespeople (see Chapter 14). Many personal information managers also allow phone dialing (see Chapter 15).

Once you choose a number and execute the one-keystroke dial command, you generally just pick up the phone handset. Some programs show an on-screen message telling you to press the space bar or another key before picking up the phone. If you have plugged a phone headset into the phone jack in back of the computer, both hands are free for typing.

Hotline—Hot Stuff for Phone Hounds

While activity trackers and personal-information managers track all kinds of information, from to do lists to phone logs, one notable piece of software that's almost exclusively a phone dialer is *Hotline* (General Information). Like the others, *Hotline* lets you call up a name from its database and dial the number (see Figure 11-1). What makes *Hotline* different is that, besides your personal directory, it presents ten thousand phone numbers for the

Figure 11-1.
If your computer is connected to the phone lines by a modem, you can highlight a phone number on the screen and dial a voice call by hitting RETURN. Shown here is *Hotline*, a phone-management program.

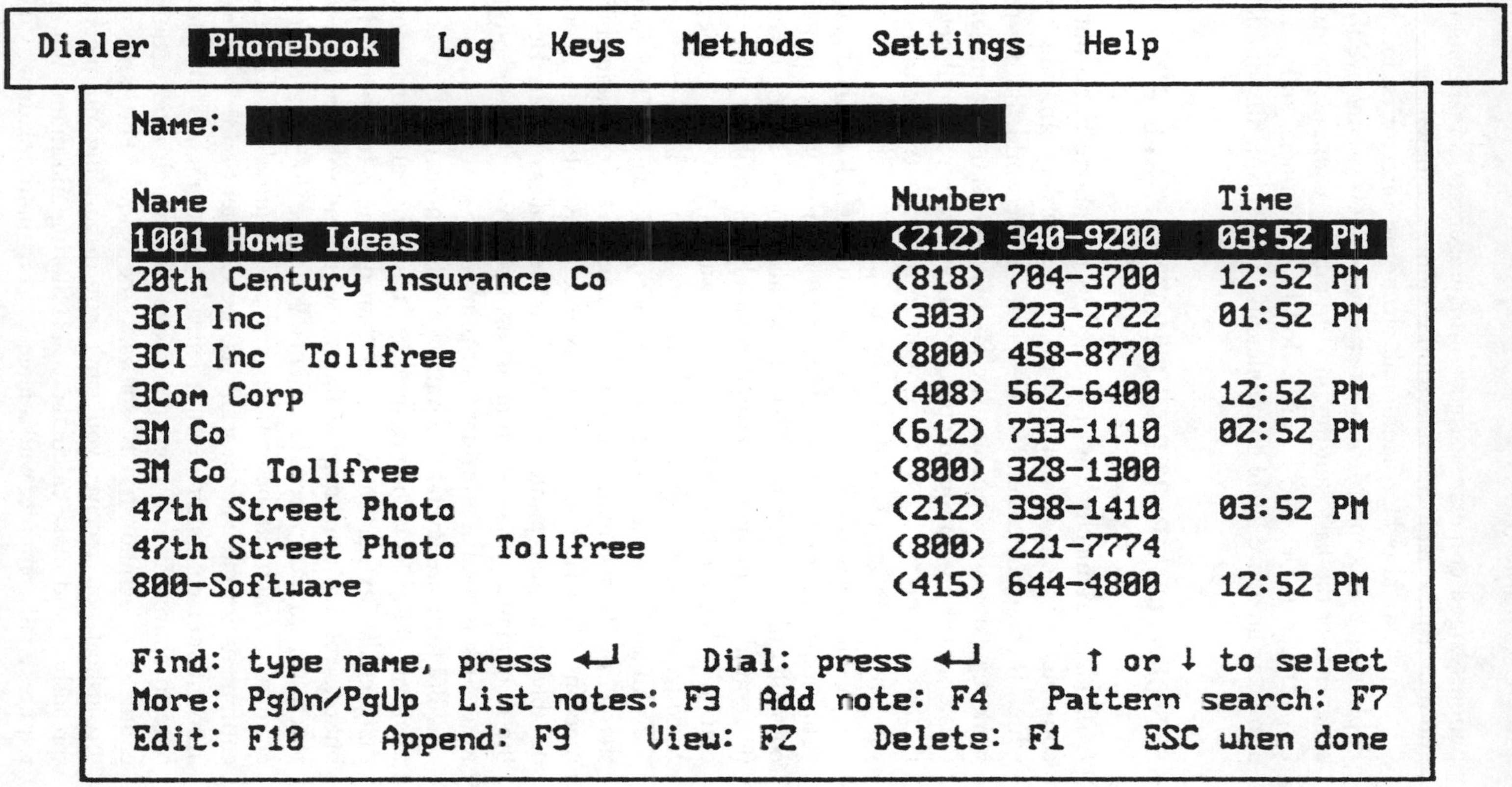

Dialer	**Phonebook**	Log	Keys	Methods	Settings	Help

Name:

Name	Number	Time
1001 Home Ideas	**(212) 340-9200**	**03:52 PM**
20th Century Insurance Co	(818) 704-3700	12:52 PM
3CI Inc	(303) 223-2722	01:52 PM
3CI Inc Tollfree	(800) 458-8770	
3Com Corp	(408) 562-6400	12:52 PM
3M Co	(612) 733-1110	02:52 PM
3M Co Tollfree	(800) 328-1300	
47th Street Photo	(212) 398-1410	03:52 PM
47th Street Photo Tollfree	(800) 221-7774	
800-Software	(415) 644-4800	12:52 PM

Find: type name, press ↵   Dial: press ↵   ↑ or ↓ to select
More: PgDn/PgUp List notes: F3 Add note: F4 Pattern search: F7
Edit: F10   Append: F9   View: F2   Delete: F1   ESC when done

nation's largest corporations, government agencies, organizations, colleges and universities, radio and television stations, and newspapers.

You can also buy additional electronic directories for Advertising, Public Relations, and Media; America's Business twenty-five thousand (an expansion of the basic ten thousand numbers); Computer and High Tech; Department of Defense; Finance; Toll-Free Numbers; and Travel. *Hotline* also keeps an active log of all phone calls, which is useful for client billing.

SENDING COMPUTER-GENERATED FAXES

A standard fax machine is connected to the phone lines, but not to the computer. As such, sending a fax isn't much harder than using a telephone, which is about the easiest tool to operate in the world. But for people who work regularly on computers, the fax machine can be a nuisance. If you create something on the computer, you have to print it out before you fax it. If you receive a fax that you want to incorporate into a computer file, you have to retype or scan it into the computer.

A solution is to use a fax/modem, which sends text and graphics from your computer to a fax machine and receives fax transmissions as a computer file. Fax/modems, which can also double as 9600-baud modems (to send files computer to computer) attach externally or internally to your computer and are driven by special software. (Also, see the description of Xpedite, and other on-line fax services, in Chapter 12.)

An additional advantage of fax/modems is that the faxes they send are sharper on the receiving end, since they haven't been scanned into the fax machine. And laser printouts of fax receptions will be sharper and more durable than those printed on standard thermal fax paper. However, since the resolution of a fax machine is less than that of a laser printer, it still won't look as good as a regular laser printout.

But there are several disadvantages to fax/modems: (1) As card-carrying members of the "emerging technology" club, they are much more complex than regular fax machines. Rather than dialing a number and pushing a button, you have to integrate the hardware and software with your computer. (2) To fax paper documents you have to scan them into your computer, which can be complex and also requires an additional piece of equipment (for more about scanners, see Chapter 6). (3) When you receive a fax in your computer—even a letter—it is a graphics file. To edit, you have to convert it to a word processing file, which often requires optical character recognition (OCR) software (see below). The same is true of a spreadsheet you receive; you can't just import the numbers into your spreadsheet and make calculations. (4) Storing and manipulating graphics requires a fast computer with a large-capacity hard disk drive. (5) Printing a received fax as a graphics file takes much longer than printing a text file. (6)

If you receive frequent faxes, it could interrupt your work flow and you may need to dedicate a separate computer to the task.

Scanning Text Into the Computer

A scanner is a perfect sidekick to a fax/modem. Without a scanner, you'll be limited to sending computer-generated files. With a scanner, you can pump both text and graphics into the computer, edit, and send them.

The standard file format for scanned images is called tagged image file format (TIFF). Desktop publishing and image editing programs will accept TIFF files. But most word processing and spreadsheet programs won't. Thus, if you scan a letter or a spreadsheet into your computer, you won't be able to edit it—unless you convert it to a file your program can read.

The missing link is OCR software, which reads pages and converts them to standard text files. Optical character recognition software scans across a line of letters, identifies them, and converts them to ASC11 text. This process can be slow (often slower than you can type!) and prone to error, but OCR software is rapidly improving. *OmniPage* (Caere Corp.), the best known OCR software, works on both Macintosh and MS-DOS machines.

"I tore a multicolumn article out of the newspaper, scanned and converted it to a text file with 98.6 percent accuracy," says David Boe, who used a Hewlett-Packard ScanJet scanner and *OmniPage* software. Such an accuracy rate still amounts to one-and-a-half errors every one hundred letters, or two lines. But it's acceptable, especially since you can correct most errors with a spelling checker.

In fact, OCR software works much like an electronic spelling checker and tries to identify characters in context. It looks at a character, tries to match it against the characters in its own library, and will distinguish a "5" from an "S" by examining the context. To be effective, of course, the software has to know what font it's reading so that it can use the proper library. If you can't identify the font, the OCR software will try to do so.

Fax, Fax/Modem, or Modem?

Despite the disadvantages outlined above, some people may find a fax/modem more practical than a standard fax machine, or at least a useful sidekick. Graphic artists who constantly fax samples to clients, for instance, are prime candidates for fax/modems. So are people who frequently receive faxes that they'd prefer in electronic form—but whose correspondents use fax machines instead of electronic mail. Writers, publicists, and others who create high-quality reports will benefit from the fax/modem's sharper output on the receiving end.

But people who send or receive frequent short memos and letters (especially those created by others), or graphics they don't need to edit, will do better with a standard fax machine.

COMPUTERIZED VOICE MAIL

An answering machine aids an individual without a secretary, but its usefulness is limited. What if you want to leave a different message for each person you expect to call? What if you want your answering machine to call you when someone leaves a message? Or to send messages to other systems? Computerized voice-mail systems do all that. And all you need to set one up is an MS-DOS computer with an empty expansion slot.

Voice-mail systems, now in widespread use in corporations, answer phone calls with a recorded message. The caller issues touchtone commands to transfer to the exact department or individual he or she wants to contact. If the person isn't available, the caller can leave a recorded message in a private voice-mailbox. A caller looking for specific information may also select from a menu of recorded messages for specialized information about a product or service.

Watson and The Complete Answering Machine

Both Watson (Natural Microsystems Corp.) and The Complete Answering Machine (The Complete PC), the two leading voice-mail systems, are MS-DOS add-on cards that connect your computer to the telephone line. You customize the system with the included voice-mail software.

Setup requires you to record messages (by talking into the telephone), indicate the touchtone codes, partition off private mailboxes with passwords for clients or colleagues, and indicate where to transfer calls. You can deliver information on your products and ask callers to execute transactions by entering keypad codes. Voice-mail systems also initiate calls, which can be useful in some telemarketing efforts.

These and other voice-mail systems theoretically work in the background while you use the computer for other tasks; unless you have an extremely fast computer, however, doing so can cause undesirable delays that will annoy callers. Thus it's more practical to dedicate an inexpensive MS-DOS clone to voice-mail operation.

Voice Mail in Action

Armando Lopez, a private investigator and hotel security consultant in West Los Angeles, uses The Complete Answering Machine to stay in immediate touch with his callers. If a client calls Lopez's home office and no one is there, a recorded announcement invites the caller to leave a voice-mail message. Clients are asked to press "3" and give their passwords. The machine takes a message and automatically dials a local computerized paging service, which in turn signals Lopez's paging device. The pager displays a number that tells Lopez which voice mailbox to call. "I usually pick up the message and get back to the client within five minutes," says Lopez.

Most people would benefit from a simpler use of voice mail. For instance, California writer and consumer electronics expert Ken Joy uses a Watson board as a supersmart answering machine. "I can leave a message that says: 'If you're returning my call, push 1; if you wish to leave a message, push 2,' and so on," says Joy. "Then if I have a personal message for a specific person I say: 'Dial the last four digits of your phone number for messages.'"

Sherry Martin, a computer training specialist and consultant in Waltham, Massachusetts, uses Watson's message forwarding feature to relay her voice mail to another number. Regular clients are assigned their own mailboxes so that they can dial back later for a response to their questions. Sometimes, Martin uses the outgoing message function to respond to clients' questions. "Watson gives me the appearance of twenty-four-hour business coverage," says Martin. "And I think the world is moving that way."

TURNING ONE PHONE LINE INTO TWO (OR FOUR)

One problem many home and small businesses encounter in setting up a fluid phone system is adding enough lines to handle their diverse communications needs. Besides a fax machine, modem, or fax/modem, most businesspeople need at least two voice lines. Often, one of these lines doubles as a fax or modem line, but that can cause problems when callers hear the annoying high-pitched squeal of electronic equipment answer the phone.

The cleanest solution is to add a dedicated phone line for each device—but that can be the most expensive way. Another solution is to use call-waiting on one line so that it does the job of two lines. But an increasingly popular choice is to use the distinctive ringing service offered by local phone companies.

Called Custom Ringing (US West), Personalized Ring (Southwestern

Bell), IdentaRing (Bell Atlantic), Call Identification Services (Ameritech), or RingMaster (Bell South), a distinctive ringing service gives you up to four different phone numbers on one phone line. Thus, you could designate 999-0000 as your voice line, 999-1111 as your modem number, and 999-2222 as your fax number. Each number has a distinctive ring, such as: two shorts, two longs, and short–long. Ideally, you can identify each call by the sound of its ring, but a modem or fax machine can't when you're not in the office.

The solution is to connect to the phone line a box that recognizes each ring and routes the call to the proper device. Then you never have to worry about a voice caller getting the fax machine's or modem's auto-answer squeal, because voice calls will be routed to the voice line.

RingDirector (Lynx Automation) and Fax Director II (Data-Doc Electronics) both decode incoming rings and route the call to the proper device. Keep in mind, though, that only one function can occur at a time; even though you may have four numbers you still have just one phone line.

TURN YOUR COMPUTER INTO A TELEPHONE SWITCHBOARD

The telephone is already the number one tool for most businesspeople, and the processing power of the computer only makes it more useful. By itself, the telephone carries voice. When attached to the computer, it carries voice, text, and graphics. By itself, the telephone connects a caller to the number dialed. A voice-mail system routes the call to other numbers, and it receives and disseminates information from and to specific individuals.

Setting up an efficient system takes some work. You have to identify your needs, find the products that meet them, and learn how to install and use them. But the potential rewards are immense. Telephone lines carry data, and computers analyze those data. Keeping the two systems separate will only cause you more work in the long run. Let your modem act as a go-between to save you the trouble of transferring data back and forth from medium to medium.

The way to get started is to change your thinking about the telephone. It's not just something you talk into. It's a pipeline that will move work in and out of your computer. Alexander Graham Bell didn't foresee that a hundred years ago, and many people don't see it now—but don't let that stop you.

COMMUNICATIONS RESOURCES

The Book of Fax, Second Edition, by Daniel Fishman and Elliot King, Ventana Press, 176 pp., 1990; $12.95. This book may tell you more than you need to know about fax machines, but it does include a chapter on "PC/Fax," which outlines the major advantages and disadvantages of using a fax/modem.

The Telephone Book, Second Edition, by Carl Oppedahl, Consumer Reports Books, 1990; $12.95. This book covers topics of interest to residential or small-business users with two or more telephone lines: wiring, long-distance dialing, dialing on the road, and cellular and fax machine use.

Also see the Resources sections in Chapters 12 and 13.

SPOTLIGHT ON: Voice-Mail Systems

Cost: $200 to $400.

Learning Curve: Steep; only people familiar with computer communications should even consider setting up a voice-mail system; however, once a system is set up, it's not difficult to operate.

Required Equipment: Fast computer with hard disk drive; modem; telephone line.

Recommended Products:

- The Complete Answering Machine (The Complete PC) is a fairly easy system to set up, with a menu and good help screens; to hear the system in action, call 800-634-5558.
- Watson (Natural Microsystems), which requires *Voice Information Systems* software, is somewhat difficult to set up, but it is quite sophisticated; it has 750 private mailboxes and stores 750 telephone numbers; to hear the system, call 800-6-WATSON; in Massachusetts, call 508-651-2186, ext. 137.

Buying Tips: Assess your needs carefully to ensure that you can't accomplish your goals with a sophisticated answering machine or by using special telephone services, such as call forwarding and remote call forward. Decide whether handling incoming calls or sending outgoing messages is more important to you, and judge a system's features accordingly.

Chapter 12

Electronic Mail: Your 24-Hour Link to Clients, Customers, and Colleagues

Send electronic memos, files, and faxes virtually anywhere in the world.

> *If you're a businessperson or professional, the question is not whether* you should use electronic mail—but how to best *implement it.*
>
> —Alfred Glossbrenner, *The Complete Handbook of Personal Computer Communications*

Electronic mail is without a doubt the fastest, cheapest, most convenient way to send computer information from point A to point B. You don't leave a phone message that says, "Please call back." You don't have to type a letter or document and then fax it. You don't run up a big overnight air bill. You send a message when you're ready—from your computer. Within minutes, it's sitting in a mailbox thousands of miles away.

"When I'm working at 6 A.M. or 7 A.M. on the East Coast and want to send a message or file to California, I use electronic mail. It'll be ready and waiting when my client starts work," says Corey Sandler, president of Word Association, Inc., a consulting and editorial services company, who uses MCI Mail. Sandler communicates regularly with about fifteen people on MCI Mail, including his business partner Tom Bladgett, who lives a thousand miles away. "When one of us is on the road we use electronic mail a lot. I send a file; he gets it when he wants it. Otherwise, I get about five messages a day, from various clients and subcontractors."

To pick up a message, your correspondent need only sign on to the same e-mail system, check his or her mailbox, and read it. Of course, e-mail works efficiently only if both you and your correspondents regularly check your electronic-mail box, just as you would check a postal mail box.

Electronic mail (often called e-mail) is an adjunct to regular use of a fax machine and telephone. Almost everyone who works with computers wants to send and receive electronic information—so it can be edited and annotated without retyping. Anyone who works for a remote client, or with a remote partner, needs a simple and reliable way to continually exchange information about ongoing projects. Electronic mail is a large part of the answer.

This chapter describes the process of sending and receiving electronic mail, how to send spreadsheet and graphics files, the most popular e-mail systems for professionals, and how to send faxes from your computer.

HOW E-MAIL WORKS

To send e-mail, you subscribe to an electronic-mail service. For a minimal start up fee, you get an identification number and a password. Depending on the system, you pay a monthly fee to cover a certain number of message units, pay each time you send a message, or pay for the time (by the minute) you spend on the system (you don't pay to receive messages). In and around urban areas, you can access e-mail systems by calling a local network number, so you don't pay long-distance charges. And some services offer a toll-free 800 number. All in all, electronic-mail bills tend to run $10, $20, or $30 a month for average users.

To sign on to a service, you dial the e-mail system's phone number; after you're connected, you type in your identification number and password (see Figure 12-1). The system notifies you if mail is waiting. You can scan the message headers—much like the *to*, *from*, and *re:* headings on a memo pad—or read the mail.

In the interest of keeping your desk clear, it's best to read and respond to short messages immediately, by typing in a response. But you can also save messages on disk or print them to be read after you disconnect from the system (to save on-line charges). To view a spreadsheet, graphics, or other binary file, you *must* save the file to disk and load it into the proper program to view it.

To send a message, you can type the text while on-line (connected to the e-mail system), or prepare it off-line and transmit the file when you sign on. You need to know the identification number or name of the intended recipient.

When composing a message on-line, you hit the RETURN key at the end of each line, as if using a typewriter. While you can edit the message when you're finished, the process is much more cumbersome than editing

Figure 12-1.

To sign on to an electronic-mail service, you dial the phone through a modem. Once connected to the service, you enter your name and password. So that others won't ever see your password, the letters don't appear on-screen as you type them. Shown here is a sample sign-on to the MCI Mail service, which also includes a link to Dow Jones News/Retrieval, a financial information service.

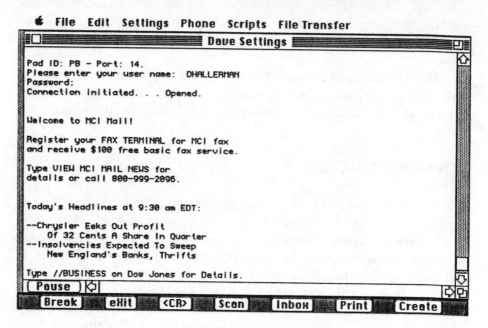

with a word processor. Thus, many communications software packages include a simple text editor to aid on-line composition.

If you save files to disk before sending, save them as ASCII text files (check your word processor's manual for instructions)—both to conform to the e-mail service's requirements and to ensure that your recipient will be able to read it, even if he or she uses a different word processing program or computer than you. That also means no boldface, special font characters, or underlining, which won't come through on the other end, or may come across as garbage. If you want to emphasize a word, frame it with two asterisks, like *this*. Use single-spacing and turn off your program's pagination feature, which can cause unwanted breaks that may be hard for your correspondent to remove.

COMMUNICATIONS SOFTWARE

Since most modems operate pretty much the same (although some are more resistant to dirty phone lines than others), it's the software controlling your modem that colors your time on-line.

Communications software controls the modem settings, tells the modem when to dial or hang up, and sends or receives files from or to your hard disk or floppy disk (called uploading and downloading, respectively). In addition to these basics, communications programs perform other tasks that might lead you to choose one program over another.

Automatic Sign-On

Rather than dialing the phone number and entering your user ID and password every time you sign on, you can write a macro, or set of steps, so that your software will automatically dial a given electronic-mail service. But writing macros can be difficult and time-consuming—too much like real software programming. Some software saves you the trouble by including a "learn" or "record" mode; you sign on, and the software records all your keystrokes (including password). Next time, just choose a given service from a menu and sit back while the software signs you on (see Figure 12-2). You can also teach your software to sign on, and look for and download new messages, while you warm up your coffee.

Figure 12-2.
Communications software stores phone numbers and sign-on sequences for services you call regularly. Just highlight the service, press RETURN, and the computer will sign you on. Shown here is the main dialing menu on *ProComm*.

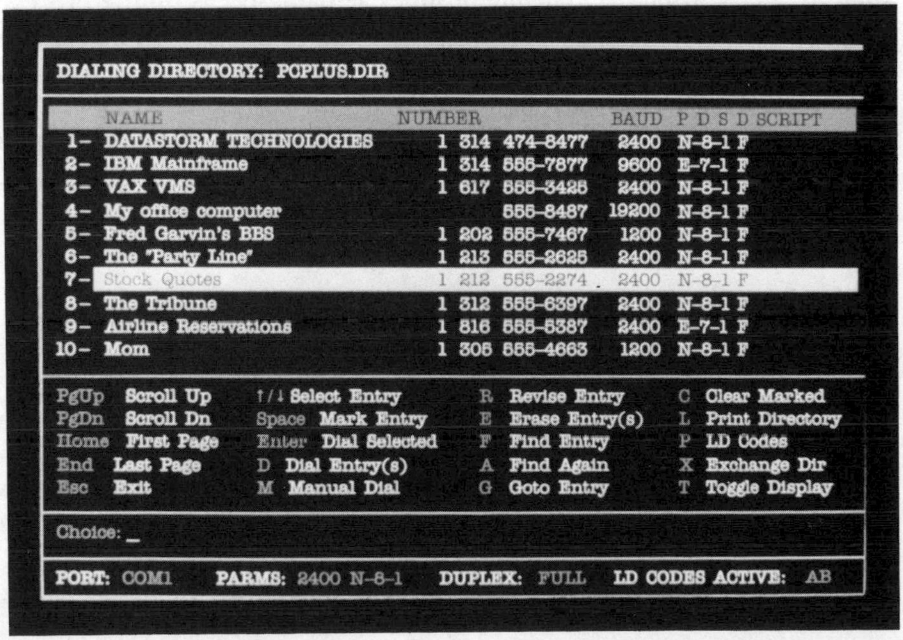

```
DIALING DIRECTORY: PCPLUS.DIR

        NAME                     NUMBER            BAUD  P D S D SCRIPT
   1-  DATASTORM TECHNOLOGIES   1 314 474-8477     2400  N-8-1 F
   2-  IBM Mainframe            1 314 555-7877     9600  E-7-1 F
   3-  VAX VMS                  1 617 555-3425     2400  N-8-1 F
   4-  My office computer         555-8487        19200 N-8-1 F
   5-  Fred Garvin's BBS        1 202 555-7467     1200  N-8-1 F
   6-  The "Party Line"         1 213 555-2625     2400  N-8-1 F
   7-  Stock Quotes             1 212 555-2274     2400  N-8-1 F
   8-  The Tribune              1 312 555-6397     2400  N-8-1 F
   9-  Airline Reservations     1 816 555-5387     2400  E-7-1 F
  10-  Mom                      1 305 555-4663     1200  N-8-1 F

PgUp  Scroll Up    ↑/↓ Select Entry    R  Revise Entry      C  Clear Marked
PgDn  Scroll Dn    Space Mark Entry    E  Erase Entry(s)    L  Print Directory
Home  First Page   Enter Dial Selected F  Find Entry        P  LD Codes
End   Last Page    D  Dial Entry(s)    A  Find Again        X  Exchange Dir
Esc   Exit         M  Manual Dial      G  Goto Entry        T  Toggle Display

Choice: _

PORT: COM1    PARMS: 2400 N-8-1    DUPLEX: FULL    LD CODES ACTIVE: AB
```

Activity Log

The phone company charges you for the time connected to an electronic-mail system, just as if you were making a voice call. You may also pay per-minute connection charges to a commercial service. Some programs automatically track your activity, creating a list of whom you called, when, and for how long. This is valuable for tallying expenses and billing clients—or when you're looking for fat to cut from your own operating budget.

System-Specific Software

You can call any e-mail system with all communications software. But if you use one system exclusively, you may not need that flexibility and might benefit from system-specific software. Instead of entering commands, you make menu choices and let the software do the dirty work. If you're new to computer communications, such software will probably cut your learning time considerably.

CompuServe Information Manager (CompuServe Information Service) is an example of such software. It adds a graphic interface with pulldown menus and icons to what is basically an old-fashioned, command-driven operating system. Besides aiding the electronic-mail process, the software helps guide you through this vast system.

Though the program makes CompuServe easier to use, using graphics can make it slower, which increases your on-line costs. A shareware program such as *Tapcis*, which is available on-line, actually speeds up the process. Both *CompuServe Information Manager* and *Tapcis* will scan your mail box for new mail, store it, and sign you off so you can read letters after you disconnect from the system.

Lotus *Express* (Lotus) for MS-DOS computers or *Desktop Express* (Dow Jones) for Macintosh computers are designed to use with MCI Mail. Besides automating the e-mail process, these programs are necessary for sending spreadsheet or graphics files.

COMPUSERVE AND MCI MAIL

The two most popular e-mail services among independent professionals are CompuServe Mail and MCI Mail. Each service has more than half a million subscribers. If you belong to CompuServe, you can send mail to an MCI Mail subscriber and vice versa, giving you a pool of over a million potential recipients.

In addition, CompuServe users can send mail to the InterNet system, which links you with government agencies, educational institutions, and corporations worldwide. MCI Mail is part of the EMS system, which connects you to AT&T Mail, Telemail, and Missive in France.

Western Union's EasyLink and AT&T Mail are other leading services, but they cater more to large corporations than MCI Mail and CompuServe do.

MCI Mail and CompuServe will laser print your electronic message and send it to a regular postal address. MCI Mail will print the letter on a facsimile of your letterhead stationary, with your signature, if you've registered it. You can request regular or overnight mail delivery. And both systems will send messages to fax machines, further widening your pool of potential recipients to all people with a fax machine.

Both systems also broadcast one message to a number of people; you could send a direct mail piece to a list of one hundred names, some with fax, some with electronic-mail boxes, and some with postal mail boxes.

While the ability to send faxes is no reason to subscribe to an electronic-mail service (unless, of course, you don't need a fax machine often enough to justify buying one), there are two advantages: You can send a file directly from you computer without printing it out, and computer-generated faxes are much sharper on the receiving end because they have not been scanned into the fax machine. (For more on computer-generated fax transmissions, see "Fax-Mail" section below, and Chapter 11.)

GATEWAYS TO ELECTRONIC LIBRARIES

By subscribing to MCI Mail or CompuServe, you also put your foot in the door of vast electronic libraries. MCI is a "gateway" to Dow Jones News/ Retrieval; that is, DJN/R is a separate service, but it is accessible via MCI Mail (see Figure 12-1). DJN/R houses a wide range of financial and corporate databases, including the full text of *The Wall Street Journal* (see Chapter 13). Since the two services are separate, the pricing is different. On MCI you pay per message unit (generally 25 to 45 cents per letter) or a basic fee of $10 a month. On DJN/R, you pay an hourly rate for usage.

CompuServe is a full-fledged information service, of which the mail service is just one component. CompuServe has many of the same financial databases as DJN/R, as well as a wide range of forums (special interest groups) where like-minded people can leave messages and files for others to read. CompuServe bills for time spent on-line; that is, from $6 to $12 an hour, depending on the time of day.

FAX-MAIL ADDS A WRINKLE TO E-MAIL

MCI, CompuServe, and other e-mail services will send your text message to a fax machine. But only through one system can you transmit graphics—

and *receive* messages from other fax machines. Xpedite Systems, Inc., lets you upload a message, using a stored graphic image of your letterhead, and send it to any fax machine. It also sends documents prepared with *WordStar*, *Microsoft Word*, *MultiMate*, *WordPerfect*, and some other leading word processors, with bold print, underlining, and other special formatting features intact.

"Xpedite is better than buying a dedicated fax machine for moderate send–receive duties," says John Konen, from Boone, North Carolina, who sends graphics created with *PFS: First Publisher*. "I send and receive about four faxes a week. I did an analysis of a three-year amortization of a $900 fax machine versus the Xpedite service, and the service won."

Xpedite receives faxes and places them in your Xpedite mail box. The fax is stored as a binary file in the TIFF used by many scanners and by drawing and publishing programs. Once you download the file, you have two choices. You can view it on your monitor, convert it to load into your word processing or publishing program, or print it on an Epson-compatible or Hewlett-Packard-compatible printer.

Using Xpedite might be a good way to send and recieve computer faxes without tying up your own computer. Let the system handle all the dirty work while you handle your own work. To use Xpedite, you first subscribe to the service, and then you pay connect-time rates when you check your mailbox or send a fax.

CONNECTING TO ANYONE, ANYWHERE, ANYTIME

There is a potential problem with MCI Mail, CompuServe, or any other e-mail service—the lack of connection between e-mail services. If you're an MCI Mail subscriber and your intended correspondent subscribes to, say, Western Union EasyLink, you can't communicate. The same is true with many other e-mail systems, whether public or corporate. With the notable exception of the links between CompuServe and MCI Mail, most e-mail systems are not connected. It's true that the barriers between e-mail systems are falling, although not nearly as fast as the Berlin Wall did.

The significance of inaccessible e-mail systems will vary with your business, but for many small-business people it's a major inconvenience and potentially a large expense. One solution is DASnet (DA Systems), which links more than sixty e-mail systems.

On the surface DASnet's operation is simple. DA Systems has an account and an electronic-mail box on each of the systems it connects. When you want to send a message from, say, MCI Mail to Western Union EasyLink, you just send it to the DA Systems MCI Mail mail box. Throughout the day, computers at DA System's headquarters in Campbell, California, sign on to each system, pick up the mail, and route it to the target system. Your message should be delivered within one to three hours—not immediately, but still quickly.

DASnet puts you in touch with more than four million electronic-mail users. In addition to U.S.-based systems—like MCI Mail, EasyLink, BIX, Telemail, Dialcom, AT&T Mail, The WELL, INET, NWI, EIES, Unison, PsychNet, UUCP (Unix), and Internet—DASnet offers a plethora of overseas connections. GeoMail connects to most countries in western Europe. The Association for Progressive Communications (APC) connects to networks in Brazil, Sweden, Nicaragua, Australia, and Canada. The TWICS network offers connections to the United Kingdom and Japan. And through Dialcom, you can reach Hong Kong, Israel, Puerto Rico, Singapore, and many other countries around the globe.

Besides electronic transmissions, you can use DASnet to send and receive telex messages and send faxes or paper mail. (The company uses EasyLink for the first two and MCI for paper printout and delivery.) And you can send a graphics file, a spreadsheet file, or a word processor-formatted document (all binary files) to any system.

ELECTRONIC PR

Most people send electronic messages to people they know, but more and more businesspeople are using e-mail to send unsolicited direct mail. It's often easier than printing labels, stuffing envelopes, and going to the post office.

Experienced entrepreneurs say there's no advertising like publicity—especially free publicity. One way to get publicity is to send a story about your business to the publication or TV station you'd like to see use it. You can send copies of these press releases to every publication in the country, which is costly and might not reach the right person.

A service called PR NewsWire will do the job for you. Send your release to PR NewsWire, by modem, fax, or mail. The service then transmits the message to the newsrooms, radio stations, wire services, and magazines you selected. You can pinpoint a marketing region for as little as $35 or blanket the country for only $325.

Bruce David, of Twinsburg, Ohio, used the service to promote his home-based advertising agency. The release he sent via PR NewsWire resulted in articles in nearly a dozen newspapers throughout the country, plus 12 minutes of airtime on national TV (NBC). David says the publicity enhanced his credibility, landed him several good referrals, and increased his sales by 10 percent.

SENDING SPREADHSEET AND GRAPHICS FILES

Letters, price lists, reports, invoices, and other ASCII text files will make up the bulk of your file transfers. You can create these on-line or off-line.

But every now and then you may have to deal with a binary file. Broadly speaking, a binary file is a file that contains nontext, or nondisplayable, characters. Examples include program files, non-ASCII word processor files (or files with formatting commands) or spreadsheet and graphics files. (To see what a machine language file looks like, key in TYPE COM-MAND.COM at an MS-DOS system prompt.)

Uploading and downloading (sending from disk to an e-mail service and saving to disk) machine language files requries using a file transfer protocol. Besides transmitting nondisplayable characters, the protocol en-sures than any errors in the transmission, such as those due to noisy phone lines, are corrected as they occur. For accuracy, many people use file transfer protocols even for pure text files when the phone connection is bad or when a minor mistake will throw a crucial number or table out of whack.

XMODEM FILE TRANSFER PROTOCOL

Using file transfer protocols for the first time can be more than a little unsettling. In fact, protocols put many people off communications alto-gether. But learning to use protocols significantly increases the types of files you send and the chances of getting them there in one piece.

The most common file transfer protocol is called XModem. It's supported by all communications software and most commercial systems (but not MCI Mail). Before uploading or downloading, you tell the e-mail system which protocol to use. Then you tell your communications to use the same protocol—and the software takes over and completes the file transfer.

If you want to send a machine language file on MCI Mail, both you and your correspondent must use Lotus *Express* or *Desktop Express*. Without this software, MCI Mail is strictly a place to exchange text messages.

COME ON, GIVE IT A TRY

Fewer computer owners use electronic mail than other main applications, such as word processing, spreadsheets, databases, and graphics. Why? First, it's not as natural as writing or calculating, which people have done for centuries. Thus people have to make a conceptual leap—the telephone is more than just a voice box.

Second, on-line systems have been notoriously difficult to use. The systems were designed on dinosaurlike mainframes and minicomputers in the 1950s and 1960s for people who were sitting in front of dumb terminals (and "dumb" is apt here). Major design improvements are made monthly, but the systems remain more primitive than modern computer software because they cannot be customized for one more type of computer.

Third, early communications software was written *by* techies *for* techies, and it continued in that vein long after the big professional software companies with the slick marketing departments began gearing other software toward the needs of average business users. That's three strikes—and many trial users were left walking back to the dugout shaking their heads.

But the climate's improving. Electronic information vendors know they have to change to widen their market, and they're doing just that. The systems add more and more plain English to their command languages, they add more and more features targeted at small-business users (such as the fax options), and software publishers soften up products with inviting user interfaces.

Any business that processes most of its information through computers owes electronic mail another chance. The initial learning curve is steep—but it quickly flattens out and drops as the productivity curve rises. The price-performance value of electronic mail is extremely high. It saves time wasted on telephone tag, and money spent on overnight mail packages. Customers and clients appreciate that today. Tomorrow, they will demand it.

Including an e-mail address on business cards, in addition to a voice and fax number, makes you more accessible and more professional. In this era of global computer communications, it's worth the effort to bring your computer system up to speed.

ELECTRONIC-MAIL RESOURCES

The Complete Handbook of Personal Computer Communications, 3rd Edition, by Alfred Glossbrenner; St Martin's Press, 405 pp., 1989; $18.95. Subtitled the "Bible of the Online World," this handbook tells you everything you need to know to enter the electronic universe, with a section on person-to-person on-line communications.

The Complete MCI Mail Handbook, by Stephen Manes, Bantam Electronic Publishing, 498 pp., 1989; $22.95. This handbook covers every detail of this popular electronic-mail service—from sending an individual message to instantly reaching huge mailing lists around the world. Money-saving shortcuts and time-savers are included.

Dvorak's Guide to PC Telecommunications, by John C. Dvorak and Nick Anis; Osborne/McGraw-Hill, 1053 pp., 1990; $45.95. This massive, comprehensive guide to telecommunications, co-authored by widely read columnist John Dvorak, should answer almost any question you have about putting a modem to work. The authors review the most popular communications software, on-line services, and electronic-mail systems. The book includes two disks: a modem tutor, and a communications package with a wide range of file-transfer protocols.

How to Get the Most Out of CompuServe, 4th Edition, by Charles Bowen and David Peyton, 323 pp., 1988; $22.95. CompuServe is such a vast system that people can use it for years without really knowing what they're missing. This handbook provides tip-packed tours of all the network's features, including electronic mail.

SPOTLIGHT ON: Electronic Mail

Cost: $10 and up a month, depending on usage.

Learning Curve: Medium to steep: E-mail services themselves are not difficult to master, especially if you're just sending and receiving simple text messages, but getting your communications software, modem, and phone to work harmoniously with a remote system takes trial and error. And learning to use file-transfer protocols to send files also takes practice.

Equipment Required: Computer; modem; telephone line; communications software.

Recommended E-Mail Services:

- *CompuServe Mail (CompuServe Information Service) gives you access to more than two million electronic-mail boxes, as well as fax machines and postal mail boxes; in addition, the system offers a wide range of financial and business databases, as well as professional forums.*
- *MCI Mail (MCI Digital Communications) reaches more than a million electronic-mail boxes and virtually all fax machines; in addition, you can send paper mail from your computer on letterhead with your own signature; from MCI Mail you can sign onto Dow Jones News/Retrieval, the leading purveyor of business information.*

Recommended Communications Software:

For IBM PC and IBM PS/2 and Compatibles

- *ProComm Plus* (Datastorm Technologies) is a solid choice for novices and advanced users; the dialing directory is large (up to 200 entries), and the program operates fluidly; it includes an excellent activity log, record mode, and text editor.
- *Lotus Express* (Lotus) sends and receives spreadsheet and graphics files via MCI Mail; it doesn't work with any other system, and it requires that correspondents use the same software—but it's the only game in town.

For Macintosh

- *Microphone II* (Software Ventures Corp.) is fairly easy to learn, with a good record mode (called "watch me"); though basic, the program has enough power for advanced users to customize and automate as they wish; it lacks a text editor.
- *Smartcom II* (Hayes Microcomputer Products) is elegant, with on-screen icons for all major functions; it includes a learn mode and text editor.
- *Desktop Express* (Dow Jones Software), the Macintosh counterpart to Lotus *Express* for MS-DOS users, sends and receives graphics and spreadsheet files on MCI Mail *only*; the correspondent must also use the package.

Buying Tips: Since you generally can communicate only with people who subscribe to the same service as you do, be sure to choose an e-mail service that co-workers, clients, or customers use. Many people subscribe to two or more proprietary services (or a wide-reach service such as DASNet) to ensure that they reach everyone they need to. If you plan on sending spreadsheet or graphics files, check in advance the requirements for doing so on a given service.

Chapter 13
Search the World's Libraries From Your Desk

Use your modem to unearth corporate and financial statistics, and newsletters, magazines, and journals covering every field.

My library was dukedom large enough.

—William Shakespeare, *The Tempest*

You may not have a good clipping or filing system, or live near a world class library—but you can use your modem to track down any squib of information on virtually any topic by signing on to an electronic information service and searching its databases.

"I did an article for my newsletter showing how the computer industry fares in relation to the rest of the economy," says Bill Vick, an independent executive recruiter. "I signed onto DIALOG, found an article from *The Wall Street Journal*, downloaded into my word processor, edited it, added a chart from *Excel*, and bingo—I had an article for my newsletter."

Steve McGowan, whose McGowan Marine consulting firm designs mechanical systems for yachts, uses the FYI database on current events to make his bids and proposal up to date. For instance, he might get a bid from a subcontractor in Holland for boat construction, sign on to FYI, check the latest exchange rate, and convert the Dutch bid into U.S. dollars for his client." "I don't have to do that—the client could check tomorrow's *Wall Street Journal*, but it's a good service to offer, and the exchange rate is only an hour old."

The catch? Finding the information you need isn't always easy—or cheap. Even if you happened to know that the full text of the *Harvard Business Review, Standard & Poor's Corporate Descriptions, Biotechnology Abstracts*, and scores of other databases are available on-line—and most people don't—you still probably don't know where they are or how to get them onto your screen. The untrained researcher prospecting for gold may end up with a pan of costly fool's gold.

Often it may pay to hire a professional information broker to search for you. That's especially true if you're always looking for a different type of information and don't want to start from scratch on every search. But if your research is focused on one general area—such as finance, medicine, or demographics—you can identify the source of information (the right database) and learn an effective foraging technique. In time, the search process will be automatic.

LET YOUR MODEM DO THE WALKING

Although electronic research can be relatively costly and difficult for the untrained searcher, it has two big advantages over traditional paper-based library research. First, from your desk you can literally reach into the libraries of the world. Not only do you save on travel time, but you can locate materials faster because you're using a computer to search. Second, when you find the information you want you can download it to your computer for editing or printing.

Pete Silver, a marketing consultant who operates out of Gainesville, Florida, once needed an article from a back issue of *Inc.* magazine. "I was about to send my assistant to the library to track it down, but thought— wait, that'll take hours," says Silver. "I signed on to Dow Jones News/ Retrieval and found it right away. I don't know how much it cost, maybe $2 or $4."

Rob Roy, an executive recruiter who works from his home in Providence, Rhode Island, routinely searches on-line databases for executive prospects and companies with employees he might want to recruit. "I can search all employers within a certain industry by state and come up with 500 companies while I shower, shave, and dress for a dinner party," says Roy. Without electronic research, Roy would have to trudge to the library, pore through volumes of resources, take notes, transfer them onto a disk, and then organize the information for his clients.

On the average, Roy estimates his searches yield successful prospects 80 percent of the time, with search sessions averaging 30 minutes. When he has the information he wants, he instantly downloads it as a *WordPerfect* file so he can further manipulate the data.

Corey Sandler, president of Word Association, an editorial services company, points out one potential drawback to electronic searching. "You lose what I call propinquity," says Sandler, who uses CompuServe and DIALOG to find back articles on the computer industry and bills clients about $100 a month for his research. "When I look up a word in a dictionary, or a catalog card in a library, I read the four or five terms and cards around it. I don't do that on-line and I lose something. Plus, when you read an article on-line you don't see the art, the tables, or captions. I often use the electronic database as a bibliography, and then get my hands on the real thing."

This chapter describes the major electronic databases for general professional use, points to other more specialized databases and professional networks, and describes how CD-ROM (a relatively new data storage medium) is becoming an alternative to on-line research.

HOW ELECTRONIC DATABASES WORK

Like a database of addresses on your hard disk drive, an on-line database holds a certain class of information. For example, MEDLINE stores literature from the National Library of Medicine; INSPEC covers electrical engineering, physics, electronics, and related information. One database may be offered by a number of information services. For example, Dow Jones News/Retrieval, CompuServe, Delphi, and GEnie all offer stock quotations. To access a given database, you need a subscription to the information service on which it resides.

You dial the service by modem, enter your password, request a certain database, and then begin your search. The process is similar to accessing an electronic-mail service to read your mail (see Chapter 12). Most electronic databases operate with different search commands. In some cases you must learn the language of information specialists—truncation, proximity operators, nesting, and Boolean logic (combining the words AND, OR, and NOT). In other cases, you can search by choosing from a series of menus or by entering keywords.

You have to be clever about picking your keyboards. If they're too specific and restrictive, the computer may find only a few occurrences or none at all, passing over crucial articles that don't happen to contain the words you've chosen. If your keywords are too broad, you'll be swamped with information, most of it irrelevant.

Full Text vs. Abstracts

The system will respond to your keywords and produce a list of related articles or files; you choose the ones you want to see. Exactly how much data you get varies, depending on the database and the system. You may get a bibliographic citation that leads you to the library. You may also get an abstract, or capsule description of an article's contents. Some systems allow you to read the whole article on-screen, and others will mail you the document upon request. A given database might offer abstracts on some articles and the full text on others.

Cost

The more specialized the information service and database, the higher the cost. You can search a general-purpose service such as CompuServe for less than $12 an hour (daytime rates). A more specialized service such as Dialog charges up to $300 an hour, depending on the database. These connect-time charges are in addition to any telephone costs or subscription costs. Many services tack on charges for each file you actually read.

Gateways

While you generally must subscribe to a given service to access its databases, there is a way to tap into a high-powered database without paying for an annual subscription. The method is to use a gateway service such as EasyNet (also called InfoMaster on Western Union and IQuest on CompuServe), which connects you with more than 700 databases from a variety of information services.

You dial a toll-free number and enter your credit card information. If you know the database you want, you can request it. If you don't, you enter search criteria, and the service chooses a database it *thinks* might hold the information you want. Then the system coughs up a list of article titles. Like a poker player demanding extra cards, you pay to see every set of ten article titles, and more to read them.

EasyNet is certainly easier to use than most of the systems it connects to, and it's a less expensive route for the occasional searcher. But once you know the database you need and how to use it, EasyNet will seem slow, cumbersome, and expensive.

NEWS, SPORTS, STOCKS, AND WEATHER

The kind of general information newspapers deliver is fairly easy to come by on-line. Stock quotes, news, sports, and weather can be found on a wide variety of information services, including CompuServe, Delphi, GEnie, Prodigy, and Dow Jones News/Retrieval. Of course, this newsy information isn't particularly valuable, since you can get it from radio, TV, or newspapers on the same day. But CompuServe's Executive News Service will search all AP articles around-the-clock to match your keywords and store articles until you sign on and read clippings.

What most searchers want is an archive of news, so they can peruse all information on a given topic published in, say, the last six months. And because that kind of information is more valuable, it's harder to come by. For example, only Nexis, an expensive and difficult system used primarily by news-gathering organizations, stores the full text of back issues of *The New York Times*. Only Dow Jones News/Retrieval stores the full text of back issues of *The Wall Street Journal*.

FINANCIAL AND CORPORATE INFORMATION

The most complete collection of financial and corporate news and information is housed on Dow Jones News/Retrieval, although CompuServe carries many of the same databases and is less expensive to use. Besides current stock quotes, which many services offer, DJN/R carries a wide range of databases that let you research the performance history of a given company. These include Dun & Bradstreet's Financial Records, with the financials of 750,000 public and private companies; Standard & Poor's Online, for earning and income estimates; Disclosure, with reports of about 12,000 publically held companies filed with the S.E.C.; and Investext, with investment-oriented news and analysis prepared by the world's leading investment banking firms (see Figure 13-1).

Dow Jones Software

Dow Jones also markets a number of software packages designed to help users interpret financial data. Once you tell the software what information you want, the package will sign on DJN/R, find the right database, download the information, and sign off. Then you can graph, chart, and otherwise analyze the information.

Dow Jones Market Manager and Market Manager PLUS track portfolios with your securities. *Dow Jones Market Analyzer PLUS* takes historical information from the Dow Jones Historical Quote database and performs technical analysis. *Dow Jones Market Microscope* hones in on companies meeting certain requirements (such as stock above or below a certain price), and *Dow Jones Spreadsheet Link* downloads data from a number of databases and stores them in Lotus *1-2-3*.

Four Hundred Plus Business Publications

Besides financial statistics, DJN/R contains the full text of more than 400 business magazines and newspapers published within the last six months.

Figure 13-1.
Dow Jones News/Retrieval is the leading source of business and financial information, with databases that give background information on all major companies. Here, Dow Jones QuickSearch goes to work to produce a capsule look at a given company *(we chose T for AT&T)*.

DOW JONES QUICKSEARCH
COPYRIGHT © 1990
DOW JONES & COMPANY, INC.

An automated method for accessing quotes, company news, financial data and profile information from eight News/Retrieval services.

Press To
1. Search by company stock symbol
2. Access a QuickSearch help menu

Or enter as much of the company name as you're sure of and hit (Return).

    1

PLEASE ENTER STOCK SYMBOL

    T

DOW JONES QUICKSEARCH AMERICAN TELEPHONE & TELEGRAPH CO.

PRESS   FOR

1. CURRENT QUOTES
2. LATEST NEWS ON T
3. FINANCIAL AND MARKET OVERVIEW
4. EARNINGS ESTIMATES
5. COMPANY VS INDUSTRY PERFORMANCE
6. INCOME STATEMENTS, BAL SHEETS
7. COMPANY PROFILE
8. INSIDER TRADING SUMMARY
9. INVESTMENT RESEARCH REPORTS

TYPE ALL FOR ENTIRE COMPANY REPORT FOR $45 FLAT FEE.

Titles include *The Wall Street Journal*, the *Washington Post*, *Fortune*, *Forbes*, and *Barron's*, as well as scores of regional business publications. DJN/R has also devised an advanced search interface called DowQuest, which makes access to these periodicals relatively easy. DowQuest, in fact, is a good example of the steps information services are taking to make their products more accessible to noninformation professionals.

Using DowQuest to search the DJN/R databases of business publications, you can pose your query in plain English. "Oil company reaction to EPA legislation," you might enter, or "Computer software for financial analysis." Within seconds, DowQuest delivers a list of articles. You can read an article or choose one that most closely matches your search needs and see more. When you read an article the paragraphs are numbered. Again, you can pick paragraphs that are close to the mark and DowQuest returns with another list of articles. You're panning for gold and with each choice get closer to it (see Figure 13-2).

TRW Credit Reports

To find the credit rating of any company that has ever applied for credit, check the TRW Business Profiles, which are available on NewsNet and CompuServe. The profile, which monitors the creditworthiness of public and private companies, features an executive summary that focuses on days beyond term (DBT), an estimate of the number of days late a firm is likely to be in paying its bills. Bankruptcy filings, open tax liens or judgments, and other information is presented, culminating in a confidence score, which represents the probability of the customer paying more or less than 30 days beyond the due date.

Telescan

One excellent investor-oriented database that you access directly—rather than through an information service—is Telescan. Telescan's combination software and database service provides data on more than 10,000 active stocks, 2,000 mutual funds, and 200 market indexes. Telescan markets two software packages—*Telescan Analyzer* and *Telescan Edge*—that turn the raw database data into vivid charts and graphs. You sign on to Telescan, select the stock or mutual fund charts you want, and download them to your computer. *Analyzer*, which offers both fundamental and technical analysis of the stock market, collects the data, constructs the charts, and performs daily updates.

Telescan Edge, an add-on to *Analyzer*, is a powerful tool for screening companies, industries, or mutual funds as possible investments. Suppose

Figure 13-2.

DowQuest allows you to search the Dow Jones News/Retrieval database of more than 400 business publications with plain-English queries. Its most powerful feature is its ability to improve a search based on examples of articles you select, as shown in the sample search below.

Assume you're a banking consultant and have been asked to prepare a marketing plan aimed at attracting deposits from older people. To begin, you decide to look at what other banks have been doing in this field. You turn to DowQuest and enter:

BANKS MARKETING TO OLDER PEOPLE TO ATTRACT DEPOSITS (RETURN)

—Press (Return) to see the starter list of headlines—

1 The Future Is Here—The Apple is history. In the 21st . . .
   WASHINGTON POST, 06/25/89 (4,997 words)

2 Banks, Thrifts in Race for Senior Citizen Dollar
   DENVER POST, 06/05/89 (1,126)

3 Legal Rainmakers Summon Money, Not Rain
   BUSINESS FIRST-COLUMBUS, 07/17/89 (1,356)

4 Banks Lose Fondness for Affinity Cards—Narrow . . .
   WALL STREET JOURNAL, 08/21/89 (1,513)

On its first attempt to satisfy your request, DowQuest has found only one article among the first four that appears to meet your needs. But that's all you need. You enter SEARCH 2 (RETURN) to tell DowQuest to look for other articles similar to article no. 2.

—Press (Return) to see the resulting list of headlines—

1 Banks, Thrifts in Race for Senior Citizen Dollar
   DENVER POST, 06/05/89 (1,126 words)

2 Geriatric Romance Prevails as Banks Woo Area Seniors
   THE WASHINGTON TIMES, 08/15/89 (1,086)

3 Your Money Matters: Gray Market: Banks Seek 50-Plus . . .
   WALL STREET JOURNAL, 07/18/89 (981)

4 Twin Cities Banks Pursue Burgeoning 'Gray Market' of . . .
   MINNEAPOLIS-ST PAUL CITYBUSINESS, 07/10/89 (1,692)

This search has quickly produced a number of good articles. In fact, still other articles on the subject are further down the list of sixteen headlines. To print the articles, you enter PRINT and the article numbers. You can then select continuous or page-by-page display.

you want to know which stocks have the highest five-year compound-earnings growth and the most insider trading; the report will list 10 to 200 stocks that best meet your investment criteria.

FULL-FLEDGED LIBRARIES

When you need more traditional library information—a catalog of all articles on a given industry or field—you turn to a service such as DIALOG. Probably the largest on-line database service, DIALOG contains more than 300 specialized databases with newspaper, journal, and magazine articles that cover virtually every professional, scientific, and academic field.

But DIALOG and other similar on-line systems—such as BRS, Orbit, and Vu/Text—are designed for library scientists. The system commands are complex, and on-line help and menus are spare. One way around these problems, of course, is to hire a professional information broker. The other is to use a "lite" version of the system, such as Knowledge Index.

Knowledge Index

Knowledge Index offers high-octane, industrial-strength information packaged and priced for the noninformation professional. You may use either menus or the systems simplified command language. (You can actually get by with just five command words: AND, OR, NOT, FIND, and DISPLAY.)

KI, as it's known, is an off-hours service (available nights and weekends) offering access to about seventy-five of DIALOG'S most popular databases. At an hourly rate of less than $30, this service is relatively inexpensive. While not all of DIALOG'S sophisticated search options are available on KI, you can satisfy all but the most complicated information needs. KI is a great way to get your feet wet without drowning in on-line charges.

KI's databases cover a wide range of subject areas. Six databases offer exhaustive coverage of chemicals and pharmaceuticals. Standard & Poor's has at least four databases on KI (news, corporate descriptions, biographical, and corporate register). Various databases cover more than 200 economic journals, and more than 500 publications dealing with banking, advertising and marketing, insurance, real estate, management, and other business topics. A cache of general newspapers and periodicals from *American Heritage* to *Yachting* are sitting on-line.

With the *Books in Print* database you can search for any book on any topic of interest. With *Marquis Who's Who* you can search for people. And with MEDLINE you can search through the exhaustive literature summaries prepared by the National Library of Medicine. Other databases are devoted to legal matters, history, art, literature, psychology, sociology, religion, sports, and the cinema.

NewsNet's On-Line Newsletters

If you're in advertising, public relations, sales, consulting, or some other information-intensive profession, you often need a quick snapshot of your client's industry or field. Often the best way to get that is by reading an industry newsletter, written by an expert who reports on important developments and trade shows. And the leader in the on-line newsletter field is the NewsNet system, with more than 350 newsletters on-line—half of which aren't available in electronic form anywhere else.

Titles cover a wide range of subjects, such as *Access Reports/Freedom of Information, China Express, Fiber Optics News,* and *Microcomputers in Education.* But you don't need to know a newsletter's title. NewsNet allows you to search by subject or industry group. Groups include Advertising and Marketing, Aerospace, Chemical, and so on. For example, to catch up on sludge issues, you would key in SEARCH CH to search the chemical group. Titles in this group include *Hazardous Waste News, Toxic Materials, Sludge Newsletter,* and others. Choose a title and then an article from a menu list and it will be displayed.

Nexis

Just as NewsNet offers the full text of hundreds of newsletters, Nexis (Mead Data Central) offers the full text of hundreds of magazines and newspapers, and transcripts of some television shows, such as the MacNeil/Lehrer Newshour. Nexis carries *The New York Times,* the *Los Angeles Times, Time, Newsweek, Sports Illustrated, Fortune, Forbes,* and other mainstream publications.

Nexis is somewhat easier to use than DIALOG and other electronic libraries, in large part because it sells the full text of articles—not just abstracts or citations. Once inside an article you can move forward or backward at will. If you don't want to read the whole article, you can enter a Keyword in Context (KWIC) and the system will move you to that spot. You can print the document on your own printer, or request Nexis to print it off-line and mail it to you.

Professional Forums

Another way to get a quick fix on a given industry or profession is by accessing a professional network. CompuServe has the largest collection and heaviest density of on-line professionals, who congregate in the forums to post and read messages on various electronic bulletin boards. For people who work outside big corporations or in areas where they don't have regular contact with professional colleagues, tapping into a professional network is an excellent way to stay in touch with new developments.

CompuServe forums include the Educators Forum, Foreign Language Forum, International Entrepreneurs Forum, Journalism Forum, Legal Forum, PR and Marketing Forum, and Working From Home Forum, in addition to a wide range of computer-related forums.

The Working From Home Forum (GO WORK), as it happens, includes a bulletin board section on information brokers. It's an excellent place to get answers to electronic research questions.

CD-ROM DATABASES

The relatively new optical storage method of CD-ROM may change the way people research volumes of data. Once viewed primarily as a gee whiz technology that would someday deliver multimedia encyclopedias with great music and art (which hasn't happened yet), CD-ROM is now seen as a practical way to deliver large amounts of data—much of it dry statistics—to business users.

CD-ROM disks, which run on CD-ROM drives and are identical in appearance to audio CDs, can hold about 550 megabytes of data. That equals 250,000 pages of text, or about 12,000 images.

By running search-and-retrieval software on your computer, which comes with each CD-ROM disk, you can search through megabytes of data in several seconds. For example, when using Microsoft's *Small Business Consultant* CD-ROM, you might enter keywords such as *franchise licencees* or *inventory control*. The search software would display a list of all entries on those topics. You could then read what you wanted, and paste portions into your word processor to print them out.

CD-ROM libraries can be a very cost-effective alternative to on-line databases because you own the database and don't pay to use it. That assumes, of course, that the database you need is available in CD-ROM format. As it happens, DIALOG offers a handful of its databases on CD-ROM disks.

CD-ROM disks are updated at regular intervals and sent to registered users. In this sense, you are not buying a static product as much as you are subscribing to an evolving electronic information service. For instance, Lotus's OneSource CD-ROMs, which hold a variety of financial data, are updated weekly and delivered to users by overnight courier.

More and more databases are being converted to CD-ROM. The 1990

U.S. Census will be available on CD-ROM, the first time the Census Bureau will have made its important demographic information so accessible.

Most CD-ROM titles, like most on-line databases, appeal to extremely vertical markets. *Nynex Fast Track* is a directory of phone numbers and addresses for every NYNEX phone exchange, which would be useful to direct marketers in the Northeast. Microsoft, a major CD-ROM publisher, offers more general titles, such as the above-mentioned *Small Business Consultant* (a collection of government-published small-business tools) and Microsoft *Stat Pack* (general U.S. government statistics).

MASTER YOUR MODEM FIRST

The first step in undertaking electronic research is to master your communications setup. You should be comfortable using a modem and all that entails—signing on to remote databases and saving text on-screen to disk—before you begin to search. Subscribing to an electronic mail service and sending and receiving messages is probably the best way to get positive results quickly.

The second step is to identify the database or databases that contain the information you need. Alfred Glossbrenner's *How to Look it Up Online* (see Resources section) is a good guide to what's available and how to find it. Alternatively, you can sign onto EasyNet, the gateway service that connects you with a wealth of databases, and start searching. Identify the databases that consistently turn up your material and subscribe to the service that houses them.

Finally, experiment with search techniques. Try to locate an article you know is in print. No doubt it will take several efforts to concoct the right combination of keywords. Keep track of the keywords that work and then try to find another article in less time. DowQuest on DJN/R (see Figure 13–2) is an excellent place to practice.

Research itself is an acquired skill, and electronic research is made more difficult because it requires mastery of computer communications. But the benefits of information on demand—just as the potential rewards in gold panning and poker—are so great that it pays to develop and hone your skills.

ELECTRONIC RESEARCH RESOURCES

How to Look It Up Online, by Alfred Glossbrenner, St. Martin's Press, 483 pp., 1987; $14.95. An in-depth look at on-line databases and how to use them. Glossbrenner profiles the major services, such as DIALOG and Knowledge Index, BRS, Nexis, ORBIT, and NewsNet, and tells you what databases to check for books, magazines, people and places, industry profiles, advertising and demographic information, and government information.

The Complete Handbook of Personal Computer Communications, by Alfred Glossbrenner, St. Martin's Press, 405 pp., 1989; $18.95. While a general guide to what a modem can do for you, this book covers both the general-purpose information services (such as GEnie and CompuServe) and the specialized database providers (such as DIALOG and NewsNet).

Directory of Online Databases, Cuadra/Elsevier, 600 pp., $75 for single copies; $175 for annual subscription. This definitive list of on-line databases is indexed a number of ways to help you find the database you need. Updated every six months for subscribers, with two quarterly update supplements. Also available on Microsoft *Bookshelf*, a CD-ROM disk.

Datapro Directory of On-Line Services, Datapro Research Corp.; $561 for annual subscription. This complete directory of databases and on-line providers comes in two thick three-ring binders and is updated monthly. Subscribers are entitled to telephone consulting via Datapro's toll-free number.

Link-Up, Learned Information, Inc.; $24/yr. A trade magazine for the electronic information field with tips, news, and reviews of more interest to general consumers than most trade magazines.

Compact Disk Products. This mail-order company sells a wide range of CD-ROM titles, including the *CD-ROM SourceDisk*, which contains listings of CD-ROM products.

Directory of Fee-Based Information Services, by Helen Burwell, Burwell Enterprises, 260 pp.; $37. If you don't want to do your own research, this book will help you locate an information broker who can help you ("information services" here refers to companies that do research, not the electronic information services that offer databases). Published annually, the book lists brokers by country, city, company name, personal name, services offered, and subject area of expertise. Nearly 700 information brokers are listed.

SPOTLIGHT ON: Electronic Databases

Cost: $10 to $300 per hour, plus subscription fees.
Learning Curve: Medium to steep. Even if you are familiar with modem communications and the lingo of information services, you will have trouble quickly finding the information you want unless you have the instincts of a librarian. But if you consistently access the same database(s), the initially steep learning curve will flatten.
Equipment Required: Computer with modem, hard disk drive and printer; to use CD-ROM disks: CD-ROM drive.
Recommended Systems:

- CompuServe (CompuServe Information Service) is the largest general information service, with something for everyone; though better known for its forums, CompuServe has excellent news, financial, and general business databases; it also has an electronic-mail service.
- Dow Jones News/Retrieval (Dow Jones) is the spot for serious investors, analysts, publicists, or business journalists who follow certain companies on a regular basis; it carries every conceivable corporate and financial database, plus the full text of more than 400 business publications; its DowQuest searching system is about the best in the business.
- EasyNet (Telebase Systems, Inc.), also known as IQuest on CompuServe and InfoMaster on Western Union, is a gateway service that puts you in touch with more than 700 databases from various vendors; it is a pay-as-you-use service, with no subscription necessary—just dial a toll-free number and enter credit-card information.

Buying Tips: Before subscribing to a given information service, experiment with several databases to make sure you will be getting what you want. If you already subscribe to an electronic mail service such as MCI Mail or CompuServe, take the MCI gateway to Dow Jones News/Retrieval or the CompuServe gateway to IQuest for a trial spin. Otherwise, dial EasyNet's toll-free number, enter your credit card information, and explore. And don't hesitate to hire an information broker to do research for you (see *Directory of Fee-Based Information Services* in Resources section).

PART IV
Office Management

Chapter 14
Managing Phone Calls, Schedules, and Follow-up Letters

Salespeople and others with long lists of contacts can turn their computers into timesaving secretaries with activity-tracking software.

Never before have we had so little time in which to do so much.

—Franklin D. Roosevelt, Fireside Chat

The independent professional, often without a secretary or assistants, has a problem: staying on top of all the day-to-day details required to run a business. Tracking contacts, phone messages, schedules and appointments, notes and to do lists, expenses and billing can be a full-time job.

The computer will collect, file, and sort this information. It will link information from a message to a certain project or client; it will time a phone call and generate a bill; it will send you a tickler beep or screen message to remind you of an appointment or phone call; it will make connections you might not otherwise make and will save you time by organizing your activities. All you have to do is find the right program to suit your particular business needs and working style.

"Before I computerized, notes would disappear or get buried at the bottom of the stack," says Mel Corbett, who runs New Horizons Management, a real estate management and investment business from his home in Brooklyn, New York. "Now, by pressing one key, I can quickly see all the things I have to do. Seeing everything organized in front of me helps me focus on the most important jobs."

Corbett uses a program called *ACT!*, a predesigned database perfect for tracking phone calls, contacts, and schedules. Such software, originally designed for salespeople, is sometimes called a sales tracker, and sometimes (because of its broadened role) an activity tracker. Better than most software, the program names describe what they do: *C.A.T.* (Chang Labs) stands for contacts, activities, and time; *ACT!* (Conductor Software) stands for activity control technology. *Sales Ally* (Scherrer Resources), *TeleMagic* (Remote Control), *Follow Up* (Xycad Group), and *Dayflo Tracker* (Dayflow Software Corp.) speak for themselves.

To track contacts, you could also use a full-fledged database, which you can customize 101 ways (see Chapter 17). But it is better suited to tracking a consistent set of data whose structure you can predict beforehand. A database isn't flexible enough to handle a torrent of unpredictable information that Post-Its, Rolodexes, and desk calendars now handle.

This chapter describes the general characteristics of activity trackers, examines in detail one advanced program designed for full-time telemarketers, and points to several memory-resident programs that can be used as trackers.

ACTIVITY TRACKERS

Activity trackers are particularly well suited to salespeople, but they are useful for any business that depends on heavy telephone contact. At its core, an activity tracker includes a strong address-management capability (or contact file) and a telephone management system. The latter includes a phone log to track who called whom and why, and any toll calls—which is useful to track both an ongoing project and its expenses.

The programs come with preset fields to record a person's name, address, phone numbers (fax, e-mail, etc.), and other particulars (birthday, spouse's name, etc.). If you have a modem, you can highlight a number on the screen and dial the telephone through the modem. (You pick up the phone handset while it's ringing and generally press the space bar or click the mouse to make the connection.) When talking on the phone, you can attach notes to that person's file (see Figure 14–1).

Besides a contact file, activity trackers also include a calendar and to do list. You can link these directories to the contact names and phone records. You can also generate printouts of to do lists that are divided into categories—such as meetings and calls. Thus you can describe the same phone call four different ways—by date, by person, by item, by length of call—providing a precise way to track your phone time and the schedule of an ongoing project.

There's a clear advantage to this multidimensional tracking method, compared to the traditional sales tracking with 3 × 5 card systems. "One problem with cards," says Rob Gilgoff, a telemarketing consultant, "is that you can only sort them one way. Either they're in alphabetical order by the name of the prospect, or they're by follow-up date or telephone number. If

Figure 14-1.
Activity trackers store contact names, addresses, and phone numbers of every call, then attach notes on phone calls and letters to that contact. The screen shown is from *Focal Point II*.

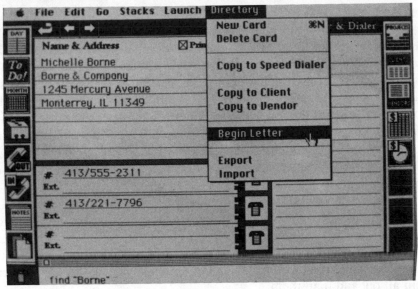

someone calls you back it's hard to find the card." An automated system can sort records any way you like. Since it can take five or more calls to close a sale, it's much easier to track a prospect with a computerized system.

Widely Acclaimed Timesavers

Almost everyone who uses an activity tracker says the systems save them time. "I don't have to spend as much time doing routine tasks, and that gives me more time to look for new business," says Tom Terry, an independent marketing consultant in Napa, California, who uses *C.A.T.* Frank Rinkus, who works for Winthrop Securities, a Los Angeles area real estate investment company, says that *Sales Ally* helps him retrieve information more quickly to answer client questions. "We can access files and shrink the turnaround time from questions asked to questions answered. It makes our use of time much more efficient and makes us look better."

All entries can be time- and date-stamped; the stamps set off a "tickler" system. When the tickler goes off, some programs bring up on-screen the calls you're supposed to make on that day. You can then check the attached notes to see what was said in the last conversation, and hit a key to dial the phone through your modem. "Everybody makes to-do lists, but with a paper list it's very easy to put things off," says Don Plumley, who operates his consulting firm, SaleSolutions Inc., from southern California. "When the computer beeps at you and tells you that you're supposed to call someone right now, it's hard to ignore."

Mailing Lists

Most activity trackers include a basic word processor so that you can prepare letters for different situations. Since an activity tracker is a type of database, you can search through your file of contacts and sort by certain criteria, which allows you to target select groups for mailings. Then you can use the mail-merge function to link addresses to letters, and print mailing labels or envelopes to send out mass mailings. "Before we got *Sales Ally*, we just weren't able to regularly target selected groups and send them personalized letters," says Jerry Jacobson, of Business Records and Consultants in Denver, Colorado.

Many activity trackers will let you indicate if a particular person should get correspondence and exactly what information is expected. For instance, Jacobson sends out different letters to prospects depending on their status. "I have about a hundred canned letters," he says. "I insert a code telling which letter to send to whom. When I'm done with all my calls, I just print them all out and mail them."

You can also use the sorting capability to generate reports. For example, if the manufacturer you represent wants to know the disposition of the 200 leads sent last week, you can immediately compile a printout.

TELEMARKETING SOFTWARE

Activity tracking software is designed primarily for salespeople. And since salespeople use the telephone extensively, activity trackers are built around telephone management. But they are not necessarily designed for full-time telemarketers, who spend all day on the phone.

Telemarketing consultants note that salespeople are considerably more productive with a computer and just the basic software packages, such as word processing and spreadsheets. With specialized sales software, however, consultants believe that the average seller can boost productivity by 100 percent or more. A computer can't close, cross-sell, or deal with objections, of course—but it can help organize a seller and the overall sales effort.

Telemagic

Telemagic (Remote Control), the best-selling telemarketing program, is essentially a top-notch activity tracker that does everything. It's designed for people who spend a good part of the day on the telephone.

Telemagic dials through the modem and supports headsets, important for hands-free telemarketing. The prospect call screen is well laid out and has seven fields that you can define for tracking information specific to your business. *Telemagic* has sales-spiel scripts that prompt you—moving to sublevels of a script with a single keystroke, depending upon the user's response.

To record details of the conversation, *Telemagic* has a large notepad area. The notepad also has automatic date- and time-stamping, a timesaving feature extremely useful for tracking conversations. It's also easy to schedule follow-up calls, which are important in building long-term relationships. Just type in a recall date and time. For example, if you want to call back in three days, you just enter "3D" and *Telemagic* will calculate the recall date. To indicate a call type, you enter a single letter that designates it as an appointment, follow-up to literature, closing, or to see how the customer is enjoying your product.

You can send a follow-up letter with just a few keystrokes (after you've set up and written the letter). Or you can quickly follow up the call with a fax, voice mail, or electronic mail. *Telemagic* allows you to set up to ten alarms per day, which include a brief message that flashes on the lower part of the screen.

To group records together for special reports or calling campaigns, *Telemagic* lets you create up to 50,000 different "filters." A filter selects records based on any field—such as city, state, or customer type—using rules of logic, such as AND, OR, EQuals, and NOT EQual.

One of the biggest problems with telemarketing is the quality of the list. Many lists that you purchase from brokers have duplicate, incomplete, or out-of-date records that need to be culled. And if a number of people are using the same list, they can inadvertently create duplicates. *Telemagic* will find and eliminate duplicates.

Even though *Telemagic* has a basic built-in word processor, a feature called Autoswap brings in any other program of your choice. When you're finished, Autoswap will automatically bring *Telemagic* back on-screen. You can export information as a comma-delimited text file (which most data-bases accept) or in *dBase* format.

POP-UP ACTIVITY TRACKERS

A potential drawback with an activity tracker is that it might not be accessible when you need it. If you plan on making a series of phone calls, you can load your activity tracker and begin ticking off names and adding notes. But if you're working on a spreadsheet, say, and you get an incoming call, you won't have your contact file at the ready. Of course, if you're running MultiFinder on the Macintosh or one of the many multitasking environments on MS-DOS (*DesqView 386, Windows 386, Operating System/2*), you can just switch to an already open program (depending on how much memory you have). But many people will have to close the spreadsheet program and load the activity tracker, which may or may not be worth the extra time it takes.

An attractive alternative for many people is to use one of the many memory-resident or pop-up programs—called terminate-stay-resident (TSR) on MS-DOS computers and desk accessories on the Macintosh. These programs are always accessible—just hit a key or click the mouse and the program pops onto the screen.

"Until I discovered *Instant Recall* (Chronologic Software) I thought I would need multitasking software just so I could jump from my proposal software to my client database to enter notes, make calls, and so on," says Lewis Mann, an independent insurance agent in Atlanta, Georgia. "Now, no matter what program I'm running I hit CONTROL and ALT and *Instant Recall* pops up instantly."

Instant Recall is memory resident (although this option can be disabled), and it takes up only 32K of memory. It organizes tasks and notes, allows you to schedule appointments, and dials the phone. Its "quick timer" allows you to track time spent on any particular task. Each set of tasks, notes, and schedules can be attached to a certain company or client.

Sidekick Plus (Borland), the MS-DOS program that popularized TSR programs, dials the phone and has a place to store names, addresses, telexes, and fax numbers. You can dial a stored number, take notes on the conversation, and tie the notes to it. The program also includes a calendar, calculator, and outliner, although they aren't as well integrated as they are in a full-fledged activity tracker (see Figure 14–2).

Prodex (Prodex Development) for MS-DOS computers and *QuickDex* (Casady and Greene) for Macintoshes are other examples of superb telephone management pop-up programs.

COMPUTERIZE YOUR CONTACT LIST

Although the phone is often considered to be distinct and separate from the computer, the two together can be a powerful combination. With a modem you can get phone numbers and addresses electronically by tying into databases of the Yellow Pages (see Chapter 16). You can use the modem to dial the telephone, thus saving time and finger exercise. (Use a telephone headset, and you save yourself the trouble of picking up the phone and leave your fingers free to type.) With an activity tracker on-screen when you call, you can track conversations, pull up background statistics, and enter sales orders.

Small businesses often succeed or fail depending on their ability to

Figure 14-2.
   SideKick Plus is a memory-resident program with many of the features of dedicated activity trackers. When working with another program, you can invoke *SideKick*, check your calendar, make notes, or place a phone call—then make *SideKick* disappear.

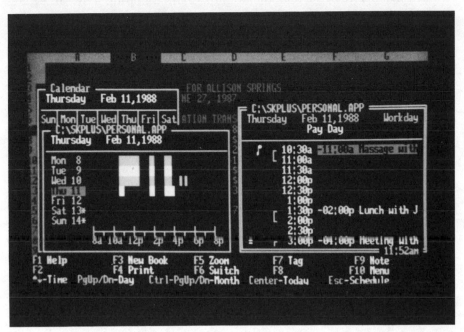

manage personal contacts. By combining your computer and your phone, and connecting people to data, an activity tracker can give you a competitive edge.

SPOTLIGHT ON: Activity Trackers

Cost: $100 to $500.
Learning Curve: Medium. No one aspect of the activity trackers is difficult to master; the secret is orchestrating all parts of the program with your everyday work flow so that you can find information when you need it.
Required Equipment: Computer with hard disk drive; modem; telephone line.
Recommended Software:

For IBM PC and IBM PS/2 and Compatibles

- *ACT!* (Conductor Software) is easy to use and customize, and fast; it's good at generating reports, but requires a lot of memory so is best used as a primary program; a favorite with salespeople.

- *Sidekick Plus* (Borland), the program that popularized pop-up TSR programs, offers less integration than full-fledged activity trackers, but is great for general background note collecting and phone call tracking.
- *Prodex* (Prodex Development Corp.), also a pop-up TSR, integrates its four directories—phone, to do, calendar, and log—and attaches a folder to each name so you can track each call (or other item) four different ways.
- *Telemagic* (Remote Control), the preferred program of professional telemarketers, does everything an activity tracker should do; it offers canned sales spiels and a form for taking orders; however, it may be overkill for general phone-tracking purposes.

For Macintosh

- *C.A.T.* (Chang Labs) organizes all activities into six types—letters, orders, meetings, phone calls, facts, and general—and can be customized to suit your work; particularly good at organizing mailings, printing mailing labels, and merging contact names with letters.
- *QuickDex* (Casady and Greene, Inc.) a pop-up desk accessory, uses the index card motif, but allows you to enter data in any form so that you can search for information without searching preset fields.

Buying Tips: Since most programs are designed for salespeople, professionals in other fields should check to see if preset categories can be customized; if you already use a database, check to see if the program will import or export data easily; make sure that it doesn't require so much memory as to be unwieldy; if you work heavily with another applications (such as a word processor or spreadsheet), choose a pop-up accessory that will always be accessible.

Chapter 15
Managing Time, Information, and People

Connect the clutter on your desk to the ideas in your head with personal information management software.

Where is the knowledge we have lost in information?
—T. S. Eliot, *The Rock*

Many business consultants like to point to the 80–20 rule, which says a person will use 20 percent of his or her files 80 percent of the time—and vice versa. The theory is that a professional works with the same basic group of contacts and information over and over again. While this appears to be an inarguable truth, it's also true that much of the 80 percent of wasted information might be used more frequently if it were more accessible. Just because it's at the bottom of the stack doesn't necessarily mean it's useless. Call it the "80/20—but" rule.

That, at least, seems to be the theory behind a relatively new class of software with a grandiose name—personal information managers. PIMs, as they're often called, are actually free-form databases. Unlike relational or flat-file databases (see Chapter 17), PIMs come with little or no field-based structure, and you don't have to add any—you just pump in information willy-nilly and extract it in different ways later. A name or note that once seemed inconsequential may present itself at the right time and set off a string of connections that lead you to new knowledge—or at least to new data.

Considered in another light, PIMs are organizers that manage text, time, clients, and ideas, much as activity trackers (see Chapter 14). The main difference between the two is that PIMs can handle more unstructured information; and since they are free-form, they can be customized to suit your work style.

At their best, PIMs are malleable tools that work the way you work—and don't force you to follow their rules. Some even have what might be called a primitive artificial intelligence and will understand who, what, and when you mean by saying, "send Bob a report next week." Many of the software titles describe the somewhat amorphous, kitchen-sink, blue-sky quality of the software: *Grandview*, *Agenda*, and *Current*.

At their worst, PIMs are confusing, memory-hungry tools that seem to be more trouble than they're worth. They are designed to work the way people want and expect computers to work—but often don't.

PIMs would be ideal for a manager who has a number of people, tasks, and dates to monitor (see also Chapter 4 for information on project management software), and for a think tank professional who is constantly gathering different types of information from different sources. But the average professional who wants to track names, addresses, and appointments would be better off with a simple activity tracker or even a pop-up accessory such as *Sidekick Plus* (Borland).

This chapter describes PIMs and how you might use them. PIMs fall into the categories of list makers/note takers, outliners, and schedulers—as do most people. (And two in particular, *Agenda* and *Current*, cut across all three categories.) Note takers use Post-Its and scrap pieces of paper stuffed into their wallets. An outliner usually has a few legal pads strewn around the desktop, each containing structured notes. And schedulers consult their appointment books and executive calendars as frequently as televangelists quote the Bible. There are no true PIMs for the Macintosh, although a program such as *Focal Point* comes close; all PIMs are MS-DOS programs.

POWERHOUSE PIMS: *AGENDA* AND *CURRENT*

Agenda (Lotus) is the product that started the whole PIM category. Lotus began developing it when then-president Mitch Kapor, inventor of the *1-2-3* spreadsheet, could find no software to handle the information that crossed his desk. Years later, after Kapor had left the company, *Agenda* emerged from the software duplicating plant.

With *Agenda*, you can build a database in as structured or unstructured a format as you want. Tools for accomplishing this goal include items, notes, categories, columns, views, and sections.

You start with items. An item can be any phrase, like "Call Sally at Acme Distribution on Friday," or "Finish marketing plans next week." An item is short (350 characters) but you can attach about seven pages of notes to each item.

From a loose collection of items and notes, you create categories and assign items to them. In other words, *Agenda's* operation is the direct opposite of a standard database, where you create a field *before* you enter information.

As your work progresses, items are automatically assigned to categories in several ways. For instance, if you had a category named after your main client, Alice Jones, every item that contained her name would be assigned to her category.

You can arrange categories hierarchically, as in an outline, so if you have a subcategory Mr. Big under the Clients category, assigning an item to Mr. Big also puts it into Clients. You can also set up categories that are mutually exclusive—such as high, medium, and low priorities on a project. Thus, you could view all sales calls you wanted to make in the coming week, or only high-priority calls.

Agenda's Sense of Time

Agenda understands a wide range of expressions, especially those relating to schedules and dates. If you type, "Finish the report four weeks from two days before the day before yesterday," *Agenda* will enter the correct date! A group of time-related predefined categories handle calendar functions: Entry Dates (the day you entered the note), When Dates (the day something is supposed to happen), and Done Dates (the day a task item is completed and removed from the database).

When you want to analyze the various notes and items you entered, you create a View, which is akin to a database report. You can, in effect, say to the computer, "Tell me whom I have to call today," or, "What are my top priority tasks for the week?"

IBM *Current*

IBM is primarily a hardware company, and few of its software products have gained wide acceptance. IBM *Current* may change that, although it's too early to tell. But it certainly will force change in the industry, since its fluid graphic interface gives users the sense that they're the captain in the cockpit when sitting at their computer.

Current operates somewhat like *Agenda*, in that you can view virtually all of the data you enter from any possible angle—but it comes with predesigned categories. Each item you enter can be related to a phone number, person, company, task, project, to do list, or other categories you create. And because *Current* runs under *Windows* (preferably with a mouse), you see graphic representations of different categories (see Figure 15-1). In fact, you can follow any train of thought by clicking the mouse to move from item to item or category to category.

Steve Miller, a computer consultant and journalist in New York City, bought a faster computer and a mouse just so he could use *Current*, an indication of the force the product exerts on the industry. "It's the first piece

Figure 15-1.

IBM *Current* can simultaneously display on-screen several ways of looking at your projects and to-do lists. Because *Current* produces Gantt charts, which project the duration of various tasks, it can be used to manage ongoing projects.

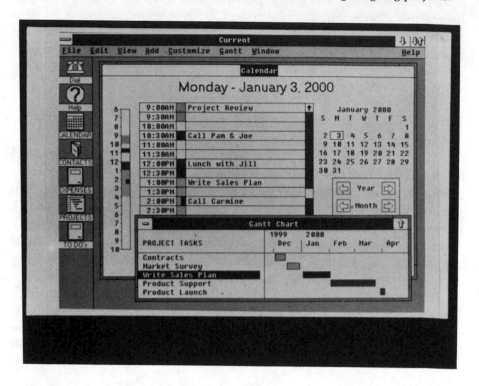

of software that convinced me I needed a faster machine," says Miller. "I always hated using a mouse, probably because most DOS software is not designed for it. But now all I do is click my way through the day."

Besides all his contact names, Miller sets up a new project category for every job he performs. When Miller clicks the mouse on one of his contact names, such as Jill Nelson, a window opens with her address, phone number, and other information. Also on the screen is the category "Working on Project," since Miller is working with her on a project he calls "Computer Funnies." He clicks on that entry and another window opens, indicating that Ms. Nelson wrote a funny piece in the *Washington Post Magazine* about how computers have replaced cars as the male macho symbol.

Following a Train of Thought

A shaded diamond icon next to the project category tells Miller there are more entries. He clicks the diamond and sees "The Dark Side." Clicking on it brings up the name of a psychologist he interviewed about negative effects of certain computer-related activities. Miller can switch from this project category to the psychologist's name and information, click on the phone icon, and (because he has a modem) *Current* will dial the psychologist's office. When the phone is connected, Miller presses the space bar and another window pops up where he can jot notes about the conversation. *Current* also automatically reads the clock/calendar in the computer and times the call. He can then paste his notes into his word processor, or print directly.

As with *Agenda*, one of *Current*'s most powerful features is its ability to view information in a variety of ways. *Current* calls it filtering. You can view everything, or just information that fits certain criteria. For example, you could view names of just the people in your database who work for IBM. You could filter that view by finding only the IBMers who are working on *Current*. You could then filter only the IBM *Current* people you've talked to since Labor Day. With any of these lists, you can create letters and generate a mass mailing.

Current's calendar tracks meetings, phone calls, conferences, and so on. Each appointment is represented by an icon that looks like your daily calendar. It tells you if you have a conflict but will let you enter the appointment anyway. When you create a project, *Current* automatically builds a Gantt chart (see Chapter 4) that tracks progress of the work.

The main problem with *Current* is that it requires a fast 386 computer to operate well. Miller has enough memory to keep *Current* open all day, so that he can switch in and out of it while he's working with other applications. However, it's possible to get many of the same results with less graphic software and a less powerful system, as is described below.

NOTE TAKING PIMS

Jack Nimersheim, an Indiana-based writer whose office is filled with notepads and napkins covered with scrawls, is a self-professed note taker who uses *IZE* (Persoft). When an editor calls to tell him that *Quick-Draw McGraw*, an imaginary graphics program needed to finish an article, will be shipped to his house the following week, he can jot a note in *IZE*. He tags several items—the names of the magazine, editor, and product, as well as the anticipated arrival date—as keywords. As he collects more information about *Quick-Draw McGraw* and other projects he enters more notes. When the software arrives, he performs a search on the keyword *Quick-Draw McGraw* and *IZE* returns a dossier on the software.

In this regard, *IZE* hasn't done anything the search-and-replace function in a decent word processor couldn't do: Nimersheim's notes are regurgitated back to him. However, he can analyze notes from a number of perspectives—even if they include dates. For instance, Nimersheim could perform a second search, asking *IZE* to show all notes relating to all magazines entered in the last two weeks. The more notes on different subjects entered, the more useful *IZE*'s ability to pick out the wheat from the chaff.

Other MS-DOS note-oriented PIMs include *Tornado* (Micro Logic Corp), *askSam* (askSAM Systems), and *MemoryMate* (Broderbund Software). All turn your computer into an electronic notepad—from which you extract data any way you want.

OUTLINING PIMS

Thom Moon, a Washington, D.C., media consultant whose two-person company, TGM Evaluations, analyzes listener trends in several major radio markets, takes an entirely different approach to organizing tasks. As a self-described outliner, Moon views the world through indented headings. As far back as he can remember, his first step in organizing any project has been to put together a rough outline. As that project progresses, he expands this initial outline to include more information. Sometimes, a one- or two-page outline for a particular project can expand to near book length before it's completed.

Moon uses *Grandview* (Symantec). Related to the earlier *ThinkTank*, a popular outline program from the same publisher, *Grandview* perfectly matches Moon's requirements. Now, whenever he starts a new project, Moon simply creates a new outline. *Grandview* lets him expand, contract, and reorganize the individual headings contained within any of its outlines. Moon edits a project file as needed—recording a meeting here, identifying a potential station contact there, and inserting important project dates.

Once an outline exists, Moon can reorganize and analyze it from a number of perspectives. For example, Moon tends to structure his original outlines around task headings—items relating to research under one major heading, reporting activities under a second, and so forth. At any time, however, he can tell *GrandView* to reorganize a given outline based on any dates its individual entries contain, a process that requires only a couple of keystrokes. Doing so allows Moon to quickly analyze the project's time line.

Although outline programs abound, *GrandView* is the only outliner with information management features. *MORE II* for the Macintosh, although primarily designed to prepare graphic presentations (such as electronic slide shows), also includes a project management feature.

SCHEDULE-ORIENTED PIMS

Tom Genslak, president of Custom Instruments Associates, a small company that designs and manufactures equipment used in genetic engineering and biomedical research, works from an office located in the garage behind his home in Bartlett, Illinois. One day, a part ordered from one of his vendors had not yet arrived, and the tool-and-die company to whom Genslak subcontracts manufacturing was on the phone wondering when to expect it. Genslak turned to his computer, looked up the part in question, verified that it had been ordered, checked its scheduled delivery date, called his vendor to confirm this information, analyzed what impact a two-day delay would have on subsequent tasks, adjusted the project's critical dates accordingly, and then passed this information on to his subcontractor. Genslak did all this from within a single package, *Who–What–When* (Chronos Software).

Genslak is a card-carrying scheduler—both he and his business tend to be driven by dates. When Genslak needs to record an important piece of information, he calls up *Who–What–When*'s Calendar Screen and uses it to record the person with whom that information is associated (who), the activity or project to which it pertains (what), and any critical dates it entails (when).

As was the case with both *GrandView* and *IZE*, *Who–What–When* demands very little in the way of planning while a record is actually being entered. For Genslak, adding information to his *Who–What–When* files is comparable to recording appointments on his desk calendar. But the program allows much more analysis than his desk calendar does.

When Genslak had to check on his missing part, for instance, a quick search brought up the record of its initial order. Then he quickly switched to a different record containing a profile of that part's vendor, which included the name of his assigned service representative. Genslak then hit a key and dialed the vendor's number by modem.

Schedulers are numerous, though most fall into the activity-tracker category. But many activity trackers are adding general information management features to their newer releases. *DayFlo Tracker* and *Primetime Personal* fall within this category. With *Primetime Personal*, for example, even though you enter records within an appointment calendar, these records can subsequently be organized by task, goal, and project.

INFORMATION AND TIME: SCYLLA AND CHARYBDIS

Information and time: Scylla and Charybdis to the small business. Too much of one, too little of the other; if one rock doesn't get you, the other will. Unless you navigate through them with a PIM.

People often complain that software doesn't work the way they do, or the way they think. This is especially true with record-keeping systems (databases), where the computer generally demands a rigid structure into which you file facts and notes as if you were a postal worker putting letters into mailboxes. But people don't think in terms of cubbyholes—they dig tunnels from one box to another to connect ideas, dates, people.

When a PIM doesn't function the way you want it to, chances are you can blame the software. Because PIMs promise so much they are often overly complex to use. But it's worth working to overcome these hurdles. When a PIM *is* functioning the way you want it to, you may feel as if the computer is earning its keep for the first time.

SPOTLIGHT ON: Personal Information Managers

Cost: $70 to $400.
Learning Curve: Medium to steep; since these programs are free-form, they require you to structure them to your liking, and it may take time to figure out exactly *how* you work best; beyond that, their command system can be difficult to master.
Required Equipment: Fast computer with hard disk drive.
Recommended Software:

For IBM PC and IBM PS/2 and Compatibles

- *askSam* (askSam Systems) is an accessible, free-form database that lets you enter information as it comes to mind instead of in a set pattern; an easy-to-use search function and ability to cross reference make the program a winner.
- *IZE* (Persoft, Inc.) lets you enter unstructured notes on a variety of topics, and it then superimposes a structure depending on how you want to view the data.
- *Tornado* (Micro Logic Corp.), a memory-resident free-form database, lets you manage notes, to do lists, calendars, memos, and messages; you can set up forms and search through and print groups of related notes with lightning-like speed: you can cut-and-paste data from or to the underlying program.
- *GrandView* (Symantec Corp) is primarily an outliner with expanded information management capabilities; for instance, you can take the dates in any outline and rearrange it to set up a time line for a project.
- *Who–What–When* (Chronos Software, Inc.) is designed to deal with time-related details; you enter information in an on-screen appointment book, starting with *when*; since you can cross-reference and link calendar entries, you can print complete reports by name, activity, and date.
- Lotus *Agenda* (Lotus Development Corp), a general-purpose PIM, will organize information from many sources and improve your

ability to make sense of it; it has keyboard functions very similar to those of Lotus *1-2-3*; it's very big, however, and requires a fast computer for efficient operation.

- *Current* (IBM), which runs under *Windows*, is a graphic information manager that operates best with a mouse and a fast computer; it is very slick and comprehensive, and it can be designed to work just about any way you do.

Buying Tips: Decide if you need an accessory that's always available, in which case you want a memory-resident program; many PIMs are weak at printing high-quality reports, so investigate that feature well if it's important to you; even though a given PIM might theoretically run on any computer, in practice it may require one with more speed, due to its size.

Chapter 16
Make Your Mailing List Your Profit Center

How to create lists, print labels, and customize standard letters to reach your target customer.

> *My mailing list is my inventory. It costs me nothing, yet it constantly appreciates.*
>
> —Bill Vick, independent executive recruiter

Every business, no matter how small, has a mailing list. The advantages of computerizing a mailing list are many. Even if you have only twenty-five names on a list, the ability to hit a few keys and print twenty-five mailing labels or envelopes certainly will save you time and money. If you also wish to send customized letters to those twenty-five people, the ability to write one basic letter and merge names and other data from a database will save you even more time. Finally, if you wish to send a selective mailing, perhaps only to clients who haven't contacted you in six months, you can search a list by certain criteria.

"I've got a prospect list of 25,000 names, but a house list with 5,000 customers who have bought in the last year. Every month, I send out a newsletter to the house list only," says Dan Poynter, who sells his self-published books on parachutes and publishing from his home in Santa Barbara, California. "Computers make it possible to deal with highly targeted lists."

This chapter describes several ways to set up computerized mailing lists, where to find mailing lists on-line, and how to write customized letters to send to select groups.

MAILING LISTS IN ACTION

For most service professionals, direct mail is a better method of self-promotion than advertising. For example, Phil Neal sends out twenty-five brochures every two days. His company, MicroServices, sells two software packages that he created—one for police departments and one for real estate companies.

By spreading out the mailings, Neal can keep things on an even keel. "In the beginning I made the mistake of sending out mailings of a thousand at a time. I'd get a lot of response for about a week and then the activity would completely die out. It also made it difficult to get the product out." And because Phil's customers generally call with questions before they buy, he was convinced that—with a single mass mailing—some potential customers were being lost simply because they couldn't get through the crush of calls.

"I have fine-tuned this now so that I know what percentage will respond, how many will call, and how many will purchase." The software sales pay to keep the business going, but what Neal is looking for is the one buyer in twenty who will ask him to customize the generic software. These are the clients who make the mailings and phone calls worthwhile. "Mailings are more work than just placing ads, but the work is worth it in the long run."

Neal now has a list of fifteen thousand names. When someone buys, the customer's name is transferred to a separate database—his "house" list. Here, a great deal of information is tracked: a running statement of calls, including the date and what was said; order dates, problems, comments, and contact names; whether callers have had programs customized or consulting services and what was done; payment and billings records; and what kind of hardware and software callers use.

The house list is also indexed by state so that it can be easily sorted to see where sales are strong. Once Neal has sent promotional material to the whole list, he will mail a second piece to the most active areas.

"The key is to experiment and keep records of what you are doing to make sure it's working. I find that if you just send out a thousand pieces, you don't know what's going to happen."

MAILING LIST MECHANICS

To set up a mailing list—so you can send the same piece to ten, one hundred, or one thousand names—you need some sort of database program. You can use either a flat-file or relational database (see Chapter 17), or you can use a dedicated mailing list program. Since many database programs need to be programmed to do the job you want, it's easier to use a dedicated mailing list program—unless, of course, you already have names stored on a standard database.

If you want to send slightly different versions of the same piece to a list of names, you need a database program and a word processor that work together to accomplish mail-merge—or one program that combines the process—a process described in detail later.

Mailing List Software

Mailing list software, or address book software, was developed because creating and printing mailing labels from a standard database can be confusing and time-consuming. Mailing list software saves you the trouble of choosing and naming fields and presents you with a simple structured database. All you do is fill in the blanks—name, address, phone, and other identifying information. Although you can't change the fields, there's generally a Miscellaneous field, or a memo pad so that you can jot your own notes about a certain contact. Then, when you're ready to print labels or envelopes, you can choose names by sorting, just as you would with a standard database.

Rolodex Live! (DacEasy, Inc.), *Address Book Plus* (Power Up Software Corp.), *Power Desk* (Software Studios), *MyAdvancedMailList* (MYSoftware Company), and *MacEnvelope Plus* (Synex Corp.) are examples of such programs (see Figure 16-1). Alternatively, you can use more sophisticated activity trackers such as *Expeed* or *Focal Point* (see Chapter 14), all of which print labels. These programs also dial and track phone calls and include calendars.

Figure 16-1.

You can use a database to produce mailing lists, but often it's easier to use a dedicated mailing list program, which requires less setup on your part. Just fill in the blanks, indicate how you want labels to print, and you're pumping out a mailing. Screen from *My Address Book*.

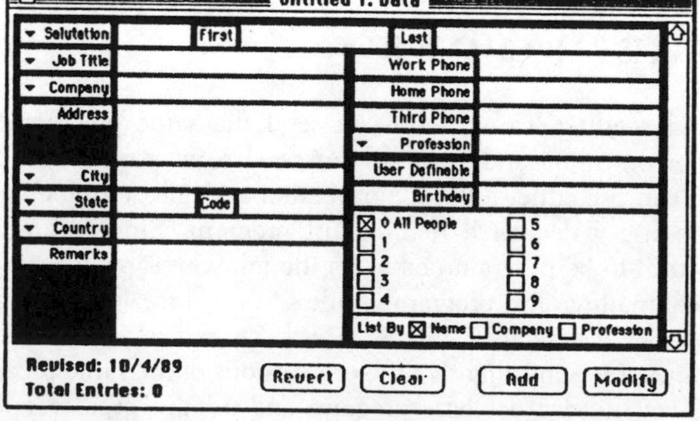

Creating a List

Before setting up your mailing list, decide what information to track. All lists should include first name, last name, salutation, address, city and state, and zip code fields, which will print out on labels. Information that will not appear on the mailing labels but which might be useful for analysis (depending on your type of business) includes: initial entry date, date of sale, amount of sale, accumulated purchases, type of purchase (if you carry more than one type of product), telephone number, and source of original inquiry.

Once your fields are set up, you can sort by one field (say, all customers who spent more than $500 in one year), and then print envelopes or labels with those addresses for a targeted mailing.

Most businesses print on standard peel-and-stick (or pressure-sensitive) mailing labels. They are inexpensive and easy to keep in zip code order when applying to mail pieces, and work with the least expensive labeling machines. These labels measure 1 inch by 3.5 inches. Printing in standard 10-pitch mode, you can fit thirty characters across with small margins. It's important to keep this in mind when specifying field lengths in your database.

Keep Three Separate Mailing List Files

Divide your mailing list into three files (each one can have different fields). The first file should be your customer (or client) list, or house list. Include as much information as possible about your customers. In addition to names and addresses, you might also include what each bought, when, why, how many times, and any pertinent demographic information.

The second file is a list of prospects; that is, any potential customers who haven't bought yet. Code each entry to indicate the source of the name.

The third file is a special list; it includes old customers who haven't recently bought anything, credit risks, and any other problem names. Code each name for easy breakout. For instance, you may want to try a special mailing to old customers that includes a special coupon for "coming back."

An alternative to the three-file approach is to keep all names in one file, but code them as "customers" or "prospects" so you can sort them whenever you wish.

Clean the Lists

The purpose of the merge/purge process is to omit duplications and thereby save money. For instance, you may have the same name on your prospect list and on your house list. A clean list is also absolutely necessary if you are going to rent out your list. Use your computer (search your file for the first thirteen or fourteen characters in a name to spot a match) to merge/purge by comparing all secondary lists to your house list.

ON-LINE MAILING LISTS

While most businesses send traditional postal mail to reach clients, customers, or prospects, there are times when it may be easier to reach people by sending electronic mail. The advantage is that you don't have to print letters and labels, or stuff envelopes. You merely write a letter, upload it to MCI Mail, CompuServe, or whatever electronic mail service you use, and enter the recipient's electronic address.

Just as you keep a mailing list file on your computer, you can keep an address file on the electronic mail system. Thus, you don't have to enter the full address every time you want to send mail to a particular person or group of people. You can send a message to another electronic mailbox, a fax machine, or a postal address. The letter will be laser printed and quickly delivered, sometimes on a facsimile of your own letterhead.

The effectiveness of electronic direct mail will vary depending on your message and your audience. It certainly isn't as formal or professional as a message on your own letterhead. But if you work regularly with the same clients or partners, the electronic method is generally quicker and easier than the paper method.

PC Yellow Pages

You can also use your modem effectively to help compile a mailing list by searching an on-line version of all Yellow Pages directories in the United States. "I've found that direct mail is much more effective for me than advertising," says Alfred Glossbrenner, noted communications author and publisher of Glossbrenner's Choice, a catalog that recommends the best shareware software on the market. "The problem is getting mailing lists. Most big houses won't deal with an individual like me, since I don't want thousands of names at a time." So Glossbrenner turned to PC Yellow Pages, a pay-as-you-use service where he's found targeted lists for different parts of the country at the cost of five to fifteen cents a name.

You access PC Yellow Pages by dailing a 900 number (1-900-860-9210) and then searching the database by zip code ranges and type of business—say, all the lawyers in Phoenix, Arizona. You will get the addresses in mailing label format (including carrier route codes for faster processing by the Post Office). The database is updated monthly.

Other services are Dun's Electronic Yellow Page (EYP) and the Online Information Network (OIN), from American Business Information. EYP is available to Dialog and CompuServe subscribers; OIN, through the American Business Information and Bell South gateways. Both services offer more addresses and information than PC Yellow Pages, but they require annual subscriptions.

USE MAIL-MERGE FUNCTION TO PERSONALIZE MASS MAILINGS

To create a personalized message for a wide audience, you can use the mail-merge function found in most word processors, some databases, and many integrated packages. Mail-merge combines a letter written in your word processor with names, addresses, and other details from a database. The mail-merge function allows you to mark places in a word processor file for insertion of material from database fields. The word processor plucks data from the database, places it into the appropriate gaps, and prints the documents as many times as necessary. Once your mail-merge system is set up, you can print out the same or slightly different letters to several people with only a few keystrokes (see Figure 16-2).

Anything that can be tracked in a database can be merged into a document. After the address and greeting, you might include account numbers, purchase information, or balance figures. Beyond that, if/then fields can be created. For instance, should a customer's balance due fall below a certain level, the phrase "thank you for your prompt payment" will follow. For those with a balance above that level, a slightly more pointed message can be inserted automatically.

In a letter to existing customers, a mail-order business might include a phrase about an earlier purchase, tying it to one of several new items. A letter to one customer might read: "If you enjoyed your recent order of our famous Belgian Chocolate-Dipped Pecans, then you'll probably find our new Honey-and-Hazelnut Butter Crunch equally palate-pleasing." A second letter might substitute "Pineapple-Glazed Almonds" and "Mandarian Orange Butter" in place of the first two products.

Mail-Merge Software Combinations

Most full-featured and even many mid-range word processors include a mail-merge function. With some programs, you set up the data file (a roster of names and addresses) with the word processor. If, however, you also want to track customer information not meant for mail-merge letters, or extract

Figure 16-2.

While the particulars of any mail-merge system may differ, the basic steps remain the same: The contents of a data file are placed into the indicated slots of a letter to create a series of personalized letters. In the representative mail-merge steps pictured here, the data file (A) was exported from a database with a return character (a field delimiter) at the end of each field—last name, address, zip, and so on.

The letter (B) reserves spaces for each data field's contents within curly braces, like this: {last name}. In the mail-merge process, the word processor takes the actual last name and fills in the blank. One of the final letters (C) is shown here. Since each customer's record in the data file was set up with both the last order and a suggested new item, each letter has been tailored for the recipient beyond the typical name and address.

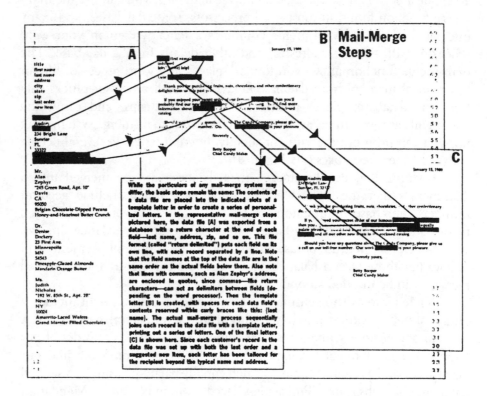

and mathematically manipulate parts of your data file for reports, you'll need a full-fledged database in addition to your word processor.

Any database can be used for mail-merge as long as the program can create files with delimiters—characters such as commas, returns, or tabs, which indicate the end of a data field (see Figure 16-1).

Most integrated software packages, such as Microsoft *Works* (Microsoft), which incorporate both a database and a word processor, provide mail-merge capability. Integrated data managers like *Q&A* (Symantec) and *RapidFile* (Ashton-Tate), which combine sophisticated databases with good, mid-level word processors, were specifically designed to unite lists with text and work well for mail-merge.

To choose your mail-merge software, begin by looking at the programs you currently use. In one possible scenario, your word processor already does mail-merge, but your customer list is growing so large that you want to add a database in order to more easily handle the list. Another possibility is that you already work with a database, but don't have a word processor with mail-merge capability, so you need one to merge and print the text. Make sure that the database's files are compatible with your word processor; that's not difficult with popular packages like *WordPerfect* and *dBase III Plus* (word processors, when boasting mail-merge scope, usually flaunt *dBase* compatibility).

Another smart mail-merge choice, particularly for salespeople, is a tracking program such as *Sales Ally* (Scherrer Resources) or *C.A.T.* (Chang Labs). (See Chapter 14.)

MILK THAT LIST

Every business has a list, but not every business uses it to full advantage. Once you compile your names and put them into computer form, don't stop here. Keep adding to the list and finding new ways to use the power of the computer to generate mailings. Once you're set up, it will cost you little in time or money to continually promote your business.

Greg Morton, owner of the Bridge Street Cafe in Dartmouth, Massachusetts, gets names and addresses from the restaurant's suggestion box, and also whenever a reservation is made. Morton then sends every name on his list a copy of his newsletter, *Cafe Communique*, that highlights new menus or performers.

Bill Vick, an executive recruiter who regularly sends his newsletter to 1,500 people, periodically tries to get a little extra from his list. Last year he took the names of fifty companies that had never called on him and were exhibiting at the MacWorld trade show in Boston. He sent envelopes marked "Confidential," so that secretaries wouldn't open them. Inside was a box of Vicks' cough drops and a four-by-nine inch card that said, "We can help cure sick sales." The mailing got a three percent response; Vick says the $200 he spent earned him $30,000 in commissions. "Anything is possible if you have the discipline and the technology," says Vick.

MAILING LIST RESOURCES

The PC Mailing List Book, by Patrick Bultema, Mike Murach & Associates, 277 pp., 1990, $24.95. This book describes how to use word processing, database, integrated, mailing list, and spreadsheet programs to prepare mailing lists, with specific references to popular programs, such as *WordPerfect, Microsoft Word, Professional Write, Q&A, dBase III Plus, Microsoft Works, Address Book Plus*, and Lotus *1-2-3*.

Getting a Good Start in a Mailing Services Business, by Steven L. Fletcher; Ad Mail Management, P.O. Box 1389, Yuba City, CA 95992-1389, 50 pp., 1989; $5 plus $1 shipping/handling. Clear, step-by-step procedures for starting and operating a mailing list service, plus a great resource section. Though the pamphlet is aimed at people who want to run a mailing list business, the information on computers should be of use to anyone who wants to computerize a mailing list.

LaserJet Unlimited, Edition II, by Ted Nace and Michael Gardner; Peachpit Press, 544 pp., 1989; $24.95. This book describes how to use Hewlett-Packard's LaserJet Series II printers with word processors, spreadsheets, databases, and desktop publishing programs. It also covers font editing programs, form design systems, and utilities for printing labels and envelopes.

SPOTLIGHT ON: Mailing List Software

Cost: $50 and up.
Learning Curve: Low to medium. Programs totally dedicated to mailing list management are easy to use, since all fields are set up and you merely enter the data. Of course, they're not as flexible as, say, a flat-file database, which requires more initial effort from the user. Beyond that, getting labels or envelopes properly lined up in your printer (be prepared for experimentation) is the most difficult task.
Required Equipment: Computer with hard disk drive; printer.
Recommended Software:

For IBM PC and IBM PS/2 and Compatibles

- *MyAdvancedMailList* (MYSoftware). See listing under Macintosh.
- *Microsoft Works* (Microsoft Corp.) is an integrated package (with database, word processor, spreadsheet, and communications) that is well suited for tracking mailing lists, generating mail-merge letters, and printing mailing labels.
- *Power Desk* (Software Studios) is a mailing-list program (with sixteen fields) with its own word processor, so that you can create mail-merged letters; it also dials phone calls through a modem.
- *LabelPro* (Avery), designed for use with Avery labels (available in office supply stores), is easy to use; it merges database records from a

variety of programs (*dBase*, *1-2-3*, *WordPerfect*), and includes its own database manager; you can put graphics on a label.

- *Reflex* (Borland), a fast flat-file database that runs under a graphical interface, excels at mail-merge and mailing list generation.
- *Rolodex Live!* (DacEasy Inc.) is an address book program where each contact entry resembles an on-screen Rolodex card; it provides room for information beside names and addresses; it prints on two sizes of labels and 7-by-9-inch continuous-form envelopes; and it can be used with a mail-merge word processor.
- *Hold Everything!* (DacEasy Inc.) is a preconfigured database program with twenty-nine fields to describe people and companies; searching and sorting is fast and fluid; it prints mailing lists in single-column format, but it doesn't allow for three or four across.
- *DeskMate Q&A Write* (Symantec), an executive-style word processor, runs under the graphic *DeskMate* operating environment; it is good for letter writing, with a built-in card to store names and addresses; it prints mailing labels and envelopes; the standard *Q&A* is also a good mail-merge choice.

For Macintosh

- *MacEnvelope* (Synex) prints all sizes of labels and shapes of envelopes; it allows you to place graphics next to return addresses and special messages in the lower left corner; and address data can be entered directly or imported from other databases.
- *Microsoft Works* (Microsoft). See MS-DOS note above.
- *FileMaker II* (Claris Corp.), a full-fledged database that can handle far more than just mailing lists, comes with a template for customer lists and sets up easily to print mailing labels three across.
- *MyAdvancedMailList* (MYSoftware) is a dedicated mailing-list program; it prints on ten types of labels, as well as Rolodex and index cards.
- *Address Book Plus* (Power Up Software) is a simple and speedy mailing list program that also prints out file cards and address books.

Buying Tips: Figure out how many data fields you want to include before buying a program, as some restrict you more than others; check to see that the software supports your printer, since a failure to communicate properly will throw labels out of whack.

Chapter 17
Get Organized!— With a Good Record Keeping System

How to choose and use a database to keep information at your fingertips.

If the house is on fire, forget the china, silver, and wedding album—grab the Rolodex.

—Harvey Mackay, *How to Swim With the Sharks*

Andy Sacks, a photographer in Chelsea, Michigan, converted his paper records to computer files several years ago when the amount of paper generated by his business began to overwhelm him. He was producing and tracking invoices, and tracking expenses paid out to suppliers, assistants, and labs. He also stored his photographic negatives and transparencies in a library so he could retrieve and resell them when needed. As his business grew he became more and more dependent on a bookkeeper, and he spent more and more time searching for photos to resell. So Sacks decided to take the reins of his business by computerizing his records.

For many people, the thought of arranging thousands of pieces of information into a coherent structure is the main reason to buy a computer. All businesses have lists: mailing lists, customer records, and inventories of possessions for an insurance policy, to name a few. By converting these into electronic form, you can search, sort, and update them easily—and incorporate them into invoices, letters, and other documents. To do so, you use a database program.

Database software is the short side of the big-three software triangle, filling in the territory that word processors and spreadsheets miss. More people use word processors and spreadsheets because they are more comfortable dealing with words and numbers than with setting up an organizational structure to store data. But databases can be more flexible because they can handle both text and numbers. Thus you can track expenses, listing both places visited and costs, or accounts receivable, filing both customers and charges. Then you can sort by trip or by customer and calculate expenses or bills.

"I store all my customers in a database, and fill in the COST field with 'C' for cash, 'N' for not paid, or a check number," says David Wilson, a tomato farmer in Massachusetts. "To get my receivables, I kick out all entries with field equal to 'N.' "

Standard database software comes in two basic flavors: file managers, often called flat files, and relational database managers, which are more difficult to use but more powerful than flat files (see Figure 17-1). There are, of course, more specialized database programs, dedicated to a specific task. These include phone or activity trackers (see Chapter 14), mailing list or Rolodex-type managers (see Chapter 16), and personal information managers or free-form databases (see Chapter 15).

This chapter describes flat-file and relational databases, memory-resident (or "pop-up") databases, and how to produce the reports (or printouts) that you want.

HOW DATABASES WORK

Electronic databases record and organize information of any kind. For instance, you might want to keep track of people (clients, business contacts, or consultants), items (inventory, equipment, or real estate), or financial transactions (expenses, income, purchase orders, or taxes).

Any object may be described by a unique set of qualities—inventories have parts numbers, for example, and clients have names. To track objects, you set up fields to describe these qualities. Each set of fields constitutes a record. Name, address, and phone number, for example, might be those fields in one record. All the records in a given file, such as Business Contacts, contain the same fields. The potential number of fields in a record, and records in a file, varies from program to program, and it depends on the amount of memory in your computer.

Once you set up the fields and enter the data, you can sort or select data from the whole file and print out reports. You search for data by certain criteria, such as all customers whose payments are more than a month late (see Figure 17-2).

After a job is finished, for example, photographer Sacks enters the name of the client, and whether or not he or she should be added to a mailing list. If the answer is yes, the program asks for the category (journalism, advertising, etc.). Then it asks for library file information, such as subject, sub-subject, location, and date shot.

Sacks retrieves this information in many ways. If a magazine requests a

Figure 17-1.

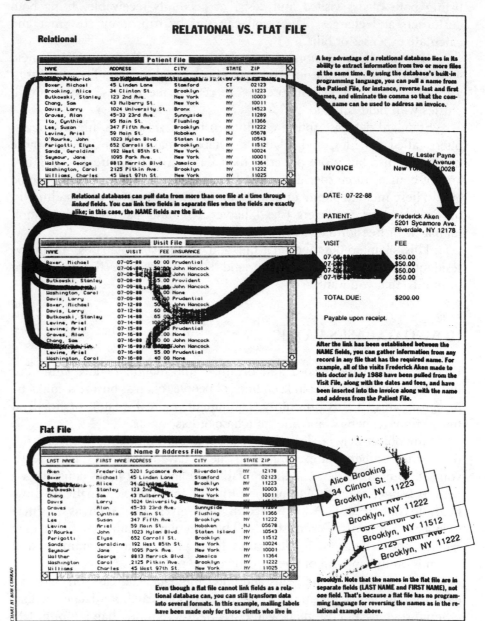

photo of an Illinois beef farmer, he looks in his agricultural file and starts his search by looking for all Illinois photos. If a supply house chief says he's got 300 rolls of such and such film at a rock-bottom price, Sacks sums up the number of rolls of black-and-white or color film charged to clients in the last six months, which lets him judge how many rolls of a given type he's likely to use in the next six months.

Figure 17-2.

Database software gives you the power to select specific information from a larger set of data. With the three selections made, this mailing list database (created with Microsoft *Works*) will select only those people whose last name is "Smith" (#1), who do not live in New York City (#2), and who were born on or after January 1, 1946 (#3).

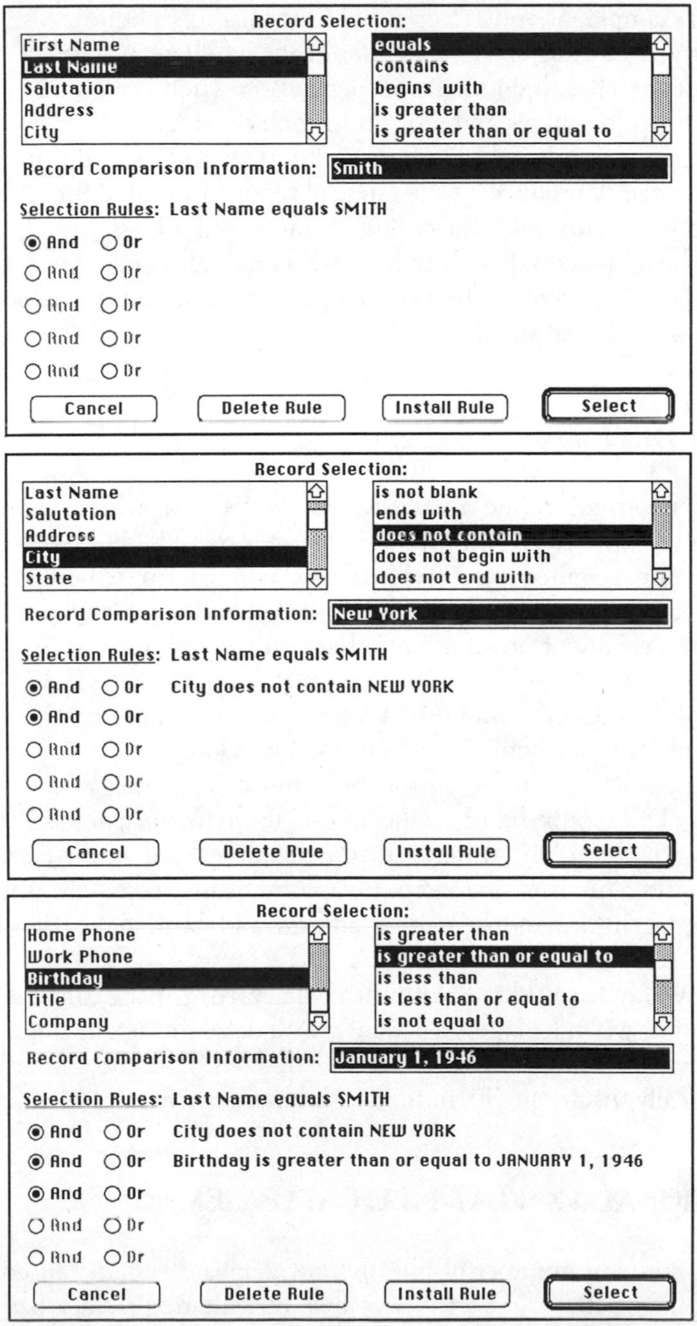

Choosing Fields to Create Reports

One of the trickiest aspects of setting up a database is choosing fields that will produce the kind of printed reports you want. To do so, you have to identify your needs beforehand, because you normally can't go back and change the structure once it's set without entering the data again.

For example, if you set up a field for business phone calls, but later find that you want to break down those calls by client or project, you may or may not be able to do so. It will depend on whether you have included separate fields for clients and projects in each record.

While you can't radically change the structure of a file once it's set, you can certainly produce a wide range of reports from that file. A customer purchase file—with fields for customer name and address, product, price, and date bought—could produce reports on total sales in the last six months, the number of customers who have bought more than once, the best-selling products overall, and so on.

Speeding Data Entry

Entering information into a database can be tedious, which is one reason why many people resist converting their paper records. But once you start, you can use advanced features such as macros (in which a series of instructions are assigned to a single keystroke) and calculated fields (whose values are dependent on values of other fields in the record) to speed data entry.

Dr. Edwin Gordy, who runs a family medical practice in Newtonville, Massachusetts, uses both these features. Dr. Gordy's database consists of two files: an active file for unpaid bills and a paid file. When payments come in, Dr. Gordy transfers the information to the paid file with one keystroke combination, using a macro he developed. And each time a patient visits, he uses a macro to automatically copy all unchanging demographic information, such as address and birth date, into the new record.

Dr. Gordy has further streamlined data entry by using calculated fields. For example, when he enters a patient's birth date, the age field is computed automatically. Typing "Miss," "Mrs.," or "Ms." in the salutation field automatically inserts an "F" in the sex field; otherwise, an "M" appears.

RELATIONAL VS. FLAT-FILE DATABASES

You can store any number of files in your database system, all containing different information. In a medical office, one file might track patients and another, doctor visits. The ability to extract information from two or more files at once is what separates relational (which can) from flat-file (which usually cannot) databases.

Relational database managers link information in one file to *related* items in other files. Relating data from various files demands extra work by the user, usually in the form of instructions written in the database's built-in programming language.

Flat-file programs, on the other hand, are invariably simpler to use than relational database managers. Flat files are akin to index cards, with one entry per card and only one set of cards per file. (The exception to this general rule is flat-file databases that offer limited linking capabilities, as described below.)

Limits of a Flat File

Flat-file records and files can get unwieldy if you try to pack in too much information. For example, a patient has a name, address, phone number, birth date, sex, date when he or she first becomes a patient, medical insurance carrier, and so on. When a patient visits, your first instinct might be to to add another set of fields that lists the date, time, length, and purpose of the visit. But what happens when the same patient makes a second visit? Do you create a new record for each visit, duplicating information such as name, address, and phone number?

You could, but it would waste time, it might cause errors as you key in the same data again (unless you automate the task as Dr. Gordy did by setting up a macro), and it would eat up hard disk space.

Another solution is to expand the structure, with a new set of fields for a second or third visit in each record. This method would work if you knew in advance how many visits a patient would make. But the number of visits varies in no predictable pattern. Also, since each additional visit could mean adding at least four new fields to your file—such as visit date, time, fee, and purpose—you might bump up against the database's limits for number of fields in a file. Even if you didn't hit those limits, too many fields containing similar data could make the structure of a database unwieldy. For example, your eye might not easily distinguish among fields called Date 1, Date 2, and Date 3.

One way to solve the problem caused by multiple patient visits is to create two data files—one that lists the qualities for each patient and another with separate records for each visit—and link them.

MAKING CONNECTIONS BETWEEN TWO FILES

To integrate these two files, both must share one parameter in common—in this case, the patient's name. The common field is called the link.

By linking two files with the same field, you can enter one record for each patient appointment in the visit file without having to repeat the information stored in the patient file. Then, as needed, you can pull data from both files for either printed reports or an on-screen view.

Relational databases use linked fields in different files to perform what's called "lookup" operations. For example, to produce a monthly invoice for each patient that includes information about each visit, a relational database would take the patient's name and address from the patient file and then use that patient's name to search the visit file for all records that contained his or her name. The combined information would create a complete description of the patient's records.

Four popular relational databases are *dBase* (Ashton-Tate Corporation), *4th Dimension* (Acius), *R:BASE* (Microrim), and *Paradox* (Borland International). All take similar approaches to creating a database, but very different approaches to relating the data files.

Most businesses that need the power of a relational database would do well to hire a consultant for two or three days to structure it; otherwise, they might spend months getting it right.

THE LOOKUP FUNCTION

An alternative to using a relational database is to use a flat-file database with a Lookup function, which gives a flat-file database many of the same linking capabilities as a relational database. *Q&A* (Symantec) and *RapidFile* (Ashton-Tate), for instance, fall into this category. (See Figure 17-3.) While they aren't quite as flexible for creating reports, flat-file databases don't require the complex programming that relational databases do.

You could use the Lookup function to develop a simple mail-order entry and invoicing system that locates and fills in prices on an ordering screen and invoice. One file contains the customer's order, and the other the list of products and prices—the link is the name of the product. You could then use the product name to adjust a separate inventory database, and so on.

Spreadsheets as Databases

Many spreadsheets also have a Lookup function and can be used as databases. For instance, Lotus *1-2-3*, *Quattro*, and *Excel* can all scan lookup tables for information. People who spend most of each day using a spreadsheet for analyzing income and expenses, budgeting money and supplies, or keeping track of inventory might rather use the spreadsheet's Lookup ability rather than creating totally new database files.

Figure 17-3.

The records shown come from two *Q & A* database files—Donors and Gifts. Because they share a common field ("Donor ID Number"), the contents of the other fields can be copied from one file to the next using the program's Lookup function. Here, first and last names are pulled from the Donors file into the Gifts file.

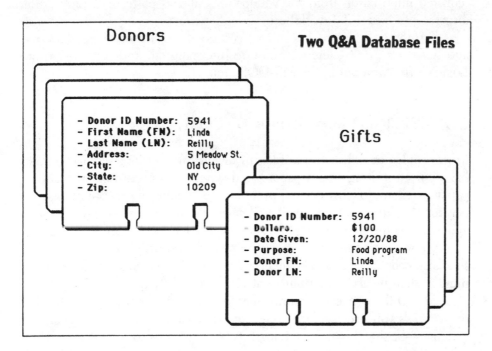

Accountants and bookkeepers find lookup functions helpful when setting up IRS tax tables. Sales managers might use spreadsheet worksheets to track sales and commissions.

Many advanced spreadsheets, such as Lotus *1-2-3* and Microsoft *Excel*, also include flat-file databases. The spreadsheets' Lookup functions can be used with the database.

POP-UP DATABASES

Switching back and forth between, say, a word processor and a database is inconvenient and time-consuming. Unless you have a multitasking setup on your computer (see Chapter 20), you have to save your document, quit your application, start the database program, load the appropriate data file, retrieve the record containing the information required, either print out or make a note of that information, close the database, reload your word processor, and (finally!) get back to work.

A solution is to use a memory-resident pop-up database manager, such as *Reference File*. Say you're creating a budget forecast with Lotus *1-2-3* and suddenly realize you need to look up the costs for several projects whose records are stored in a database. Simply press ALT-F (the default "hot key" that calls up the program), and your spreadsheet temporarily moves to the background as the database window pops up. You can then retrieve the required information from the window or cut and paste that information directly into your *1-2-3* worksheet.

DAtabase (Preferred Publishers) is a good Macintosh desk accessory, and *Reference File* (Reference Software International) and *Tornado* (Micro Logic Corp) stand out in the MS-DOS arena.

CONVERTING FROM PAPER TO COMPUTER

Most people must clear two hurdles to successfully set up a database. First, having lived so long with a paper-based system and accumulated reams of paper, you have to convince yourself that the benefits of computerizing will pay for the time and energy it will take. While this is true with many applications, the problem is more acute with databases.

Second, you can automate only a process you fully understand. Since so many people have helter-skelter record keeping systems, or keep many files "in their heads," describing that structure is difficult.

To start the conversion from paper to electronic records, study the type of materials you use regularly to decide what kinds of reports you want to generate—be they invoices, pricing lists, sales records, or client lists. Then work backward, on paper, to figure out what fields you need to sort through data and create these reports.

Next, choose between a relational and flat-file database. Most small businesses, especially service businesses, do well with a flat file that has a lookup function. Larger businesses, or those that sell product and stock inventory, probably need the power of a relational database.

However you go, create a few test files and use them long enough to make sure that they suit your needs. Then enter your data. It's a tough mountain to climb, but the view from the top is commanding.

DATABASE AND RECORD KEEPING RESOURCES

Douglas Cobb's Paradox 3 Handbook, 2nd Edition, by Douglas Cobb, with Jeff Yocom and Brian Smith, Bantam Electronic Publishing, 880 pp., 1989; $27.95. This book provides an explanation of *Paradox 3.0*, *Paradox 386*, and *OS/2 Paradox*. It discusses the basics of database design and focuses on ways to use PAL (Borland's programming language) to produce results fast. Detailed coverage of generating forms and reports is included.

Mary Campbell's dBase IV Handbook, by Mary Campbell, Bantam Electronic Publishing, 960 pp., 1989; $26.95. A detailed look at all the features of *dBase IV* for intermediate-level users. Full of tips, hints, and techniques, plus ideas on database organization.

dBase IV Power Tools, by Malcolm C. Rubel, Bantam Electronic Publishing, 992 pp. with two 5.25-inch disks, 1989; $49.95. This book/disk package provides well over 150 preprogrammed functions and procedures to extend the power of *dBase IV*. These utilities add pop-up menus, custom help functions, and financial analysis tools.

The First Book of Q & A, by Jack Nimersheim, Howard W. Sams, 275 pp., 1990; $14.95. The author provides the novice computer user with a "once over lightly" treatment of the fundamentals of installing and using this highly regarded software. Quick Steps sections and end-of-the-chapter questions will help get you going.

SPOTLIGHT ON: Database Software

Cost: $100 to $500.
Learning Curve: Medium to steep. Setting up a paper filing system that works well is tough; setting up a computerized filing system is a little tougher—although flat-file databases are easier than relational databases.
Required Equipment: Computer with hard disk drive.
Recommended Software:

For IBM PC and IBM PS/2 and Compatibles

- *Reflex* (Borland), a flat-file database, is very fast, runs under a graphical interface, and is packed with features, including calculated fields; it can view files in six ways; it approaches the power of a relational database; it is great for mail-merge and generating mailing lists.
- *Q&A* (Symantec) is one of the friendliest programs in any field; it integrates a full-featured flat-file database with a solid word processor; it links files with Lookup function; it is one of the best values around.
- *RapidFile* (Ashton-Tate) combines a flat-file database with a word processor; no single quality makes it outstanding—it just has a superb combination of features and ease of use.
- *DBXL* (WordTech Systems, Inc. is a relational database that can do anything *dBase* can do, for one-third the price; it has a very intuitive menu system.
- *PFS: Professional File* (Software Publishing Corp.) offers flexible data organization, entry, and retrieval; it allows variable records that can run for thirty-two pages; it lets you include a screenful of data in a single field, which makes it ideal of organizing blocks of text, such

as notes for a proposal; the on-line help is so good you'll need to look at the manual only once.

- *Microsoft Works* (Microsoft), an integrated program with several modules, includes an excellent flat-file database that is easy to set up and use.
- *Reference File* (Reference Software International is a pop-up memory-resident flat-file database; press ALT-F4 from within any application and the *File* window pops up; you can cut and paste information from *File* into your application and then make it disappear; the program is a breeze for novices to master.

For Macintosh

- *DAtabase* (Preferred Publishers), a pop-up desk accessory, is a graphic flat-file manager that allows calculated fields.
- *Microsoft Works* (Microsoft). See notes under MS-DOS.
- *Filemaker II* (Claris Corp.) excels at generating reports (with graphics), because you can move fields around on-screen to print where you like; timesaving pop-up data-entry lists enhance operation.
- *Panorama* (ProVUE Development Corp. is extremely fast; when you enter data, should the particular entry already exist in the same field in a previous record, *Panorama* will automatically suggest it for you; it produces graphic reports.

Buying Tips: If you merely want to record lists (such as addresses or products), look at flat-file databases. If you want to link these lists to other lists (such as names to product purchases, or products to suppliers), look at flat-file databases with a lookup function. And if you have a series of lists that are all interrelated (such as names, products, and suppliers), look at relational databases.

Chapter 18

Financial Record Keeping: The Key to a Stable Business

Track business expenses and accounts receivable with check writing, personal finance, or accounting software.

> *"If you take one from 365, what remains?" asked*
> Humpty Dumpty,
> > *"364, of course," said Alice.*
> > *Humpty Dumpty looked rather doubtful. "I'd rather*
> *see that done on paper," he said.*
>
> —Lewis Carroll, *Alice in Wonderland*

The two main tasks of financial record keeping are to record financial information to comply with tax laws and to track profit and loss. You might also want to track money due (accounts receivable), money owed (accounts payable), inventory, payroll, and your checking accounts. And you may need to generate periodic reports for tax purposes or for presentation to a bank that has loaned you money.

If you're running a small business, you might jump to the conclusion that you need an accounting program. But that's not necessarily true, especially if you're a one-person operation. If you don't already understand accounting principles, the time it takes to learn the software and the mistakes you might make will outweigh the benefits.

"We never knew where we stood month to month. I never knew how much I owed or how much was in my account. We didn't know until October how we did the previous summer! And then we only knew by looking at the checkbook," says Greg Morton, owner of the Bridge Street Cafe in Dartmouth, Massachusetts, who now uses *One Write Plus* (Great American Software) to track his accounts payable and to write checks. "Now we can generate a profit-and-loss statement any time. Plus, we can write thirty checks in a couple of minutes."

Financial management software of every stripe squirrels away your transactions into neatly defined cubbyholes. Like database programs, financial software allows you to retrieve and sort transactions in different ways. If you write an expense check, the software will debit a chosen expense category. At the end of the year, or at any given posting period, you can sort expenses by category, which has obvious value for tax purposes.

Like spreadsheet programs, financial programs allow you to calculate and recalculate according to different formulas. If you want to see how much money you have coming in, you have to add up all the entries in accounts receivable. You can do that by hand, of course, but it's much faster by computer. The larger your business, the more time you'll save.

Unlike either database or spreadsheet programs, however, financial management programs are set up and are nearly ready to go. You just have to customize them with your own chart of accounts and expense categories.

This chapter describes the main features of check writing, personal finance, and accounting programs, and discusses how to write checks and pay bills electronically, which saves addressing, stamping, and mailing.

THREE TYPES OF FINANCIAL SOFTWARE

The beauty of all automated bookkeeping is that you don't have to record the same entry in two or more files. While there's no doubt that an automated bookkeeping procedure saves time, the choices among check writing, personal finance, and accounting software is not so clear. Bear in mind that these software categories are not mutually exclusive, but are the terms manufacturers use to describe their software.

In fact, check writing, personal finance, and small-business accounting programs perform many of the same functions. All three let you write checks, record deposits, group expenses and income by category, keep tabs on credit card expenses, and manage your bank accounts. Check writing and personal finance programs are in many ways accounting programs in disguise. They've been sweetened to reach a wider market.

Many home and small businesses can be run perfectly well with the combination of a good check writing program, such as *Quicken* (Intuit), *Money Matters* (Great American Software), or *CheckWrite Plus* (MECA), and outside help from an accountant or bookkeeper. This approach might be the simplest.

Small-business owners who want to track both business and personal finances, including investments, might be better off with a personal finance program, like *Managing Your Money* (MECA) or *Dollars and Sense* (Monogram), which allows you to track full portfolios. And business owners who want to track inventory or who have more than five employees probably need accounting software.

CHECK WRITING SOFTWARE

Check writing programs perform the basic financial chores quickly and easily. If writing checks and keeping a register that lets you code payments are the main functions you need, a check writing program is your best bet.

Since these programs are extremely simple to set up and operate, they're good to use if you have limited time and patience for financial record keeping. You can always hire an accountant for tax preparation or business forecasting, but you'll be able to hand him a detailed list of your financial transactions.

Before you start using a check writing program, you customize it for your business by setting up your checking accounts, the names and addresses of monthly payees, and expense categories (business supplies, rent, etc.). Then you order tractor-feed checks for your printer, a process described in each program's documentation.

When you're ready to write a check, you load checks into the printer and boot up the program. You see an on-screen check (see Figure 18-1) and enter the numerical amount (the program automatically writes out that amount). You enter one or more expense categories. For example, you could split a phone bill into business and personal, or among several clients. You then enter the payee or choose a name from your preset list. If you have windowed envelopes, the program will print the address. If you write any checks manually, you must record the transaction on-screen to keep the account in balance.

While check writing programs are designed to be simple computerized versions of your regular checkbook, companies are slowly adding features to compete with more full-featured financial software. Some check writing programs, such as *Quicken*, have accounts receivable and accounts payable sections so that you can track what you're owed and what you owe. A program such as *Money Matters* generates invoices and has a special version for professional consultants who want to produce slick bills. Both print reports, such as tax summary and net worth reports.

Many check writing programs can transfer data to popular spreadsheets, and to personal finance or tax preparation programs. For instance, *Quicken* sends data to *TurboTax* (Chip Soft), *J. K. Lasser's Your Income Tax* (Simon & Schuster), *SwiftTax* (Timeworks), and *MacInTax* (SoftView). *CheckWrite Plus* (MECA) sends data to *Managing Your Money* and *TaxCut* (MECA). *Money Counts* (Parsons Technology) sends data to *Personal Tax Preparer* (Parsons Technology).

Figure 18-1.

The backbone of many financial programs is the check writing screen. As you fill in the check, all information will automatically be recorded in the proper cubbyhole. The program shown here is *One Write Plus*.

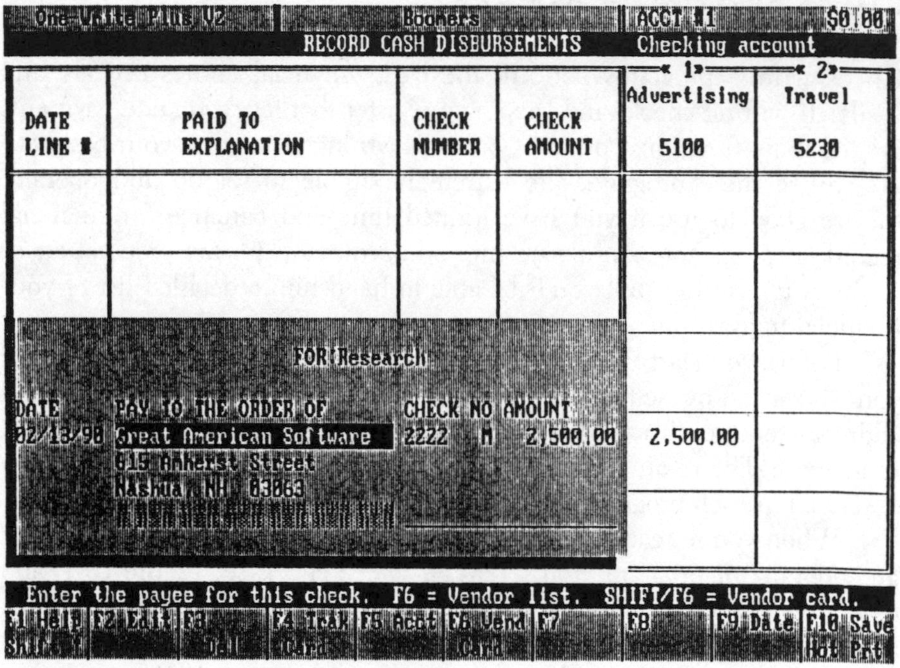

ELECTRONIC CHECK WRITING

One problem with check writing software is that you have to get special printer-ready checks made, and then load them into your printer whenever you want to write a check. To make the system work smoothly, you ideally want a printer dedicated to check writing. You can write checks manually, of course, but then you have to record the transactions in your computer program. And if you do that too often, you negate the value of the software, which is supposed to save you from recording transactions more than once.

One solution to the printer problem is to write your checks electronically through CheckFree (CheckFree Corporation), the national electronic banking service. No matter what bank you use, or whether your payees accept electronic payments, you can pay bills through CheckFree (if you have a modem). The advantages are that you don't have to load checks into your printer, nor do you have to address envelopes or mail them. Furthermore, you enter information for fixed monthly payments only once and indicate when they should be mailed; CheckFree will pay the bills automatically from then on.

With the program, you create a list of merchants to receive your payments. You then write checks to these merchants on the screen and instruct your computer to dial the CheckFree on-line service. CheckFree automatically stores all your bill paying information in its central computer system.

Depending on the facilities of the receiving merchant, CheckFree prints and mails a paper check or transmits payments electronically through the Federal Reserve System's Automated Clearing House, which is connected to all banking institutions.

Every time you write a check, CheckFree enters the date, payee, and amount into the register and adjusts the balance. Similar actions take place when you enter withdrawal and deposit data, although CheckFree doesn't handle those transactions directly.

In many respects, CheckFree substitutes for a check writing program. It tracks your balances and codes expenses by tax and budget categories. However, CheckFree data also feed into both the *Quicken* and *CheckWrite Plus* programs. The CheckWrite service is available for a minimum of $9 a month (depending on how many checks you write).

PERSONAL FINANCE SOFTWARE

Personal finance programs do everything check writing programs do, and then some. They track investments and loans. They produce statements of net worth: what you own minus what you owe. Many can be set up to produce a balance sheet, a statement showing income and expenses often required by banks managing business loans. Most personal finance programs help you calculate loan payment schedules, project cash flow, budget expenses, and estimate taxes. They will produce basic bar graphs of your data so you can view your financial status graphically (see Figure 18-2).

At the basic level, personal finance software works the same way as check writing software: You set up accounts and payees, put checks in your printer, and fill out on-screen checks with assigned expense categories. Of course, you can also track your stock, bond, and bank investments by setting up separate accounts. Just as your checking accounts won't stay in balance unless you record every transaction, the portfolio sections won't stay current unless you enter the various rate changes and stock and bond price changes.

Personal finance programs can send data to accounting and tax preparation programs. *Managing Your Money*, the preeminent personal finance program, feeds into *TaxCut* (MECA) and *SwiftTax*. *Money Matters* (Great American Software) sends data to *One-Write Plus* (Great American Software).

What really distinguishes personal finance programs from check writing programs are the bells and whistles. *Managing Your Money*, for instance,

Figure 18-2.
    Graphs produced by your check writing or personal finance software show at a glance how your income, expenses, or cash flow is going. Here, a screen from *Dollars and Sense* compares monthly income this year with income the previous year.

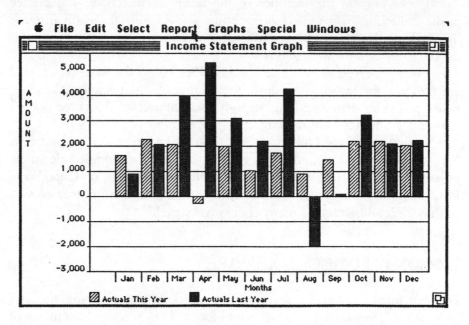

includes a buy-rent-lease analysis and life insurance planning. It allows you to set up budget categories that flow into specific lines of tax forms and schedules. *Dollars and Sense* (Monogram Software) produces consolidated reports on more than one business. Most programs perform loan repayment calculations or plan how much you have to invest at what rate and for how long to reach a given goal.

GENERAL ACCOUNTING SOFTWARE

Small-business accounting programs aren't designed as alternative check-books, though some have check writing ability. They aren't designed as personal portfolio managers, although they can manage bank accounts and credit cards and track investments and loans (which they often term assets and liabilities). They are designed to keep a very tight and highly structured account of your business's financial situation—including payroll and inventory.
    Check writing and personal finance programs group income and expenses by category. Accounting programs call this list of categories a *chart of accounts*. They produce reports that your accountant, the government, and your bank loan officer will understand and sometimes require.

Typically, small-business accounting software lacks many features—pop-up notepads, easily accessed category lists, and calculators—that helped make check writing and personal finance software so popular. Some don't even have help screens. And—with the exception of *DacEasy Light* and *One-Write Plus*—they require some knowledge of double-entry accounting.

Double-Entry Accounting

Double-entry accounting forces you to keep your books in balance. The larger the sums you deal with and the larger potential errors, the more you need double-entry accounting. Also, when a business that carries inventory switches from cash to accrual accounting to meet IRS requirements, it will have to switch to double-entry accounting.

In double-entry accounting, every transaction involves two sides—debit and credit (left and right)—that must always be equal. For example, when you pay a bill for stationery, you debit (increase) your office supply account and credit (decrease) your checking account. However, when you make a bank deposit, you credit your sales/income account and credit your checking account. In this instance, that means you'll increase them both. Finally, when you pay a loan installment, you debit your loan account and credit your checking account, thereby decreasing them both. Because of these varying meanings of debit and credit, nonaccountants often become hopelessly confused with double-entry accounting.

The summary of all debits and credits is kept in a general ledger—the summary of all business transactions. A general ledger lists assets (property you own); liabilities (debts); net worth (the value of the business); and sales, costs of goods, and operating expenses. Most accounting software won't let you move on to another task until your records balance, or "zero out."

One-Write Systems

One way around double-entry accounting is to use a one-write system. This is a check writing system in which each transaction is recorded on a ledger automatically as you write checks (which have built-in carbon paper). *One-Write Plus* (Great American Software), based on the One-Write manual system, effectively executes double-entry accounting even if you don't understand the principles. *DacEasy Light* disguises double-entry accounting as check writing and deposits/withdrawals—but it also allows a traditional general ledger system if you want one. Some people argue that even simplified check writing programs such as *Quicken* are actually double-entry accounting programs, because they automatically record a cash payment to an expense account.

Who Needs Accounting Software?

When should you graduate to traditional accounting software? Certainly not until you understand the principles of accounting. If you rely on accounting software to teach you how to keep books, you'll get into hot water the first time you run into a problem. For instance, listing sales tax you collect as an expense rather than as a liability is a common error made by beginners.

Generally, if you have more than thirty sales coming in, or write more than sixty expense checks or more than ten payroll checks each month, you probably need accounting software. If you file W-2 forms or need sales tax automatically incorporated into invoices you also need accounting software.

HOW ACCOUNTING PROGRAMS WORK

Accounting software is sold in modules, or sections, that work in concert. Most packages come with three basic modules: accounts receivable, accounts payable, and general ledger. Data from the first two modules flow into the general ledger (see Figure 18-3).

Other modules include invoicing, inventory, and payroll. Many of these same modules are available in personal finance programs, but in accounting software they are designed for those with heavier needs. There's no point to using a payroll module, which can be used for recording withheld FICA and federal, state, and local taxes from your own or an employee's payroll checks, unless you have at least five employees. And an inventory module is useful only if you carry a large inventory; it allows you to find out at a glance when it's time to reorder, the average cost per reorder, and how much inventory you're carrying.

Since accounting software isn't as simple for the untrained user as personal finance software, all publishers provide telephone training. However, it will cost you anywhere from $20 to $60 an hour, so it's definitely not the way to learn accounting.

Evaluating Accounting Software

Some accounting programs offer total integration. For example, an entry in accounts receivable is automatically recorded in the general ledger, and so on. With most software, integration is an advantage (such as a word processor with a hot link to a spreadsheet), but with accounting it's sometimes best to keep the modules separate. With integrated software, if a mistake is made and goes unnoticed too long, you'll have a hard time undoing it without messing up your books.

Figure 18-3.

In a full-fledged accounting system—used by any business that operates on an accrual basis, carries inventory, or has more than five employees—all data roads lead to the general ledger. And all posting, balance sheet, and income statements derive from the general ledger.

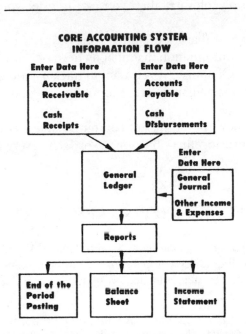

Some programs won't allow you to make any changes to the preestablished formats that are part of the program. You have to make accounting decisions at the beginning and stick with the system, which is fine if you're an experienced accountant—but not so good if you're learning as you go.

Finally, some programs allow you to enter or erase data in the general ledger, rather than just taking it from the accounts receivable or accounts payable modules. Good programs require you to remove errors with a reversing entry—one that undoes the mistake. Because the more expensive and sophisticated programs allow you to fix mistakes and change formats more easily, they are better for novices. With most types of software, of course, the reverse is true.

START SIMPLE

When you switch from a manual to a computerized bookkeeping system, you should run the two systems side by side for three to six months, to make sure you obtain the same information from both systems. And since virtually all financial software packages are geared on some level to tax preparation, it makes sense to start your computerized bookkeeping at the beginning of a tax or fiscal year.

Most small businesses do best to start small with a simple check writing or one-write system and move up to a more powerful package if their needs aren't met. If you choose a program that is upwardly compatible with more powerful accounting software, then you can transfer your data files when you upgrade.

Using a program that's too big for your business can mean wasting a lot of time creating information that nobody needs—not you, your accountant, or your bank. Of course, if you want to track payroll or inventory, then you need a personal finance or accounting program with the proper modules.

A small business should master computers and accounting separately, before tying the two together. But sooner or later, every business must tie the knot.

FINANCIAL RECORD KEEPING RESOURCES

The First Book of Quicken, by Gordon McComb, Howard W. Sams, 300 pp., 1990; $14.95. Written for the novice computer user running a home or small business, the book provides step-by-step guidance on setting up accounts, printing checks, and balancing accounts.

The Best Book of DacEasy Accounting, by Clifford D. Philip, Jr., Howard W. Sams, 500 pp., 1990; $24.95. This book is a nontechnical guide that teaches the basics of using *DacEasy* for accounting. It is heavily illustrated.

Training for Accounting, Individual Software Inc., 1985; $69.95. This tutorial disk for MS-DOS computers teaches the basic accounting principles: understanding a balance sheet, reading a financial statement, deciphering a chart of accounts, and posting transactions. It has a section that discusses how to use computers effectively in accounting. The content is as solid as a good accounting textbook, but the colorful screens, sound effects, charts, graphics, and animation make the learning much easier and more enjoyable.

Still! The Only Investment Guide You'll Ever Need, by Andrew Tobias, Bantam Books, 179 pp., 1983; $3.95. Tobias, who wrote books before software (*Managing Your Money* and *TaxCut*) makes the preservation of capital seem like the most fun game in the world. But he also imparts general rules of financial management that will help you think clearly in good times and bad.

Small-Time Operator, How to Start Your Own Business, Keep Your Books, Pay Your Taxes & Stay Out of Trouble, by Bernard Kamoroff, Bell Springs Publishing, 190 pp., 1979; $6.95. The book does what its title promises and does it well. It doesn't tell you how to computerize your business tasks, but it should give you a good understanding of the basic financial processes all businesses undergo, which is just as important.

SPOTLIGHT ON: Basic Financial Software

Cost: $50 to $300.

Learning Curve: Slight to medium, depending on the category you choose and exactly what you want to accomplish. Check writing programs operate like computerized checkbooks; accounting programs require a knowledge of accounting principles. In between are personal finance programs, which do a bit of everything.

Required Equipment: Computer with hard disk drive. To print checks: printer. To pay bills electronically: modem.

Recommended Software:

For IBM PC and IBM PS/2 and Compatibles

- *CheckWrite Plus* (MECA), a spinoff from *Managing Your Money*, is a check writing program that also handles accounts payable and receivable, invoices, loan tracking, and amortization schedules.
- *Quicken* (Intuit), a popular check writing program known for its simplicity, generates reports for income/expense statements on rental properties, W-2 employee reports, and other tricky maneuvers.
- *Managing Your Money* (MECA) is a popular personal finance program, with useful life insurance and financial planning sections; it's fun to use because its on-line help screens were written by author Andrew Tobias.
- *Money Counts* (Parsons Technology) is the least costly personal finance program; although it lacks an accounts receivable section, it has such extras as a mailing list manager.
- *Dome Simplified Bookkeeping* (Great American Software), a computerized version of the manual system, cannot write checks, handle more than one checking account, or track accounts receivable; yet it offers one of the clearest ways to keep records in a ledger format; the manual is especially good for beginners.
- *One-Write Plus Accounting System* (Great American Software), based on the manual one-write system, is probably the easiest double-entry system to use; it also offers accounts receivable and payable, with an optional payroll module; excellent documentation is provided.
- *DacEasy Accounting* (Dac-Easy) is an accounting program that's relatively easy to set up, because it includes a sample chart of accounts; modules include general ledger, accounts receivable, and accounts payable.

For Macintosh

- *Dollars and Sense* (Monogram) is a powerful personal finance program that is particularly good for rental property owners and investors.

- *Quicken* (the same check writing program described above) is a winner on the Mac as well, with a great link to *MacInTax* (SoftView), the popular tax preparation program.
- *Managing Your Money* (described above) has better graphing capabilities than the MS-DOS version; double-entry accounting is explained in the manual and it can be used directly if you want; the software gives you updates on your current tax situation throughout the year.
- *AtOnce!* (Layered, Inc.), a full-fledged accounting program, takes advantage of Macintosh interface; it includes accounts receivable and payable, general ledger, and payroll modules. Setup is easy, aided by an interactive *HyperCard* tutorial.
- *M.Y.O.B.* (Teleware) is an integrated accounting system (with accounts receivable and payable, inventory, general ledger modules) that also writes checks; it provides good step-by-step help and is a good value.
- *Bedford Simply Accounting* (Bedford Software) is a thorough accounting program for the bigger small business; it's relatively easy-to-use, and lets you allocate income and expenses to individual projects, which is perfect for job costing; a similar program from the same publisher for MS-DOS computers is called *Bedford Integrated Accounting*.

Buying Tips: Start with a simple package that has an upgrade option; you can upgrade to a more powerful package once you've figured out exactly how to set up your accounts. If you have specific needs that might not be met by a general package (such as managing rental real estate), seek out software with such a specialty.

Chapter 19
Easing Tax Preparation

Organize and speed file, and prevent mathematical errors with tax preparation software.

> *It was as true as turnips is. It was as true as taxes is. And nothing's truer than them.*
>
> —Charles Dickens, *Dombey and Son*

Self-employed people are taxed more heavily than employees. Business owners and freelancers can pay out in taxes about 50 cents of every dollar of net income. To make up for this heavy taxation, the self-employed can take far more deductions than employees.

The self-employed, most of whom classify themselves as sole proprietors and file a Schedule C, are also more likely to be audited, especially if they report above-average incomes. Taxpayers with $100,000 or more of total gross receipts who file a Schedule C are more than four times as likely to be audited as the average taxpayer. And even low-income taxpayers (with total gross receipts of less than $25,000) who file a Schedule C are about 50 percent more likely to be audited than the norm.

Taxes can or should be a consuming passion for the self-employed. Every business purchase, meal, trip and repair has a possible tax consequence. No matter how well you understand your tax situation and plan for it, there's no substitute for keeping up-to-date records that you can sort and tabulate at will. And the computer is perfect for such a task.

"If you file a Schedule C, you should have an accounting system," says John Tyler, a CPA from Cambridge, Massachusetts. "You can do that manually but there are many reasonably priced accounting and tax-preparation programs that make the maintenance of records much easier."

This chapter describes several methods of record keeping, how tax preparation programs work, and how you can get quicker refunds by filing your tax returns electronically.

YEAR-LONG RECORD KEEPING

"People with good procedures for keeping track of their business deductions get more back than the person who waits until the end of the year," says

Dick Moore, a licensed tax preparer and small-business bookkeeper in Escondido, California.

The best way to keep financial records during the year is with a checkwriting or personal finance program (see Chapter 18) that allows you to set up tax-deductible expense categories. Some programs, such as *Quicken*, allow you to split expenses in several ways. For instance, you might want to divide expenses for Schedule C into distinct classifications, beyond those supplied on the tax form. You could split telephone expenses into subcategories (such as business travel, direct client calls, and general research) and then into classes (breaking down calls into categories for specific jobs).

You don't necessarily need a personal finance or accounting program to track business expenses. Some people might find it easier to set up a simple spreadsheet worksheet tailored to their own situation. For instance, Linda Stern, a freelance writer who lives in Takoma Park, Maryland, set up a template on the spreadsheet in Microsoft *Works* to track her expenses. (See Figure 19-1.)

Since you won't have a computer with you at all times, you still need a good paper-based system. In addition, you need to keep all receipts and paper records, because your electronic records won't survive an audit. Peter Samelson, a magician from New York City who travels extensively, uses a Day Runner book to record "where I am, the date, and expenses for travel, food, dealer supplies for shows, transportation, taxes, and hotels. Each information category is documented day by day and is transferred to my computer when I get home."

Even if you don't prepare your own taxes, good records make it easier to deal with an accountant or tax preparer. The interpretation and application of tax law usually make up less than half of an accountant's fee. The major portion of the billing is for record keeping, filing, and paper handling. With good records, your accountant can focus on saving money on your taxes—and charge you less at the same time.

Export to Tax Programs

One of the promises of the computer is that it will prevent you from retyping the same words and numbers over and over—and that certainly is true during tax preparation. If you use the right combination of software, the expense records you keep all year long in your electronic checkbook or personal finance software can be transferred into your tax preparation program.

The easiest method of transfer is when you use two programs from the same company, such as *Andrew Tobias' Managing Your Money* and *Andrew Tobias' TaxCut* (both from MECA). *TaxCut* will take an *MYM* file, pick up

Figure 19-1.

If you don't want to write checks on the computer and track spending with a check writing or personal finance program, you can use a basic spreadsheet worksheet to tally expenses. Shown above is the worksheet Linda Stern developed to monitor spending for her freelance writing business.

	A	B	C	D	E	F	G	H	I
1	Date	Notes	Auto Miles	Prof. Serv.	Dues. Pubs	Home Office	Entertainment	Supplies	Phone
2	1/13	copying	2	$0.96					
3	1/09	NY Times			$19.50				
4	1/20	lunch at GW					$21.00		
5	2/03	mailing labels	4					$37.80	
6	2/17	magazine	4		$3.95				
7	2/17	copying	2	$5.50					
8	2/08	wastebasket	4			$12.50			
9	2/17	cable							$19.95
10	2/10	magazine	4		$12.50				
11	2/20	envelopes	12					$12.38	
12	2/21	calls to NY							$33.40
13									
14									
15									
16		Totals	32	$6.46	$35.95	$12.50	$21.00	$50.18	$53.35
17									
18		Deductible Miles	$7.20						

entries, and place them in the proper lines on the tax form. *TaxCut* will also take data from other programs—such as *Quicken* and *Lotus 1-2-3*—but you have to select the data and indicate where it should go. A powerful combination for the Macintosh is *Quicken* (Intuit) and *MacInTax* (Soft-View).

Even if you don't transfer data, however, you can print out totals for various expense categories and enter them in a given tax prep program. That certainly is preferable to sorting through a shoebox of receipts and totaling them yourself.

TAX PREPARATION SOFTWARE

Tax preparation software, which takes you step by step through the numerous forms and schedules you've grown to hate, can save time and anguish in early spring. Most tax preparation packages can handle any joint or individual federal income tax form, from plain old Form 1040 through Schedule W (deduction for working couples) and Form 2441 (credit for child care expenses).

Modules to complete state tax returns are sold separately by the same publisher; however, most companies offer packages only for the larger states (New York, New Jersey, Massachusetts, California, Illinois, and Pennsylvania are the most common). *TurboTax Federal Personal Series* (ChipSoft) is an exception and has supplements for most states.

Publishers release updates of their tax programs each year to reflect changes in the tax laws; registered owners buy the updates for about half the price of the original. Tax preparation programs, of course, are tax deductible.

Electronic Advisors

Besides performing many of the calculations that you'd otherwise perform by pencil or calculator (such as adding sources of income together), tax prep programs prevent you from entering the same information twice (such as a charitable contribution on Schedule A and on your 1040). Alternatively, tax prep programs *save* you from entering the same information twice. For instance, when you prepare your tax gains or losses on Schedule D, the program automatically inserts the final tabulation in the proper line on Form 1040.

Many programs insulate you from filling out tax forms directly, instead prompting you for information that is then routed to the proper line on the tax form. The best example of this is *Andrew Tobias' TaxCut* (MECA). For items with receipts you can use the "shoebox" function. The computer will ask you for, say, medical data, and route it to the proper line on the proper schedule. It also presents on-screen a W-2 form; you just copy data from your paper form onto the screen and the software puts the data on the proper line.

For trickier items that aren't directly dependent on receipts—such as business use of a computer, business use of the home, or business travel—the computer's built-in expert (Dan Caine) asks a series of questions that become more and more focused as he learns more about your particular situation. Caine will then recommend, say, how much you can depreciate your computer in a given year (see Figure 19-2).

Other programs offer help in different ways. *MacInTax* which became well known several years ago because it was the only program whose tax form printouts the IRS would accept, includes disk-based IRS instructions for each line of a schedule or form. *Swifttax* (Timeworks) includes the *Price Waterhouse Personal Tax Advisor Book*.

If you're comfortable with tax forms, most tax preparation programs also present on-screen facsimiles of the IRS tax schedules and forms. You fill in the blanks, just as you would manually. A few years ago, the IRS wouldn't accept printouts of these computer forms as legal tax returns, but now it generally does (although it pays to check each program to be sure).

Figure 19-2.

Many tax preparation programs offer on-line help, but none quite as good as that from accountant Dan Caine in *Andrew Tobias' TaxCut*.

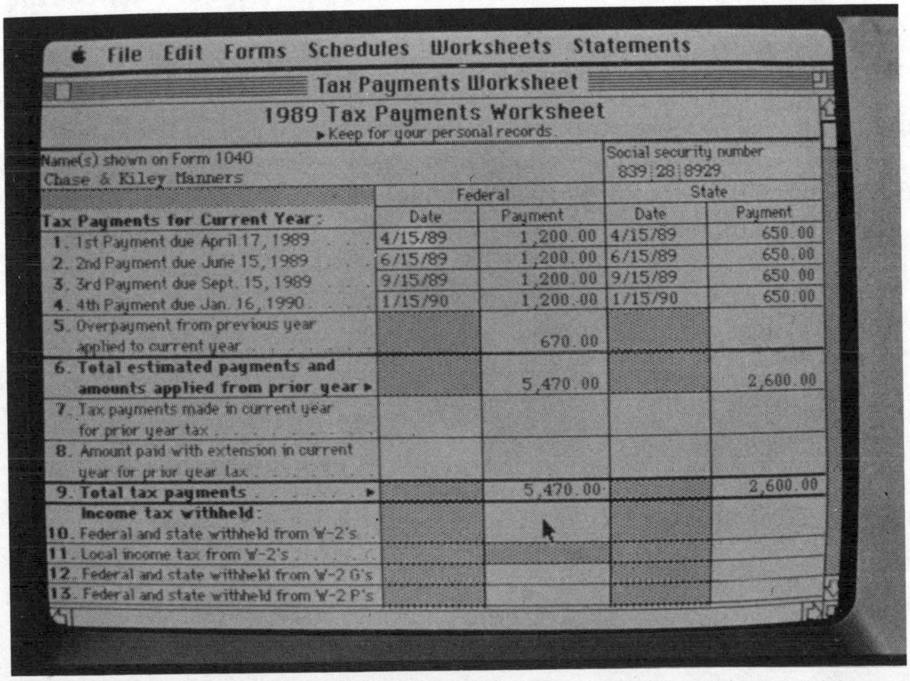

If the IRS accepts printouts from a certain program, it generally accepts dot-matrix printouts.

Calculations

The most common mistakes on tax returns occur in calculations—and computers are great calculators. If you've used a finance program during the year to track expenses, you'll already know your total telephone, utility, and other business expenses. But the real mistakes are made during actual tax calculations.

Anyone who's ever completed a Schedule G for income averaging will instantly understand the joys of computerized tax prep. Requiring tedious calculations, income averaging allows you to save taxes by averaging this year's higher income with lower earnings in the prior three years. Working by hand, Schedule G requires fifteen calculations to fill twenty-eight lines. With most tax programs, you simply enter three figures from your old returns and watch the other numbers fall into place. Nothing else is required.

Tax preparation programs also execute more basic additions, such as combining income from different sources, which can be a great help. *MacInTax* (SoftView), the popular Macintosh tax prep program, has an itemization window (see Figure 19-3). Wherever you are on the tax form, you can open a window that lets you enter a series of items; the program tabulates them and enters the amount on the tax form.

Most tax programs keep a running tab of your tax bill. After entering data about your income and capital gains or losses, the program will make the basic calculations and place the proper numbers on the right line of the 1040 form. Then, before you've completed your other deductions, the program might show that you owe the IRS a whopping $15,000! Every time you add a deduction or change a figure, the amount of taxes due is recalculated from the appropriate tax table.

The virtue of this constant tax-due calculation is that you can play what-if games with your deductions to see how they might affect your final tax bill. You could see, for instance, how much a Keogh contribution or higher mortgage interest payment would affect overall taxes.

DacEasy Rapid Tax (DacEasy, Inc.) simultaneously calculates three ways of filing—joint return, married filing separately, and single—then you decide which will benefit you most.

ELECTRONIC FILING

If you complain about how long it takes to get your tax refund, you're going to have to find something else to gripe about. The IRS now allows electronic filing—by disk or modem—and promises fast refunds in return.

Figure 19-3.
MacInTax shows exact replicas of the IRS tax forms on the screen.

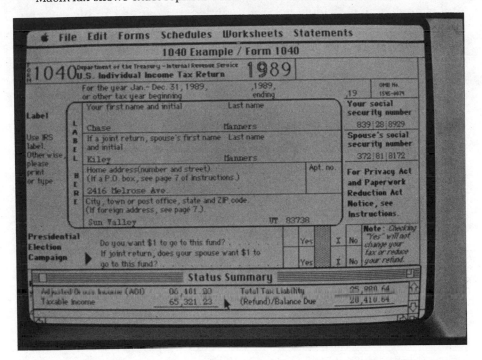

The IRS began electronic filing as a pilot project in the 1987 tax year in three metro areas, with about 77,000 electronic returns filed. The next year, it added five more areas, and the number of returns rose to over 580,000. Now that it's been implemented nationally, the IRS expects more than 2 million electronic returns for tax year 1989.

To file electronically, you have three choices. You can use a tax preparation software package that supports electronic filing; go to an IRS-approved tax preparation firm (such as H&R Block); or search for a CPA who files electronically.

When you use the right tax prep software, you prepare your return and then, for a small fee, send it electronically (via modem) or on a floppy disk to the IRS-authorized transmitter (a third party) that accepts output from your particular software. The transmitter— who's contracted by the software publisher—will recheck the return for accuracy and forward it to the IRS. Thus electronic filing theoretically reduces the chances of computational errors—and audits.

Once the IRS receives the return, it is checked again for accuracy. Unlike paper returns that can get lost in the shuffle, the IRS acknowledges it has received the return within forty-eight hours.

Some notable tax prep programs that support electronic filing are *Tax Shop 1040* (TenKey Publishing, Inc.), *Andrew Tobias' TaxCut*, *DacEasy RapidTax*, and *MacInTax*.

Who Can File Electronically

At this time, only individual taxpayers entitled to a refund can file electronically. In 1991, the IRS plans to accept balance-due returns, payable by credit card. Of course, if you're not getting a refund, there's not much incentive to file electronically. And if your return requires supporting documentation, you're amending a previously filed return (even if the original was filed electronically), or you're married and filing separately, you have to file on paper.

The IRS now accepts all forms and schedules, with just a few exceptions. Considering the complexity of IRS procedures and rules, there are surprisingly few restrictions. For details, read IRSD Publication 1345 or call 800-424-1040.

Even if you file electronically, one thing remains the same. The IRS still wants your signature. You or your tax preparer must mail Form 8453 with your signature and other basic information.

"The IRS is committed to electronic filing of tax returns," says Chips Maurer, an IRS public affairs officer. Eventually, you'll be able to send your tax return directly to the IRS from your computer on April 15 and get a refund less than a week later. By the mid-1990s, the IRS projects that half of all tax returns will be filed electronically.

TIMESAVERS, NOT MONEYSAVERS

Tax preparation software doesn't promise to save you money, although it can. If your math is sloppy, the software will take care of the calculations and perhaps prevent costly errors. And if you hire an outside tax preparer, the software will do much of the organizing that you would otherwise pay for. Of course, you have to factor in the cost of the software and the cost of your own time.

But tax prep software does promise to reduce the amount of time you spend on taxes, because it will do the math and will enter data from the various schedules onto Form 1040. Tax preparation software really shines when you use it as part of a consistent financial record keeping system. Good paper records make manual tax preparation easier, and good electronic records speed up electronic tax preparation. So don't buy a tax program to organize your records; start with a checkbook, finance, or accounting program, and ice the cake with a tax program.

TAX PREPARATION RESOURCES

IRS Publications, free; call 800-424-3676 for more information.

The only true authority on taxes is the written word from the IRS. The best sources for information are the free IRS publications, which are full of information. The titles listed below are most pertinent for business owners.

Order from the Forms Distribution Center nearest you: Rancho Cordova, Calif. 95743-0001; P.O. Box 9903, Bloomington, Ill. 61799; P.O. Box 25866, Richmond, Va. 23289.

Publication 334, Tax Guide for Small Business; 463, Travel, Entertainment, and Gift Expenses; 505, Tax Withholding and Estimated Tax; 527, Residential Rental Property; 533, Self-Employment Tax; 534, Depreciation; 537, Installment Sales; 541, Tax Information on Partnerships; 544, Sales and Other Dispositions of Assets; 548, Deduction for Bad Debts; 550, Investment Income and Expenses; 551, Basis of Assets; 560, Self-Employed Retirement Plans; 561, Determining the Value of Donated Property; 587, Business Use of Your Home; 589, Tax Information on Subchapter S Corporations; 917, Business Use of a Car; 926, Employment Taxes for Household Employers.

SPOTLIGHT ON: Tax Preparation Software

Cost: $20 to $100 (some annual updates are free; others cost up to $100).
Learning Curve: Slight. Certainly, figuring out how to use tax preparation software is easier than figuring out IRS tax forms.
Required Equipment: Computer with hard disk drive; printer.
Recommended Software:

For IBM PC and IBM PS/2 and Compatibles

- *Andrew Tobias' TaxCut* (MECA) includes tax advice from accountant Dan Caine, making it one of the most helpful tax packages; it allows electronic filing; it imports data from Lotus *1-2-3*, *Managing Your Money* and *Checkwrite Plus*; it prints IRS-approved 1040 forms, even with a dot-matrix printer.
- *MacInTax for Windows* (Softview), the PC version of the popular Macintosh program, shows exact replicas of IRS forms and schedules on-screen; it runs under *Windows* for ease of use; it offers electronic filing.
- *Swiftax* (Timeworks Inc.) offers a taxpayer interview that helps you figure out which schedules and forms to use; it includes *The Price Waterhouse Personal Tax Advisor Book*; it imports data from *Quicken*, *Dollars and Sense*, *Managing Your Money*, and Lotus *1-2-3*; it prints an IRS-approved 1040, even with a dot-matrix printer.

For Macintosh

- *MacInTax* (Softview), which shows exact replicas of IRS forms and schedules, is one of the most fluid tax packages on the market; it imports data from *Quicken*; it prints IRS-approved forms; on-screen itemization windows allow quick calculations when you're filling out a form; it supports electronic filing.

- *Personal Tax Templates* (Hcizer Software), a set of spreadsheet templates primarily for Microsoft *Works* plus a few for *Excel*, covers about thirty-five tax forms; it is very popular and inexpensive.

Buying Tips: If you use check writing, personal finance, or accounting software, choose a tax program that accepts data from that software. If you must file a specialized schedule or form, be sure that the tax software includes it; likewise, if you want to file electronically or file computer-generated tax forms, check to see that the software has those features. Finally, most tax software includes separate state tax forms only for the largest states.

Chapter 20
Getting More Out of Your (Old) Computer

Work more efficiently with a graphic interface, extra memory, a better-organized hard disk drive, or timesaving utilities.

> *Though I look old, yet I am strong and lusty.*
>
> —William Shakespeare, *As You Like It*

When you first use a computer, you worry less about the machine's performance than your own. The computer works so much faster than other office tools that its performance isn't an issue. But once you've established a system and a daily routine—once you start typing the same keystrokes every day—you begin to think of ways to streamline the work. You want better software, a better file management system, more speed, and so on.

There are 101 ways to improve computer performance, depending on the type of work you do and the software you use. For instance, adding a thesaurus, spelling checker, or outliner to a basic word processing program may turn it into a completely different beast; using *Allways*, a so-called spreadsheet publisher, with Lotus *1-2-3* may help you see the same old numbers in a new light.

But no matter what software you use, you can apply some general remedies. By using a graphical interface and a mouse, or a wide range of utilities that copy and delete files, MS-DOS users can circumvent the operating systems they love to hate. All users can add memory to run software more efficiently, run new software, or add memory-resident programs. All users can rearrange their hard disk drive filing systems to make files easier to retrieve and improve the way the hard disk stores files. And many users can set up their systems to perform two tasks at once.

This chapter describes the general improvements that will upgrade any computer's performance, as well as number of superb software utilities that will help upgrade your own.

GO GRAPHIC, FOR EASE OF USE

The major trend in the MS-DOS world today is to emulate the famous Macintosh graphical user interface. A GUI (pronounced "gooey"), as the interface is sometimes referred to, is an on-screen environment with pulldown menus, icons, and dialog boxes. Most require or recommend that you use a mouse, which you move to control the cursor on-screen and click to invoke a menu choice (see Figure 20-1).

When operating within a graphic environment, you don't have to remember or type commands. You move the cursor to the menu bar across the top of the screen, depress the mouse key, and pull down a menu. Slide the mouse to highlight the action you want, and release the key. In another

Figure 20-1.

The move to a graphic user interface (GUI) is one of the major trends in the MS-DOS world today. A GUI generally speeds operation, especially for new users, and it shortens the learning curve for a new product.

Using a mouse, you point the cursor at one of the general headings on the top menu bar and pull down a menu; you then choose an option by releasing the mouse. Shown here is *Ami Professional,* a word processor that runs under *Windows,* the prevalent MS-DOS graphic interface.

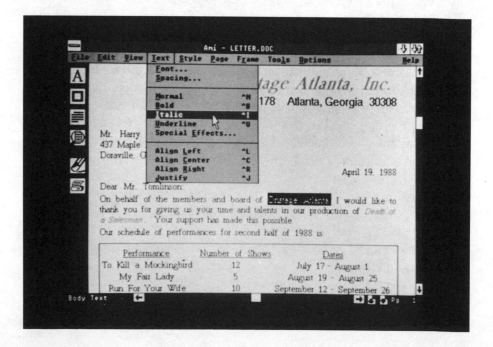

case, you point at an icon such as a printer, and click the mouse button. The action (such as saving or printing a file) is executed automatically.

Often a dialog box appears on the screen that prompts you to set options. In this box, you might choose the word to find, indicate what print mode (high-quality or draft) to use, or indicate the number of columns you want to create.

Because a GUI doesn't force you to learn commands or remember all possible options, and because most GUI software operates in a consistent fashion, these graphic environments promise to help you get work done faster. With a shorter learning curve, you're more likely to try new software that will make you more efficient. To run effectively, a GUI requires computer speed and memory, and software that runs under the given GUI.

Windows—The Dominant MS-DOS Graphic Interface

Windows (Microsoft) is a graphics-based, mouse-oriented desktop environment that allows an MS-DOS computer to operate much as a Macintosh does. Windows lets you open several applications at once and move instantly between them, cutting and pasting information from one to the other (as long as the applications are designed to work with Windows). Windows Dynamic Data Exchange (DDE) allows hot links between different Windows applications; when you change figures in an Excel spreadsheet, for example, those figures will be updated in any part of your spreadsheet within the word processing document.

Windows has been available for years, but has begun to make sense only recently. Older computers weren't fast enough to do it justice. Consequently, software developers didn't design their programs to run under Windows (with the notable exception of PageMaker).

Now that 286 and 386 machines dominate the MS-DOS world, Windows is coming into its own. Word for Windows (Microsoft) and Ami Professional (Samna), for example, are considered two of the best word processors on the market.

A competing MS-DOS graphic interface is GEM (Digital Research, Inc.), though fewer programs run under GEM. Xerox Ventura Publisher, the leading MS-DOS desktop publishing package, runs under GEM.

Presentation Manager—Making OS/2 Graphic

If Windows running under MS-DOS represents the present, Presentation Manager running under IBM's OS/2 is the future. To run this combination you need at least 4 MB of RAM, but as memory becomes cheaper such a combo will make more sense. As with Windows in the early days, not enough users have high-powered systems to justify too much software development. But it's coming. Designers for *WordPerfect for PM* (WordPerfect Corporation) and Lotus *1-2-3/G* (for graphical) worked together to make sure their respective programs looked and operated alike. And, of course, Microsoft has updated its *Windows* products to produce *Excel for PM* and *Word for PM*.

DeskMate—Graphics for Slow Computers

What if you have an older PC or XT computer that is *not* blessed with memory and speed, but would prefer to work with graphic interface? Tandy's *DeskMate* is the answer. The early *DeskMate* was a no-frills integrated package (with a word processor, spreadsheet, database, communications, and desktop organizer) that Tandy gave away with every Tandy 1000 computer. *DeskMate* empowered new owners to use the computer right out of the box, without rushing off to buy expensive, full-featured programs. Since then, Tandy has turned *DeskMate* into a slick GUI interface with pulldown menus, dialog boxes, and a DOS shell. What makes it particularly attractive is that it runs on older computers and doesn't require a 286 or 386 machine (see Figure 20-2).

Figure 20-2.

DeskMate, a simpler GUI than *Windows*, provides many of the same functions, but runs on PC and XT computers. Several major software packages, including Lotus *Spreadsheet for DeskMate*, run under *DeskMate*.

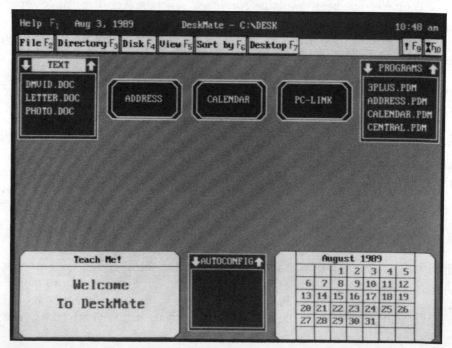

Even better, major software publishers have developed special versions of their programs that run under *DeskMate*. The *Lotus Spreadsheet for DeskMate* (Lotus), a lean version of *1-2-3*, is the big name in the lineup. But *Quicken*, *DacEasy Accounting*, *MemoryMate*, *PFS:First Publisher*, *Print Magic*, and *Venture: The Entrepreneur's Handbook* are all available in *DeskMate* versions.

IMPROVE YOUR MEMORY

There was a time when people wondered how they'd ever use more computer memory. Now people always complain about not having enough memory. Adding more memory helps most software run faster, especially graphics-based software. Extra memory can be used for so-called memory-resident utility programs, which sit in the background until you call them up with a keystroke or a mouse click. And extra memory may allow you to run two or more programs at once, or to create larger files (if you want more rows on your spreadsheet, more records in your database, or more detailed graphics).

The memory problem is most acute for MS-DOS users, since that operating system cannot address more than 1MB of RAM. The OS/2 and Macintosh operating systems, on the other hand, can address 16MB or more; if you need more memory you simply add the chips.

With MS-DOS, no more than 640K of the 1MB maximum can be used to run programs, including DOS itself. The remaining 384K is reserved for system functions like video memory. But there are ways around the problem.

Extended Memory

MS-DOS computers sold with more than 1MB of memory use extended memory. For example, a system with 2MB of RAM has 1MB of conventional memory and 1MB of extended memory. Extended memory improves system performance in several ways: (1) as a RAM disk—a chunk of RAM functioning as a disk drive; (2) as a print spooler—a chunk of RAM in which a data file can be dumped and fed to a printer, freeing up conventional memory; (3) as a disk cache—a chunk of RAM in which information from frequently accessed parts of a disk are stored. Since the contents of a disk cache and a RAM disk are stored in the computer's memory, it can access those data much more quickly than it could if it were on the disk drive.

Expanded Memory

Under certain circumstances, software can trick the computer into using extra memory for normal computing functions. To do so, you add memory on a plug-in EMS board, specifically, a board that adheres to the Lotus-Intel-Microsoft (LIM) Expanded Memory Specification. The designers of these *expanded* memory boards have devised tricks that fool DOS into seeing blocks of expanded memory as conventional memory (see Figure 20-3).

You can add anywhere from 512K to 8MB of RAM through EMS boards. But it's important to note that EMS works only with software that supports LIM.

MANAGING A HARD DISK DRIVE

If you don't have a hard disk drive, adding one is probably the single easiest way to improve computer performance. You can store all your application programs and all the files you create in one place, without ever having to switch (or care for) floppies. In addition, accessing files from a hard disk drive is much faster than from a floppy.

A 40MB hard disk drive is standard on most computers today. For most users, that's plenty of storage space. As applications move from text-based to graphics-based, however, a higher-capacity disk drive becomes more important. If you plan to use OS/2 or *Windows/386*, or to store graphics files, seriously consider an 80MB drive or larger.

Despite its many advantages, a hard disk can create its own problems. You can easily amass thousands of files, which can be an organizational nightmare. Who wants to spend half an hour looking for a file whose name you can't remember? The larger the disk, the more acute the problem, especially if you use an older version of DOS. Until MS-DOS 4.0 came

Figure 20-3.
Expanded Memory Specification (EMS) borrows addresses from the "Other System Function" portion of conventional memory and assigns them temporarily to blocks or "pages" of additional memory. DOS then sees the pages as part of conventional memory and can address them.

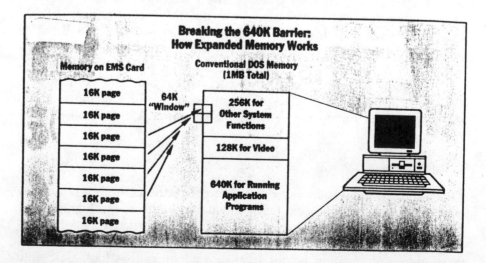

out, DOS could support only a 32MB partition; thus, a 40MB drive required two partitions and an 80MB drive three, which makes it confusing to organize files.

There are two solutions to the problem, and they aren't mutually exclusive. You can reorganize your files in a more logical pattern that fits the way you work. And you can use file-searching software, which searches megabytes of data in seconds, looking for keywords that point to files.

Setting Up a Filing System

Whether you use MS-DOS or the Macintosh Hierarchical File System (HFS), you store files in compartments and subcompartments—called root directories and subdirectories (MS-DOS), or disk names and folders (HFS). You can easily set up too few or too many of these groupings, each of which may complicate your retrieval process. One approach is to organize your files by application; that is, all spreadsheet files in one folder, all word processing files in another, and so on. But that can lead to confusion. Over time, you'll have hundreds of files in the same compartment. Another approach is to organize files based on the way you work.

Often this procedure entails subdividing your files by project instead of by application. If all the files for a single paper, report, or publication are in a subdivision dedicated to that project, however, your search becomes much easier. For example, when a newsletter is being put together, all the art, word processing, and database files related to one issue could go into a clearly labeled subdirectory. Within that subdirectory, you could set up such additional divisions for article text, correspondence, and graphics.

To help organize your files, consider a DOS "shell" program such as *Norton Commander*, which displays a listing of subdirectories and files whenever you start the computer. You don't need to remember which command is needed to change directories, and which is used to create a new one. Just press the listed function key, and the commands are executed. To copy files between subdirectories or to delete files, merely highlight the files and press ENTER. Like the above-mentioned GUIs, *Commander* and other DOS shells insulate you from the computer's operating system.

Another option is to upgrade to the latest version of MS-DOS, that is, 4.01 or higher. This latest incarnation of the operating system that Microsoft designed about a decade ago includes several improvements, including a DOS shell that gives menu choices when a user is working with files. The latest version also supports a mouse for DOS functions, and on-line help.

File-Finding Software

Even if you organize your files to suit your work patterns, there will be times when you can't put your fingers on a file you need. And there will be times when you want to find a phrase or fact or note that is buried among millions of other phrases and facts and notes.

Because so many people suffer from the same inability to locate data they worked so hard to collect and create, a whole class of disk-searching software has emerged. Notable packages include *GOfer* (Microlytics), which runs on both MS-DOS and Macintosh; *Magellan* (Lotus), for MS-DOS; and *OnLocation* (On Technology), for Macintosh.

GOfer

GOfer (for both MS-DOS and Macintosh) will search for file names or text within a file. Say you're looking for a letter written to the law firm of Hammond, Hammond, and Smith—but have no idea what you named the file. Use *GOfer* to search for Hammond and sit back.

GOfer allows sophisticated search criteria. You can specify a search for two text strings appearing together or near each other. If you don't remember how many *m*'s there are in Hammond, you can ask for all file names starting with "Ham." You can read a file once *GOfer* finds it, but you can't edit it without opening the application that created it.

A real *GOfer* advantage is that it can be run as a memory-resident utility that pops up when you need it, no matter what other application you're using.

Magellan

Magellan does everything *GOfer* does and more. To begin with, it's extremely fast, even on a slow computer. Rather than searching through 40MB or so to find a file, it first creates a compressed index of all data on the disk—and then searches the index. Indexing a 40MB hard disk drive takes about thirty minutes, but you do it only once (and then update it periodically to reflect additions). Because the index is compressed, it takes up less than 5 percent of hard disk space.

Magellan's real advantage is that it lets you scroll through a directory of files on one side of the screen and view each file on the right side (see Figure 20-4). Ordinarily, you view an MS-DOS directory but then have to open a file to view it. With *Magellan*, as you move the bar-shaped cursor down the list highlighting file names, the View Window changes nearly instantly to display data. If you want to see more of the file, just press the right-arrow key to move the cursor into the View Window. And you can launch the application that created the file with a keystroke.

OnLocation does for the Macintosh what *Magellan* does for MS-DOS users. It creates a compressed index of all data on your hard disk drive and searches it within seconds. Double-click the mouse on the file's name and it will open, and from there you can launch the program. Alternatively,

Figure 20-4.
With Lotus *Magellan*, a hard disk organizer and file finder, you can scroll through a directory in one half of the screen and view the file in the other half. When you are cleaning out a hard disk, this process allows you to quickly examine a file before deleting it—without loading the application that created it.

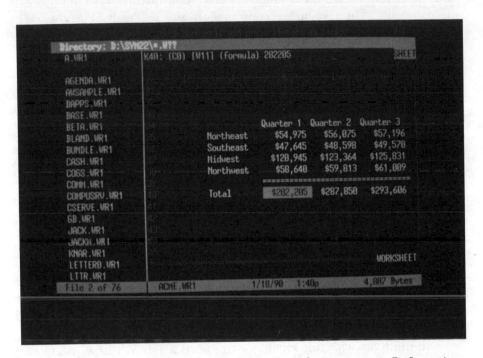

you can move or copy text without opening the program. *OnLocation*, however, doesn't offer the split-screen directory listing that *Magellan* does.

HOW TO PRINT AND CHEW GUM (AT THE SAME TIME)

You're printing out a long file, staring at the message on your computer screen, "Busy Printing." You're downloading a long file from CompuServe, staring at the changing message on your screen, "15 blocks received, 16 blocks received. . . ." You wonder how many blocks are in the file. Should you go get a cup of coffee or check the mail?

If you find yourself in this predicament time and again, you should take steps to free your computer from such bondage. The printing problem can be solved by adding a print buffer or print spooler, which stores text while the printer cranks along. For instance, a 50K buffer will take a 50K document out of your computer and restore power to you, saving you perhaps thirty minutes of downtime.

Many printers come with built-in buffers, and the manufacturers generally sell additional memory. Alternatively, you can use extended memory on an MS-DOS computer (see above) as a buffer or add print-spooling software.

A solution to the modem problem is to use communications software that operates in the "background" mode, thus freeing the computer for other tasks. Some MS-DOS programs have their own background processing capability. Hit a keystroke combination and you're back at the DOS prompt, ready to run other software while the communications process continues. These programs include *CrossTalk* (Digital Communications), *Mirror III* (SoftKlone Distributing Corp.), *Relay Gold* (Microcom Software Division), and *Smartcom III* (Hayes Microcomputer Products).

There is a price to be paid for attempting background communications, however. Since both programs running simultaneously share the same microprocessor, neither works as quickly as it would running alone. In some cases, you may slow the file transfer process, encounter a higher error rate, or lose the connection entirely. But it's worth trying.

Multitasking

Another potential solution to the overworked computer is to set up a multitasking environment, in which you open and run several programs at the same time. Depending on your computer's speed and memory, you can search a database, calculate a spreadsheet, and write a letter on the word processor all at the same time.

To multitask with true efficiency you need a 386 MS-DOS computer, or a Macintosh with a Motorola 68030 microprocessor (used in the SE/30, IIcx, IIci, and IIfx). In addition, you need enough memory to open several programs at once; generally that means a minimum of 2MB of RAM.

386 Computers

The 386 microprocessor was designed for multitasking. Because of its speed, the 386 appears to be operating several programs at once; in fact, the microprocessor alternates from one job to the next. True multitasking, also called multiprocessing or concurrent processing, is found mostly on mainframe computers. There are now parallel processors that can actually execute two tasks at once.

Although both 286 and 386 computers are capable of multitasking when running OS/2, the beauty of 386 computers is that they can multitask when running MS-DOS, which is ordinarily a single-task operating system. On a 386 computer, programs such as *Windows/386* and *Desqview 386* set up several imaginary DOS computers; each imaginary computer can use 640K, and together they can run several MS-DOS programs at the same time.

With OS/2, which is designed for multitasking, you can simultaneously operate several programs of any size up to the limits of available memory. You can run MS-DOS applications under OS/2, but you cannot multitask; software must be written specifically for OS/2.

Macintosh

The situation is more clear-cut in the Macintosh arena. All Macintoshes are sold with MultiFinder, a part of the operating system that allows multitasking. And most new software is written to work with MultiFinder. Thus the major issue is how much memory you have. One major drawback to MultiFinder, however, is that it allows only background printing with a laser printer; ImageWriter owners still face the "Busy Printing" message.

UTILITIES

A good utility is like a good night's sleep—when you need it, nothing else can substitute. Utilities are programs that fill in the cracks when your regular programs or operating system can't do what you need done—or won't do it easily. For instance, you could back up your hard disk drive by using MS DOS alone, but that's often a tedious process. Instead, a well-designed utility such as *Feedback Plus* (Fifth Generation Systems) can ease this vital task.

One of the most widely used MS-DOS utilities is *Norton Utilities* (Peter Norton Computing). This set of programs won't prevent your files from being destroyed, but it will bring files back if they are somehow damaged. Included is a utility for data recovery; another for format recovery; and a third that can find "lost" files on your disk. You may be surprised and comforted to know that a deleted file is rarely deleted—it is merely renamed and rendered invisible.

Disk Optimizers

The longer you use a hard disk drive, the slower it gets, because the computer's operating system puts files wherever it finds free sectors on the disk. Those sectors often aren't next to each other, so each time you read a file, the drive's head may go to various sectors to find the data in one file. A good hard disk utility will rewrite all your files so that they're contiguous on the disk. By using such a disk optimizer periodically, you'll ensure that your hard drive is operating as fast as it should.

A popular general-purpose Macintosh utility is *SUM II* (Symantec), a complete data protection and recovery program that also speeds up hard disks by optimizing files (see Figure 20-5). *SpinRite* (Gibson Research) is a good disk optimizer for MS-DOS computers.

THE UPGRADE DECISION

When you are looking for ways to boost computer performance, you should first troubleshoot by trying to identify the root of the problem. It could be your hardware, your software, or both. The first step is to clean up your hard disk drive. Erase unwanted files and reorganize the rest with a disk optimizer.

While it's true that almost any software will perform better with more memory and speed, it's also true that one software package may outperform another package on the same system. If you're not satisfied with your software, make sure you're using the latest version of the program. Publishers sometimes make radical changes from version to version.

Also, assure yourself that you're not asking a given package to do something it's not meant to do. Often, adding a memory-resident TSR (on MS-DOS machines) or a desk accessory (on a Macintosh) will solve your problem by adding a function or two. Finally, don't be afraid to switch to a

Figure 20-5.

The computer user's toolkit should include a data recovery program that can restore files that have apparently disappeared. *SUM II*, which is shown here, is one of the major recovery programs for the Macintosh; *Norton Utilities* is the big name in the MS-DOS world.

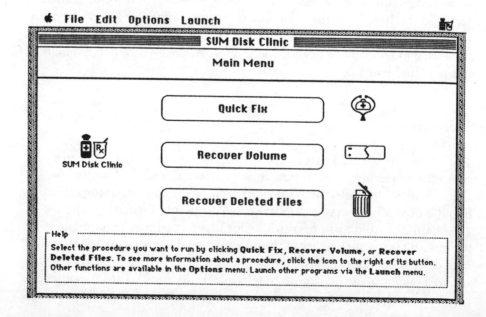

new program you think will be better. Every generation of software is easier to use, so the learning curve is shorter. In addition, the new program will probably accept your old files.

If you determine that your equipment needs a shot of Geritol, be cautious not to invest too much in an outmoded computer. For instance, while you can add speedup boards to an XT computer, you'd probably be better off investing the money in a new 386 machine. Speedup boards don't always integrate well into your system, and even if they do, much of the software being written today won't run on an XT computer. With a 286 computer, adding expanded memory and *Desqview* (for multitasking) will breathe new life into an old machine.

As far as upgrading a Macintosh, it's not worth investing too much money in a computer unless it uses the Motorola 68030 or higher microprocessor. It's not that older machines are nonfunctional—but many new products won't run on them. The action, as always, is at the high end of the spectrum. You don't have to be in the center of it, but you want to stay close enough to reap the rewards.

YOUR POWER TOOL

The computer is one of the most versatile tools ever designed. It automates tasks of every description and allows you to produce work you never could before. It empowers you to work faster and better. You don't need the latest model to work effectively. But just as a carpenter oils and sharpens tools for maximum performance, you should keep your power tool up to speed.

COMPUTER PERFORMANCE RESOURCES

PC Magazine DOS Power Tools, by Paul Somerson, Bantam Computer Books, 1,296 pp., 1988; $44.95 (includes disk). This package provides dozens of undocumented tips and shortcuts, as well as sections that show how to surmount common trouble spots. The disk contains more than 200 utilities for DOS versions 2.0 through 4.0. More than 350,000 copies are in print.

PC/MS DOS 4.0 For Hard Disk Users, by David D. Busch, Bantam Computer Books, 384 pp., 1989; $22.95. This is one of the few DOS books written specifically for hard disk users, with analysis of each disk management function. It covers all DOS commands and is current with version 4.01.

Glossbrenner's Complete Hard Disk Handbook, by Alfred Glossbrenner and Nick Anis, Osborne/McGraw-Hill, 450 pp., 1990; $39.95. A comprehensive volume that covers everything from buying a hard disk drive to installing and tweaking it for maximum performance. It includes two disks packed with tutorials and utilities.

Hard Disk Management for the Macintosh, by Nancy Andrews, Bantam Computer Books, 256 pp., 1989; $34.95 (includes disk). This book is a guide to selecting and installing a hard disk drive, as well as a discussion of three programs that help users find lost files, create backups, and ensure security in multiuser situations.

Running MS-DOS, by Van Wolverton, Microsoft Press, 423 pp., 1989; $22.95. Anyone who uses MS-DOS could use a copy of this classic book, which describes in simple step-by-step terms how to make the world's most popular (and confusing?) operating system work for you.

The Macintosh Bible, by Dale Coleman and Arthur Naiman, Goldstein & Blair, 418 pp., 1987; $21.00. This classic book of tips, tricks, and shortcuts to using a Macintosh fills in the many gaps in Apple's documentation and adds tips for using popular Macintosh software.

The Best Book of Microsoft Windows 3, by Carl Townsend, Howard W. Sams, 600 pp., 1990; $24.95. This book is an in-depth tutorial and reference on *Windows 3.0*, the latest version of the dominant DOS GUI. It includes tutorial exercises and advanced techniques for power users.

The Best Book of Desqview, by Jack Nimersheim, Howard W. Sams, 450 pp., 1990; $24.95. This book is a nontechnical guide to *Desqview*, the operating environment that allows you to open several programs and switch between them. It includes tips and tricks on automating the program, as well as a resource listing of third-party products that can be used with it. It covers *Desqview/386*.

The First Book of The Norton Utilities, by Joseph Wikert, Howard W. Sams, 275 pp., 1990; $14.95. Aimed at the computer novice, this guide offers a series of "quick steps" to various tasks, and includes end-of-chapter review questions. Topics such as file backup and recovery and working with batch files and TSRs are covered in detail.

The First Book of DeskMate, by R. K. Swadley, Howard W. Sams, 275 pp., 1990; $14.95. This book describes how to get the most out of the ten built-in programs in *DeskMate*, using the "quick steps" approach. It also discusses *DeskMate*'s role as a GUI that other major applications, including Lotus *1-2-3*, run under.

Macintosh Repair & Upgrade Secrets, by Larry Pina, Hayden Books, 351 pp., 1990; $32.95 (includes disk). If your Macintosh isn't performing up to snuff, you may be told by a dealer that you've got to replace the whole logic board. But if you use the diagnostic disk enclosed with this book, you may find that you can fix the problem yourself with a few standard electrical parts. If not, you'll at least be able to point your Apple dealer in the right direction.

The Brady Guide to Microcomputer Troubleshooting & Maintenance, by Henry F. Beechhold, Prentice-Hall Press, 324 pp., 1987; $4.95. The author, a long-time tinkerer, takes the novice by the hand and says, "This is what could happen and here's what to do about it." He also describes how to install disk drives and memory boards, which is useful knowledge for those without the support of a friendly dealer.

SPOTLIGHT ON: Software Utilities

Cost: $50 to $200.
Learning Curve: Medium; utilities are designed to insulate you from your computer's operating system, but often require that you understand the operating system.
Required Equipment: Computer with enough memory to run memory-resident programs as well as regular applications (in some cases).
Recommended Software:

For IBM PC and IBM PS/2 and Compatibles

- *Magellan* (Lotus) navigates through hard disks the way its namesake navigated the oceans; it is extremely fast at finding text and files; it displays a list of files with most occurrences of a given word; it displays a given file in a split-screen window as you tab through a directory; the software is a pleasure to use.
- *Norton Utilities* (Peter Norton Computing) is the program that smart computer users always seem to pull out when the going gets tough; like life insurance, it's worth buying before it's too late.
- *GOfer* (Microlytics) quickly searches through jam-packed hard disks to find files or bits of text in a file; it can be run as a stand-alone program or as a memory-resident utility. Also for the Macintosh.
- *Fastback Plus* (Fifth Generation Systems) is about the easiest backup program on the market, with windows and pulldown menus; it compresses data so that fewer disks are needed for a backup. Also for the Macintosh.
- *SpinRite* (Gibson Research), an impressive hard disk organizer, determines the best patterns of file distribution on your disk and then reformats the drive without harming data; the program actually restores formerly unusable disk sectors.
- *PRD+* (Productivity Software International, Inc.), whose full name is *Productivity Plus*, lives up to its name; type a short abbreviation in any program and *PRD+* automatically enters a longer word or phrase that you've previously recorded; for example, *vty* can become *very truly yours.*

For Macintosh

- *QuickKeys* (CE Software), a marvelous macro program that's always in memory and saves repetitious keystrokes by allowing you to set up hundreds of keyboard shortcuts for inserting text, choosing menu items, clicking and moving the mouse, and many more procedures; it is almost indispensable once you start using it.
- *Symantec Utilities for Macintosh (SUM II)* (Symantec), a collection

of utilities unified by an easy-to-use interface, recovers data, optimizes files, diagnoses disk problems, and more.

- *DiskTop* (CE Software), a desk accessory that greatly expands on the Mac's desktop capabilities, lets you copy and delete files from within nearly any program; it also finds any files or launches an application from a menu so that you can jump quickly from program to program; it incorporates *GOfer* for text searches.

- *Suitcase II* (Fifth Generation Systems) lets you surpass Apple's limit of only 15 desk accessories and 200 fonts per system file by loading any DA or font on disk.

- *OnLocation* (On Technology) marks the return of Mitch Kapor, founder of Lotus, to the computing scene; his new product does for the Macintosh what *Magellan* does for MS-DOS users: It finds files and text fast.

- *Fastback* (Fifth Generation). See MS-DOS description.

- *GOfer* (Microlytics, Inc.). See MS-DOS description.

Buying Tips: Computer users in general depend on word-of-mouth recommendations, and in no category is this more true than utilities; talk to others who have encountered and overcome the problems you now face, and take their advice.

Appendix:
Manufacturers' and Publishers' Phone Numbers

Adobe Systems   (800) 833-6687
Aldus   (206) 622-5500
Alpha Software   (617) 229-2924
Apple Computer   (408) 996-1010
Ashton-Tate   (213) 329-8000
askSAM Systems   (904) 584-6590

Bantam Electronic Publishing   (800) 223-6834
Bitstream   (617) 497-6222; (800) 522-3668
Borland International   (408) 438-8400
Broderbund Software   (415) 479-1700; (800) 521-6263
Burwell Enterprises   (713) 537-9051
Business Forecast Systems   (617) 431-6855

Caere   (408) 395-7000
Casady and Greene   (408) 624-8716
CE Software   (515) 224-1995
Chang Labs   (408) 246-8020
CheckFree   (614) 898-6000
Chronos Software   (415) 626-4244; (800) 777 7907
Claris   (415) 960-1500
Compact Disk Products   (212) 737-8400; (800) 634-2298
The Complete PC   (408) 434-0145; (800) 634-5558
Compugraphic   (800) 622-8973
CompuServe   (614) 457-8600
Computer Associates   (408) 432-1727
Conductor Software   (214) 929-4749
Consumer Reports Books   (212) 983-8250
Cricket Software   (215) 251-9890

DACEasy   (214) 248-0205
DA Systems   (408) 559-7434
Data-Doc Electronics   (512) 928-8926
Datastorm Technologies   (314) 474-9468
Delrina Technology   (416) 441-3676
Deneba   (305) 594-6965
DIALOG Information Services   (415) 858-2700; (800) 982-8319
Digital Composition Systems   (602) 870-7667
Digital Research   (408) 649-3896
Dow Jones/News Retrieval   (609) 520-4000
Dragonfly Software   (212) 334-0445
Dubl-Click Software   (818) 700-9525

Eighty/20 Software   (612) 587-8020

Fifth Generation Systems   (504) 291-7221
FlipTrack Learning Systems   (312) 790-1117
FormMaker Software   (205) 633-3676
Formworx   (617) 890-4499
Fox Software   (419) 874-0162

Gibson Research   (714) 830-2200
GoldMind Publishing   (714) 785-8685
Goldstein & Blair   (415) 524-4000; (800) 982-8319
Great American Software   (603) 889-5400; (800) 388-8000

Hayes Microcomputer Products   (404) 441-1617
Heizer Software   (800) 888-7667
Home Office Computing   (212) 505-3580; (800) 678-0118
Horizon   (205) 633-3676; (800) 888-8423

IBM Desktop Software   (203) 783-7000
Individual Software   (800) 331-3313
Informix   (415) 926-6300
Intel   (800) 525-3019
Intuit   (415) 322-0573; (800) 624-8742

Layered   (617) 242-7700
Learned Information   (609) 654-6266
Letraset USA   (201) 845-6100
Lexpertise US   (801) 350-9100; (800) 354-5656
Logitech   (415) 795-8500
Lord Publishing   (508) 651-9955
Lotus Development   (617) 577-8500

Lynx Automation   (206) 285-1754

The Marketer's Bookshelf   (215) 247-2787
Marketing Graphics   (804) 747-6991; (800) 368-3773
McGraw-Hill Publications Online   (212) 512-2000
MCI Digital Information Services   (800) 444-6245
Mead Data Central   (800) 227-4908; (416) 591-8740
MECA   (203) 226-2400
Microcom   (617) 551-1999
Metro ImageBase   (800) 525-1552
Micro Logic   (800) 342-5930
Microlytics   (716) 248-9150
MicroPro International   (415) 499-1200
Microsoft   (206) 882-8080
Microsoft Press   (800) 677-7377
Monogram Software   (213) 533-5120
MySoftware   (415) 325-9372

Natural Microsystems   (800) 533-6120
NEC Technologies   (708) 860-9500; (800) 746-6363
NewsNet   (800) 345-1301; (215) 527-8030

On Technology   (617) 225-2545
Osborne/McGraw-Hill (800) 227-0900

Palo Alto Software   (800) 336-5544
Parsons Technology   (319) 395-7300; (800) 223-6925
PC Publishing   (213) 556-3630
Peachpit Press   (415) 527-8555
Persoft   (608) 273-6000; (800) 368-5283
Peter Norton Computing   (213) 453-2361
Power Up Software   (415) 345-5900
PR Newswire   (800) 326-8169
Prodex Development   (206) 527-2898
Productivity Software International   (212) 967-8666
ProVUE Development   (714) 969-2431

QMS   (408) 986-9400; (800) 635-3997
Quicksoft   (206) 282-0452

Reference Software International   (415) 541-0222; (800) 872-9933
RightSoft   (800) 888-4437

Samna   (404) 851-0007; (800) 831-9679

Scherrer Resources   (215) 242-8751
Simon and Schuster Software   (212) 373-8882
SimpleSoft Products   (303) 444-8771
Softview   (805) 385-5000
Software Publishing   (415) 962-8910
Software Studios   (703) 978-2339
Software Ventures   (415) 644-3232
Star Software Systems   (800) 242-7827; (213) 533-1190
Survivor Software   (213) 410-9527
Symantec   (408) 253-9600; (800) 228-4122
Symmetry   (602) 844-2199
Synex   (718) 499-6293

Tandy   (817) 390-3011
T-Maker   (415) 962-0195
TenKey Publishing   (407) 351-0966
Timeslips   (800) 338-5314
Timeworks   (708) 948-9200

Ventana Press   (919) 942-0220
Venture Software   (617) 491-6156
VideoTutor   (512) 328-3721

WordPerfect   (801) 225-5000; (800) 526-5017
WordStar International   (415) 499-1200
WordTech Systems   (415) 254-0900

Xpedite Systems   (800) 227-9379; (201) 389-3375

Index

[Italic page numbers refer to figures.]